From perversion to purity

Manchester University Press

From perversion to purity
The stardom of Catherine Deneuve

edited by
Lisa Downing and Sue Harris

Manchester University Press
Manchester and New York

distributed exclusively in the USA by Palgrave

Published by Manchester University Press
Oxford Road, Manchester M13 9NR, UK
and Room 400, 175 Fifth Avenue, New York, NY 10010, USA
www.manchesteruniversitypress.co.uk

Distributed exclusively in the USA by
Palgrave, 175 Fifth Avenue, New York,
NY 10010, USA

Distributed exclusively in Canada by
UBC Press, University of British Columbia, 2029 West Mall,
Vancouver, BC, Canada V6T 1Z2

British Library Cataloguing-in-Publication Data
A catalogue record for this book is available from the British Library

Library of Congress Cataloging-in-Publication Data applied for

ISBN 978 0 7190 7338 0 *hardback*

First published 2007

16 15 14 13 12 11 10 09 08 07   10 9 8 7 6 5 4 3 2 1

Typeset in Sabon by
Koinonia, Manchester
Printed in Great Britain by
Biddles Ltd, King's Lynn

Contents

List of illustrations

List of contributors

Andrew Asibong is a Lecturer in French at Birkbeck College, University of London.

Bridget Birchall is a doctoral candidate in French film studies at the University of Exeter.

Lisa Downing is Professor of French Discourses of Sexuality at the University of Exeter.

Peter Evans is Professor of Hispanic Studies and Film Studies at Queen Mary, University of London.

Fiona Handyside is a Lecturer in European Film at the University of Exeter.

Sue Harris is Reader in French Cinema Studies at Queen Mary, University of London.

Cristina Johnston is a Lecturer in French at the University of Stirling.

Bill Marshall is Professor of Modern French Studies at the University of Glasgow.

Pauline Small is a Senior Lecturer in Film at Queen Mary, University of London.

Susan Weiner is a Teacher and Fellowship Adviser at the University of the Pacific, Stockton, California.

Introduction

Lisa Downing and Sue Harris

She who for almost four decades has symbolised, represented, person-
ified, both in France and beyond its borders, not only French cinema
but France itself; its classical elegance, haughty charm, its innumerable
paradoxes.

(Celle qui, depuis pas loin de quatre décennies, symbolise, représente,
personnifie, dans et hors de l'Hexagone, non seulement le cinéma français,
mais la France elle-même, son élégance classique, son charme un peu
hautain, ses innombrables contradictions.) (Fache 2004: 9)

Few screen icons have provoked as much commentary, speculation
and adulation as the 'she' of this plaudit, Catherine Deneuve. In
the printed media and the annals of cyberspace the most hackneyed
and superficial myths of Catherine's celebrity are circulated and
recycled. Her ubiquity in popular discourse has not been equalled
by scholarly attention, despite the recent efflorescence of work in
the field of French star studies. This, then, is the first full-length
academic volume to analyse the significance of Deneuve's myth in
modern screen culture, both in and outside France.

The volume begins with a brief overview of Deneuve's career,
followed by a critical survey of the field of theoretical star studies,
highlighting its potential and limitations for European, and particularly French, film scholarship. We argue the need for the single-star
case study as a model for understanding the multiple signifying
elements of transnational stardom, particularly as embodied by
one of Europe's most enduring and exportable star commodities,
Catherine Deneuve.

1

Being Catherine Deneuve

Catherine Deneuve, as legend demands, was born in proximity to stage lights and cameras. The third of four daughters, Catherine was born in Paris on 22 October 1943 to actors Maurice Dorléac and Renée Deneuve. Maurice was already a well-respected stage actor, and would go on to become a veteran of supporting roles in the 'quality tradition' of French cinema of the 1940s and 1950s. Later in his career he became the director of the Paramount–Paris dubbing operation, thereby finding himself at the heart of an industry in full post-war, pre-new-wave bloom. Renée Deneuve, Catherine's mother, had been a stage actress since her childhood, and by the age of 18 was already a permanent member of the celebrated Odéon theatre company. Just as Renée had followed her own mother into the world of Parisian theatre, so by 1960, both Catherine (now armed with her mother's maiden name) and her elder sister Françoise had abandoned their *baccalauréat* studies to embark on careers as actresses. Deneuve's rise to stardom was swift and uncompromising: in 1961, still a relative unknown, she was part of a delegation of ten 'promising young actresses' selected to represent French cinema on the international stage; by 1968, the American magazine *Look* was proclaiming her 'the most beautiful woman in the world' (Fache 2004: 26–9). And by the mid-1970s, a series of personal relationships with high-profile directors, actors and artists (Roger Vadim, François Truffaut, Marcello Mastroianni, David Bailey) had endowed her with the dynastic credentials of European screen aristocracy: Catherine's children Christian Vadim and Chiara Mastroianni have conformed to family type, going on to establish premium screen careers in their own right.

From the outset, Deneuve was engaged in provocative screen roles that highlighted questions of female sexual identity. Her first role, at the age of 13, was a brief appearance as a schoolgirl in André Hunebelle's *Collégiennes/The Twilight Girls* (1956), a soft-erotic fantasy starring the semi-notorious Gaby Morlay. Her second film *Les Petits Chats* (Jacques Villa, 1958), was banned until 1965, as censors deemed the story of a planned murder within a group of schoolgirls too disturbing for general release. Deneuve's trademark blonde hair was first seen in Marc Allégret's *Les Parisiennes* (1961), in which she played a schoolgirl seduced by rising 1960s pop idol Johnny Hallyday's youthful charms. Off-screen, the roles she

embraced were no less complicated; Catherine's romantic attachment to the scandalous Roger Vadim, fresh from his marriage to
Brigitte Bardot, established a level of press interest in her private life
that would never diminish: 'it was a rare interview indeed that didn't
make mention of Deneuve's status as a young unmarried mother, a
situation considered abnormal in pre-1968 France' ('rares sonts les
interviews où l'actrice n'est pas renvoyée à son statut de jeune mère
sans mari, situation jugée anormale dans la France d'avant 1968')
(Fache 2004: 62).

Deneuve's first serious success came with her role in Jacques
Demy's contemporary musical fable, *Les Parapluies de Cherbourg/
The Umbrellas of Cherbourg* (1964). Eclipsing her sister's screen
success (Dorléac was much admired in Truffaut's *La Peau douce*,
released at the same time), the film won the prestigious Prix Louis
Delluc and the Cannes Palme d'Or in 1964. With the achievement
of the Academy Award for best foreign-language feature film in the
same season, Deneuve found herself projected onto the international stage in a role that confirmed both her talent and her ability
to take performance risks. The film proved to be a turning point
for her screen persona, opening up the next years of her career to
major auteurist film projects such as *Repulsion* (Polanski, 1965),
Belle de jour (Buñuel, 1966), *La Sirène du Mississippi/Mississippi
Mermaid* (Truffaut, 1969) and *Tristana* (Buñuel, 1970), as well as
more work with Demy (*Les Demoiselles de Rochefort/The Young
Girls of Rochefort*, 1967), in which she co-starred with Dorléac. She
was even slated to work with Hitchcock on a film entitled *The Short
Night*, a project which came to nothing, and which Deneuve has
described as one of the greatest regrets of her career (Fache 2004:
153). By the beginning of the 1970s, Deneuve's already substantial filmography attested to her range and versatility as well as her
growing celebrity. This celebrity, however, had been accelerated in
a uniquely tragic way by Françoise Dorléac's very public death in a
car accident in June 1967.

As her career advanced into the 1970s, Deneuve grew secure in
her choice of projects, both on-screen and off-screen, and began to
build significantly on the international profile she had begun to
establish. Outside France she was a regular in Italian productions,
a relationship cemented by her marriage to Mastroianni, and her
relationship with Marco Ferreri. Her work in English-language films
was also significant, particularly in terms of her collaborations with

high-calibre transatlantic stars. In *The April Fools* (Stuart Rosenberg, 1969) Deneuve shared the screen with Jack Lemmon, while *Hustle* (Robert Aldrich, 1975) saw her paired with Burt Reynolds. *The Hunger* (Tony Scott, 1983), a neo-gothic vampire fantasy, saw her cast alongside David Bowie and Susan Sarandon. In France, she consolidated her career in home-grown dramas by French favourites like Jean-Pierre Melville (*Un Flic/Dirty Money*, 1972), Jean-Paul Rappeneau (*Le Sauvage/The Savage*, 1975) and Claude Lelouch (*A nous deux/An Adventure for Two*, 1979), among others. From the 1980s onwards, she found commercial success on a new scale with work in big-budget French costume drama (*Le Dernier Métro/The Last Metro*, Truffaut, 1980; *Indochine*, Régis Wargnier, 1992; *Est–Ouest/East–West*, Wargnier, 1999). Meanwhile, critical approval was consolidated in an ambitious return to the kind of auteurist projects with which she was identified in the first decade of her career: she has produced performances with directors such as André Téchiné, Lars von Trier, Raúl Ruiz, Nicole Garcia, Léos Carax and Arnaud Desplechin. These projects have conferred an enduring air of gravitas on the actress, bringing her acclaim and awards, and confirming her standing as an ambassador of French cinema on the world stage. Her celebrated selection as the model for the republican emblem Marianne in 1985, coupled with high-profile associations with Chanel, L'Oréal and Yves Saint-Laurent have cemented the popular perception of her as an ideal expression of the desirable qualities of French femininity. Her recent movement into more popular performance and broadcasting modes, including film comedy (*Belle Maman/Beautiful Mother*, Gabriel Aghion, 1999; *8 femmes/8 Women*, François Ozon, 2002; *Palais Royal*, Valérie Lemercier, 2005); made-for-TV dramas (*Les Liaisons dangereuses*, Josée Dayan, 2003; *Princesse Marie*, Benoît Jacquot, 2004) is evidence of her continued versatility, as well as a desire to evade the late-career categorisation that is the lot of so many actors. In Deneuve's case a mature foray into new territory is rarely a risk, but, instead, a reiterated confirmation of stature and enviable longevity.

Deneuve's public profile has evolved in tandem with her film career. From her first public declaration as a signatory to abortion rights in the 1971 'Whores' manifesto' (*Le Manifeste des 343 salopes*), her commitment to political causes has remained in the public eye. Her energies have been directed into causes as diverse as AIDS research, homelessness, mental health, children's rights and 'Reporters without frontiers'.[1] She has been a particularly vocal supporter of Amnesty International, and famously donated the proceeds from the use of her image as the Marianne to its campaign against the death penalty. In 1989 she provided the voiceover to an Amnesty documentary on this subject, and in January 2001 she delivered a petition of 500,000 signatures opposing the death penalty to the American Embassy in Paris. She opposed the 1996 'loi Debré' which sought to deport illegal immigrants from France, a cause to which many in the French arts world lent both voice and funds. In 1994 she was appointed as a goodwill ambassador for UNESCO, a position from which she resigned in 2003 following the controversial nomination of French businessman Pierre Falcone to the organisation.

The protection of her image has been a key concern of the actress, and France's strict privacy laws have worked to her advantage on many occasions. She has never feared litigation, suing the magazine *Lui* over publication of unauthorised images in the January 1973 issue (images that had previously appeared in *Playboy*), and taking Vadim to court in 1986 over the publication of his memoirs. She famously prevented the US lesbian magazine from using the name 'Deneuve' as a title. Being Catherine Deneuve – the person, the brand, the industry – is clearly a full-time job, both on-screen and off-screen.

As her recent forays into unexpected territory would suggest, Deneuve's capacity for self-reinvention and for undermining her familiar star image is undiminished by the longevity of her career. If stars exist primarily as fantasy images whose fixed construction is sustained by the apparatus of narrative, then Deneuve's rare capacity for visible self-deconstruction is perhaps the single most compelling aspect of her stardom.

Deneuve among the stars

This book takes as its methodological basis – and also, we will argue, significantly extends the remit of – the branch of film and cultural studies known as star studies. It is worth considering briefly here the history of star studies as a field of academic inquiry and the preoccupations and omissions of existing work in the domain, particularly where it concerns European and French stardom, in order to demonstrate the significance of this book, a single-star case study of Catherine Deneuve.

Studies of stars and stardom have tended to focus on Hollywood cinema, whose traditional studio system moulds, brands
and markets individual stars as commodities whose personae are
subject to rigid regulation and control.[2] The American studio-
based star system provided the paradigmatic model of a signifying
system of commodities moving within the capitalist marketplace,
to allow Edgar Morin in 1957 to develop the first work of star
studies, heavily influenced by a Marxist analytic framework. It is
true that Morin also refers to French stars (mainly Brigitte Bardot),
but he does so without analysing the material differences between
the American and French systems. It is somewhat anomalous that it
should have been a Frenchman who first analysed Hollywood stars
since, subsequently, star studies has been primarily a facet of film
and cultural studies within the Anglo-American tradition. The bias
towards aesthetic and formal analyses in French academic studies
of film has been, at least until recently, at the expense of any consideration of the significance of film texts and star texts as signifiers of
cultural meanings and of national, gendered and ethnic stereotypes.
Jacqueline Nacache points out that the absence prior to 2003 of
a French translation of Dyer's seminal work of 1979, *Stars*, may
account for the differences between the development of the study of
actors in France and in the UK/USA (Nacache 2003: 155).[3]

In *Stars*, Richard Dyer developed Morin's idea that stars consist
of an amalgam of on-screen and off-screen personae. (Morin distin-
guished the 'actor' from the 'star' on the basis of the latter's possession of this extra-filmic dimension.) Dyer took this further and
argued that these personae reflect those fantasies of identity that
are particularly pertinent to the culture and epoch that create and
consume the star image in question. The idealised and glamorised
star image exudes 'charisma', by means of which ideological contradictions and tensions are smoothed over and appear to be reconciled.
However, the meanings of star texts are not unambiguous or straightforwardly readable and sometimes their function of 'managing'
contradictions fails and flips over into subversion. Moreover, as
they move from one film text to another, or bear sometimes incon-
gruous on-screen and off-screen associations within the same image,
star texts are unstable and polysemous. Later in *Heavenly Bodies*
(1987), Dyer foregrounded the importance of audience reception
in shaping the signifying power of star images, and in particular
subcultural audience recuperation of the star images of such actors

as Judy Garland, for queer purposes. Thus, if stars articulate the ideals and anxieties of the mainstream, they are also available for readings against the grain, for viewings awry.

More recently, British scholarship within French film and cultural studies has turned its attention to the question of stars in French culture. The first full-length work on this subject, Ginette Vincendeau's *Stars and Stardom in French Cinema* (2000), offers a series of readings of French star texts, from Max Linder to Juliette Binoche, including a chapter on Catherine Deneuve. Vincendeau argues that the French star is a symbol of the nation, at once remote and aspirational on the one hand, and 'of the French people' on the other (she cites Alain Delon's claim that he likes to enjoy a baguette in his local café, much like any Frenchman). Vincendeau historicises French stardom citing Max Linder as the first star in the 1930s and positing that the rise to hegemony of US stars over their French counterparts occurred in tandem with the more general eclipse of French (European) power by American influence at the global level. Guy Austin's *Stars in Modern French Film* (2005) makes a different argument for the specificity of French stardom, arguing that it begins in 1950 (and thereby refusing to account for the widespread influence prior to that date of figures such as Linder and Gabin). Austin's argument, which is heavily indebted to Kristin Ross's *Fast Cars, Clean Bodies* (1996), contends that the birth of the French star is a product of the relatively late arrival of modern capitalism in French culture. The moment of French stardom for Austin, then, is specifically aligned with decolonisation and the rise of consumer society associated with the Gaullist presidency.

While acknowledging that France lacks a structured 'star system' such as that of Hollywood, both these studies of French stardom are principally concerned with the functioning of a 'national cinema'. They analyse the signifying function of French stars within a specifically French context, contributing to an understanding both of processes of national identity and of the economic and aesthetic workings of the French film industry. However, the 'national cinema' approach does not fully do justice to the analysis of stardom, particularly when it is a question of European star images, which, unlike their Hollywood counterparts, tend to float across a series of national cinemas, bearing the weight of representing their own nationality, often in a clichéd or stereotypical form (e.g. Deneuve as the internationally recognised face of 'French chic' (Vincendeau 2000: 198)).

The tendency of European stars to cross national boundaries and, where they appear in US films to portray a stereotyped image of their national character, suggests that a model for reading European star images may be needed which is not reducible to an analogy with the 'star system' as it exists in America; nor to a national cinema model.

The single star case study may be this method. It allows for a careful analysis of the way in which a given star text signifies in a number of contexts: (1) inside and outside their own national cinema; (2) within and between the cinemas of a series of directors; (3) as the object of mainstream and subcultural audience reception; and (4) as off-screen as well as on-screen personae. The model which considers stars only in the context of a national cinema risks perpet-uating a hermetic idea of 'the nation' within and through which the star is uniquely understandable. It thereby risks closing down the meaningful potential of each of the four crucial star contexts listed above.

A single-star case study of Catherine Deneuve is a particularly rich endeavour. Previous accounts of Deneuve's stardom have focused on single elements of her star persona (in Austin's account, her associ-ations of icy, clean 'whiteness', in contrast with Jeanne Moreau's earthy 'redness'); or have acknowledged the transformations and contradictions of her star persona, but without being able to account for the precise factors leading to the developments, breaks and lines of continuity that constitute her image over the course of a career (Vincendeau 2000: 196–214). Such accounts of Deneuve's persona run the risk of dividing Deneuve's career neatly into two phases: the innocent beauty tainted by misogynistic representations of nympho-mania, madness and masochism in the early days ('from reverence to rape rolled into one image' (203), as Vincendeau puts it, neatly paraphrasing Molly Haskell); and the stately, maternal *grande dame* of the French nation in her maturity. While these associations and images do indeed represent Deneuve at given moments, the division they posit is a less than absolute one. A careful look at Deneuve as star image, both on-screen and off-screen, over a period of forty years, reveals previously undiscussed instances of prescience, lines of continuity and ignored fractures in her trajectory. Several of the chapters of this book read against the grain of accepted scholarship to highlight the ways in which the seeds of the later persona are sown in early works. In the first chapter of the book, Lisa Downing argues that already in *Repulsion*, Deneuve's image functions to trouble discourses of female madness and frigidity and to foreground female subjectivity as a lens through which to critique the fantasies and neuroses of culture. A part that has been almost universally associated with misogyny by critics is reassessed in the light of a close reading of the film and a retrospective contextualisation of the Polanski-created role in light of Deneuve's later career.

Contributions by Peter Evans (Chapter 2) and Susan Weiner (Chapter 3) grapple with the young Deneuve's associations with extreme aspects of female sexuality, here perversion (particularly masochism) and idealised virginity, showing how the two apparently contradictory labels are almost – but not quite – reconciled within Deneuve's on-screen persona, as constructed and directed by Buñuel and Demy. Evans's chapter also offers insight into a moment in Deneuve's career when the 'Frenchness' of her star image is both placed in relief and troubled by its location in a Spanish setting or tradition. Weiner, on the other hand, returns to an archetypal French narrative (Demy's *Peau d'âne/Donkey Skin*, 1970), in which the purity associated with the young Deneuve is placed in the realm of enchantment and fairy tale. Via a discussion of costume and setting as cinematic masquerade, Weiner reveals the artifice of purity at the heart of Deneuve's spectacle.

Pauline Small's contribution (Chapter 4) revisits Deneuve's association with masochism, most usually linked to her work with Buñuel, via an exploration of the cinemas of Ferreri and Monicelli. Deneuve's Italian career has been largely ignored in previous critical accounts. Small highlights how these Italian directors, the first a maverick, difficult to classify in terms of Italian national cinema, the other a national veteran, both make use of Deneuve's status as a sophisticated actor of auteur cinema to break with the trend for largely popular filmmaking in the Italy of their epoch.

The films that Deneuve made during the 1970s, the period on which Bridget Birchall's chapter focuses, are seriously underrepresented in published accounts of Deneuve's career, despite the fact that some of her most interesting work dates from this decade. Deneuve's 1970s persona oscillates between the arch feminine (on-screen) and the actively feminist (off-screen). However, despite being aligned with certain women's debates of the age (abortion rights, marriage laws), Deneuve refused to commit to the label of feminist. Her inconsistent approach to feminism is read by Birchall to reflect the wider conflicts regarding women's roles in France in the light of the burgeoning women's movement.

Moving beyond the obvious political ambiguities of the 1970s, Sue Harris turns in Chapter 6 to the 1980s, the decade when Deneuve was acknowledged both commercially and critically as the *grande dame* of French cinema. In adopting the vehicle of the heritage film (*Le Dernier Métro*, François Truffaut, 1980; *Indochine*, Régis Wargnier, 1992), she appears to embrace the most conservative version of screen femininity and the most exportable ideal of Frenchness. The idea of Deneuve as the embodiment of Frenchness was consolidated by her selection as model for the emblematic national figure of Marianne. Harris argues that the apparently implacable conservative agenda that Deneuve embodies both on-screen and off-screen is held in tension by the controversial qualities of her earlier screen images.

Chapters 7 and 8 – by Bill Marshall and Cristina Johnston, respectively – explore Deneuve's work with a new generation of international auteurs. Marshall's investigation charts Deneuve's associations with André Téchiné, worked out over a series of five films. For Marshall, Téchiné's are 'narratives of change, transformation, plurality and becoming'. He argues that in her collaboration with Téchiné, Deneuve's status moves from that of star to *acteur fétiche*; she becomes a site on which the director inscribes a continuity of meaning internal to his project. However, this deliberately deglamorised image is not untouched by the pre-existing meanings of Deneuve as a more mainstream star. Marshall's readings signal the emergence of Deneuve as ageing female actress, a concern picked up and developed by Johnston in Chapter 8. This chapter demonstrates how Deneuve's work in the 1990s with a range of directors (Lars von Trier, Gabriel Aghion, Philippe Garrel) offers a series of portraits of ageing; focusing on stereotypes of maternal and sexual relationships, as well as challenges to these. These roles offer an unusual level of exposure for an actress held by cinematic discourse to be the celebration of youth and beauty.

The final two contributions to the book – by Andrew Asibong and Fiona Handyside, respectively – treat elements of Deneuve's off-screen persona and the subtle relationships between her filmic and extra-filmic images. They engage in detail with the discourses surrounding reception of her multilayered persona. Following Dyer's assessment in 1987 of the importance of queer audiences in shaping the meaning of a star persona, Asibong assesses Deneuve's status as lesbian icon, identifying at least two types of lesbian persona in Deneuve's career – a titillating but ultimately 'safe' presentation of vanilla lesbianism (in Téchiné's *Les Voleurs* and in the kiss with Fanny Ardant in Ozon's *8 femmes*) and a more complex lesbian persona, involving overtones of sadomasochism and power play in *Belle de jour*, *The Hunger* and Deneuve's character's relationship with Emmanuelle Béart's maid in *8 femmes*. It is this second mode, Asibong argues, which reveals the way in which Deneuve's persona can be read to reveal the ideological interplay between sexuality and class. The book reaches its conclusion with Handyside's chapter on Deneuve as fashion icon. This chapter examines the crucial part played by *haute couture* in defining Deneuve's persona and highlights how her apparently immaculate and glamorous off-screen image paradoxically includes elements of disruption and play that irreverently reference her more eccentric on-screen roles and disrupt the constricting image of 'perfection'.

While it is generally accepted since Dyer that stars embody paradoxes and resist linear or unitary meanings, it is by showing in detail how these characteristics function with regard to one star – in this case Catherine Deneuve – that we may be afforded a new and deeper insight into how star images *in general* function in culture. Until recently, very few single case studies of stars existed in the field of academic publishing. The appearance of Graham McCann's *Marilyn Monroe* (1998), Rachel Moseley's book on Audrey Hepburn (2002) and Susan Hayward's monograph on Simone Signoret (2004) bears witness to a currently nascent academic interest in the signifying power of individual stars in culture.[4] This is perhaps unsurprising since, as Richard Dyer put it in 1987, 'being interested in stars is being interested in how we are human now' (Dyer 1987: 17). This may be truer in the first decade of the twenty-first century than ever before. In a Europe that is increasingly obsessed with celebrity and fame, the task of analysing the relationship between the glamour of stars and everyday culture becomes increasingly urgent. In the mass media (popular TV interviews, celebrity magazines, online fanzines), stars are often sites around which normative and mainstream discourses of gender, beauty, class, ethnicity and sexuality are shored up. Popular discourses about stars offer an aspirational and commodified ideal of masculinity or femininity, wealth, style and capitalist values. Politically informed star studies, on the other hand, can offer a powerful corrective tool with which to show up the workings of these ideologies and may offer alternative and resistant readings of star images that also cast fresh light on the workings of the cultures that produce them. The star text 'Catherine Deneuve' emerges in the set of readings that follow as an unstable and shifting sign that problematises as much as it perpetuates the associations that accrue to the image of this beautiful star.

Notes

1 Deneuve was the first celebrity to broadcast a message of support on French TV for abducted journalists Christian Chesnot and Georges Malbrunot, in September 2004.
2 So rigidly enforced was James Stewart's 'nice guy' persona in 1960s Hollywood, for example, that he could not be cast a murderer, with the result that Hitchcock's *Vertigo* had to be made with an alternative ending to the murderous denouement of Boileau and Narcejac's novel *D'entre les morts*.
3 In a review article of recent scholarship in French film studies (Handyside, 2003), Fiona Handyside notes that Martine Beugnet's *Marginalité, sexualité, contrôle dans le cinéma français contemporain* (Beugnet, 2000), by importing the English terms 'star studies' and 'cultural studies' into her French-language book, and by putting the concerns of these Anglo-American inquiries into dialogue with more traditional French analytic methods, may have inaugurated a long-awaited and significant *rapprochement* between the Anglo-American and European models of film analysis.
4 A precursor to these titles that deserves acknowledging, not least because it is a French study of a French star, is Claude Gauteur and Ginette Vincendeau's *Jean Gabin: anatomie d'un mythe* (1993). (Republished by Le Nouveau Monde, 2006.)

Works cited

Austin, Guy (2003), *Stars in Modern French Film*, London: Arnold.
Beugnet, Martine (2000), *Marginalité, sexualité, contrôle dans le cinéma français contemporain*, Paris: L'Harmattan.
Dyer, Richard (1979), *Stars*, London: BFI.
Dyer, Richard (1987), *Heavenly Bodies: Film Stars and Society*, London: BFI.
Fache, Alexandre (2004), *Catherine Deneuve: une biographie*, Paris: Presses de la cité.
Gauteur, Claude and Ginette Vincendeau (1993), *Jean Gabin: Anatomie d'un mythe*, Paris: Nathan.

Handyside, Fiona (2003), 'Une certaine idée du cinéma français: contemporary French cinema criticism', *French Cultural Studies*, 15(3), October, 311–18.

Hayward, Susan (2004), *Simone Signoret: the Star as Cultural Sign*, London: Continuum.

McCann, Graham (1998), *Marilyn Monroe*, New Brunswick: Rutgers University Press.

Morin, Edgar (1957), *Les Stars*, Paris: Seuil.

Moseley, Rachel (2002), *Growing Up with Audrey Hepburn: Text, Image, Resonance*, Manchester: Manchester University Press.

Nacache, Jacqueline (2003), *L'acteur au cinéma*, Paris: Nathan.

Ross, Kristin (1996), *Fast Cars, Clean Bodies: Decolonisation and the Reordering of French Culture*, Cambridge, MA: MIT Press.

Vincendeau, Ginette (2000), *Stars and Stardom in French Cinema*, London: Continuum.

1

Polanski's Deneuve: 'frigidity' and feminism

Lisa Downing

By 1965, 22-year-old actress Catherine Deneuve had featured in seven films. Of those roles, only one had brought her serious critical recognition: the part of the fresh, innocent heroine of Jacques Demy's musical extravaganza *Les Parapluies de Cherbourg/ The Umbrellas of Cherbourg* (1964). It was in 1965 that Roman Polanski would cast her in *Repulsion*, described by one critic as a 'one-woman show' (Johnson 1966: 44), in a role that would effectively create a persona which would resonate throughout her future film career. Polanski put on-screen the qualities of youthful beauty and guilelessness that had characterised both her role with Demy and her earlier part as 'Virtue' in Roger Vadim's Sadeian adaptation *Le Vice et la vertu/Vice and Virtue* (1962), but only in order to suggest the fissures of psychical disturbance, resistance and violence that could underlie them. As Johnson put it: 'Polanski has chosen fragile Catherine Deneuve to play his schizoid heroine, infusing Demy's princess with a stark witchcraft nature, alternately catatonic and violent' (44).

The British-made *Repulsion* was Polanski's first English-language film and his second feature (after a series of Polish-made shorts and the critically acclaimed *Knife in the Water* (1962)). Polanski first met Deneuve on the set of *Les Parapluies*, and contacted her with the offer of working together on a project soon after seeing the finished film. After Deneuve rejected his initial suggestion of a part in the screen adaptation of Roland Dubillard's *The Swallows*, they settled on the screenplay that would become *Repulsion* (Deneuve [2004] 2005: 161). The film tells the story of a young Belgian beautician, Carol (Deneuve), who lives in London and shares a flat with her older sister Helen (Yvonne Furneaux). Carol is emotionally withdrawn and reacts with disgust to the very prospect of men and the intimate rituals of heterosexuality; while her sister Helen, by contrast, is a sexually active extrovert. Left alone in the flat while her sister is on holiday, Carol becomes increasingly delusional. She ends by murdering both the young man who has attempted to court her and the sexually predatory landlord who calls to collect the rent, before finally succumbing to a catatonic state.

Commentary of the film, in both reviews written at the time of release and subsequent scholarly works, has tended to dwell upon its impressive atmospheric and formal qualities and, to quote one critic, its 'visual eloquence' (Dyer 1965: 146). The figure of Carol and the film's treatment of female madness and murder, however, have elicited a mixed reaction. While some critics find the film's subject matter simply unpleasant and disturbing (Dyer, 1965), others go further and accuse it of a pathologising misogyny (Bisplinghoff, 1982). In what follows, first, I will assess and critique the reception of Polanski's film with regard to its portrayal of female subjectivity, arguing that Deneuve's presence in the film works to disrupt rather than to confirm straightforward stereotypes and codes of femininity, and, second, I will discuss the significance of this film for the development of Catherine Deneuve's screen persona.

Repulsion: 'irresponsible fiction' or 'indictment of society'?

In his damning review of the film in *Sight & Sound*, Peter John Dyer described it as 'an irresponsible fiction' and added 'its possible effect on anybody going through a period of crisis or depression doesn't bear thinking about' (Dyer 1965: 146). For this critic, the elements borrowed from the horror genre (frightening fantasy sequences and graphic murders) are more significant in determining its effect than the understated, slow and careful consideration of Carol's mental state against the backdrop of modern society that the film undertakes.

Some feminism-informed criticism has made its objections on different grounds. The character of Carol has been read as the symptom of a masculine fantasy of femininity as always-already pathological. In her article, 'Codes of feminine madness', for example, Gretchen Bisplinghoff argues that *Repulsion* 'use[s] Freudian conformist psychology in defining and portraying insanity' such that 'a female character deviates from the norm by the fact of being female, which in itself is defined as a deviation from the male standard' (1982: 37). In this reading, Polanski's representation of Carol's schizoid and murderous behaviour is simply the extreme logic outcome of culture's pathologisation of women. In her seminal work on the horror genre and its construction of the 'monstrous feminine' Barbara Creed offers a more nuanced understanding of the relationship between femininity and madness than that posited by Bisplinghoff. She evokes the dimension of beauty that changes pathology into evil within representational codes. Beauty for Creed is the double-edged sword which assures that woman on-screen is desired but also feared and damned by those who desire her: 'it is this stereotype of feminine evil – beautiful on the outside/corrupt within – that is so popular within patriarchal discourses about woman's evil nature' (1993: 42). It hardly needs to be stated that beauty is one of the primary associations that Deneuve's name evokes and which characterised her star persona from its earliest days. We may wonder, then, whether what may initially seem to be a striking paradox – Deneuve's angelic appearance (the film was originally to be called *Angel Face* (Deneuve [2004] 2005: 161) coupled with Carol's homicidal behaviour – is actually the most deep-rooted and reactionary of stereotypes: the seductive mask worn by the fatal woman?

However, Polanski's choice of profession for the protagonist of *Repulsion* – that of beautician – must be read as significant. Deneuve is shown in the film applying facial treatments to women clients. By creating on-screen the mask of beauty, using modern cosmetic techniques and in a commercial setting, Carol's work shows up the artifice of femininity in commodity culture; drawing attention to rather than erasing the traces of the surface–depth division that characterises cultural constructions of femininity; particularly cinematic femininity. Moreover, in a discussion of *Repulsion*, Creed goes on to point out that Deneuve's character is not only an example of this masculine stereotype of archetypal beauty that kills. She can also be read as exemplifying the rather more active and subjective role of the vengeful woman, a figure that will become familiar to cinema audiences in later decades via feminism-inspired rape-revenge movies, such as *Thelma and Louise* (Scott, 1991) (Creed 1993: 123). Significantly, Carol hallucinates that she is being raped numerous times in nocturnal fantasy sequences, but these are not the only rapes alluded to in the film. Her murderous attacks on the two men only occur when the first one breaks into her flat against her will (a metaphorical violation) and the second one forces himself upon her physically, rendering inaccurate the words of certain critics who suggest that heterosexual male aggression is just a figment of the insane woman's desiring imagination in this film.[1] Creed gestures towards the idea, though she does not develop it, that Polanski's Carol, by bridging two modes of cinematic femininity with very different ideological connotations, may be a symbolic figure bearing political meanings that go beyond stereotypes of that embodiment of masculine masochism and misogyny, the monstrous feminine.

Of the reviews of *Repulsion* that appeared at the time of release, I could only find one that suggested Polanski's agenda was anything

other than exploitative and sensationalist. Albert Johnson wrote in
Film Quarterly that the film constituted 'a thematic indictment of
society' (45). The society in question is that of mid-1960s London,
the hey-day of the so-called sexual revolution. Johnson goes on: 'the
acceptance of beautiful women as physical objects of desire and the
complete indifference of modern society towards the bizarre [...]
makes it easy for insanity to flourish, undetected by mothers, sisters,
prospective lovers and employers' (65). While Johnson's point may
sound slightly conservative or normative, I am interested in his
suggestion that *Repulsion* constitutes a critique on Polanski's part of
the ethics and social codes of an epoch that styled itself as liberating
for female subjectivity and sexuality, all the while exhorting women
to be beautiful objects for male sexual enjoyment.

Readers of Michel Foucault will be familiar with the idea that
the notion of sexual repression is a historically constructed 'hypoth-
esis' rather than a given fact. In the first volume of his *Histoire
de la sexualité/History of Sexuality* (1976), Foucault attempts to
think sexuality outside of a model of repression and liberation. He
shows that the pursuit of knowledge about sexuality – such as the
creation of diagnostic categories of sexual perversion and mental
disorder on the basis of a person's attitudes and behaviours with
regard to the pleasures of their bodies – is not a disinterested or
neutral pursuit. Sexuality is always highly politicised and carries
meanings that function within a network of power and knowledge.
The notion of a 'sexual revolution' is thrown in doubt by Foucault's
formulations.

In her revisionist historical reading of the sexual revolution,
separatist lesbian feminist Sheila Jeffreys uses a different ideological
and political framework to that employed by Foucault, but similarly
argues against an understanding of the culture of the 1960s as 'liberating'. She contends that the apparent increase in women's sexual
freedom actually had the opposite effect of exerting even more
restrictions on their behaviour. For the first time in history, economically empowered women were entering the workforce, living the
lifestyle of single women, often sharing flats together, removed from
the control of parents and husbands. They thereby constituted an
economic class that threatened traditional patriarchal patterns.
Jeffreys posits that economically independent women would no
longer have had an investment in replicating family structures. The
potential female revolution – entailing a rejection of the subordinate

status of married women – never took place, Jeffreys argues, because the discursive force of the sexual revolution acted as a counter-measure to any emergent female militancy.

According to this argument, the single woman in the 1960s occupied her mind and time with the paraphernalia of sex and dating, which prevented her becoming a truly revolutionary social agent. Hence the proliferation of advice on sexual matters that suddenly became available to her. Jeffreys cites Gurley Brown's influential sex-advice manual of 1962, *Sex and the Single Girl* which taught young women how to lure men into marriage – using varied and skilful sexual techniques as bait, rather than virginity, as had been recommended by manuals of the 1950s. The suspicion of frigidity rather than of promiscuity became the most unattractive reputation that could accrue to a woman, as it removed her commodity value in the new sexual 'free' market. Thus, women were encouraged to grow their hair: 'lots of hair is sexy'; efface their personality: 'being able to sit still is sexy. Talking all the time about anything is unsexy'; and to perform a docile benevolence: 'smiles are sexy' (Cited in Jeffreys 1990: 106).

In the course of his career, Roman Polanski's directorial output has been associated with a glorification of sado-masochism, a satanic vision and misogyny. He is not the most obvious candidate to exemplify the radical anti-heterosexual, anti-S&M agenda of Sheila Jeffreys. Moreover, critical analyses such as that by Gretchen Bisplinghoff would put Polanski in the camp of those proliferating discourses of truth about norms and deviations of sexuality, repeating the pathologising logic of the psychological professional. However, my contention is that *Repulsion* can be read against the grain to offer a surprisingly sympathetic account of what happens to a young woman of the sexual revolution generation who rejects the imperative of heterosexual activity. Deneuve does not simply function in this film as a seductive and deviant female monster, designed to create a frisson of masochism in the male spectator. Rather, Polanski offers us a chance to look awry at the ideology of the time, precisely by means of our proximity with Deneuve's character.

Through Carol's eyes

Carol's perception is foregrounded in the film in several ways. The opening credits role over a close-up of Deneuve's eye. In the first frame of the film, the camera pulls back to reveal her whole face, strikingly immobile, and then cuts to the face of a reclining woman. The woman has closed eyes and a thick white substance covering her face. Her immobility and pallor rhyme with Deneuve's. Suddenly, the stillness and silence are interrupted by her sharp words to Carol in a pinched twanging voice: 'Have you fallen asleep, then?'. The woman is a client in the beauty parlour where Carol works; her strange appearance a face mask. As the sinister opening becomes understandable for the viewer, we witness the shift in perspective from grotesque and horrifying (Carol's habitual perception of the world) to comfortingly familiar. By experiencing this initial alienation, followed by a comforting shift back to our perspective, the filmmaker encourages the viewer to empathise and sympathise with the perception of Deneuve's character for whom the world is habitually grotesque. She is not a monster who remains wholly other to us: while embodying alterity in a number of ways, she is also a locus of subjectivity, a subjectivity that we are invited to share in.

The film, then, is not just a prurient voyeuristic glimpse inside the mind of a beautiful female psychotic, but something considerably more intimate and sympathetic, an effect that is achieved by numerous means. Several times in the film, we are shown close-ups of Deneuve's eye before cutting to objects or scenes that we know she is watching. The many suggested subjective shots place the 'real', 'normal' 'naturalised' world under the gaze of one who is profoundly alienated, in order to bring to consciousness a larger sense of alienation. In French, Deneuve's native language, *un(e) aliéné(e)* is both an alienated person and an insane person, 'alienisme' being the nineteenth-century term for the medical specialism that would become psychiatry. In American English, an alien is an ethnic immigrant. The shifting associations of alienation and familiarity are thus played with in multiple ways by Polish *immigré* Polanski. Carol's construction as 'other' in the film is multivalent, and is achieved through an amalgam of the characteristics of the fictional character and of the actress, Catherine Deneuve. Carol is a French-speaking Belgian woman living in London. Her name, however, is not the French-sounding Carole, but the strangely English Carol. (Her sister is not Hélène but Helen.) By playing a Belgian with an English name, Deneuve, who will one day provide the model for the archetypal French woman Marianne, whose statue can be seen in town squares all over France, adopts a role in which she is removed from her national identity, an ambiguous figure whose ethnicity lacks cohesion in the same way as her mental state is fragmented.

Carol's difference is also signalled by physical appearance. She is the one blonde in a strikingly brunette London. The two female figures she associates with, and with whom we visually compare her, her sister Helen and colleague Bridget, have dark, short hair in contrast to Deneuve's thick, long, blonde hair which often hangs over her face obscuring her features. The two brunettes with their fashionably cut bobs signify an ease with the lifestyle of their epoch. They both have lovers (Helen's is married), and enjoy sex with their partners. The association of icy blondes with frigidity or perversion and of brunettes with a more earthy sexuality will become a cinematic cliché, exploited most strikingly by Hitchcock, and it is suggestive that Deneuve has stated in an interview that she would have loved to play the role of Hitchcock's Marnie, a role bearing all the associations of Polanski's Deneuve: blondeness, frigidity and criminality (Guardian Unlimited Film/Interviews/Catherine Deneuve, 2005). In *Repulsion*, however, the significance of the blonde among the brunettes is not simply meant to be archetypal, as in Hitchcock, but also to reflect dislocation from cultural and historical specificity.

Several times in the film we are shown how Carol is almost, but not quite, able to perform the role of the modern young woman about town that is dictated to her by her peers. Recent scholarship on French new-wave cinema has focused on the cultural meanings of 'walking in the street' for a woman in modernity (see especially Handyside 2002). Jean Seburg in Godard's *A bout de souffle* (1960) exemplifies this principle; she is a *flâneuse*, with short hair and trousers who is mistress of the sidewalk. Deneuve walks in the street three times in *Repulsion*, her progress followed by a hand-held camera in new-wave documentary style. The jaunty tones of Chico Hamilton's American Jazz accompany her progress each time. In the first walking scene, she is watched avidly by men on the street and a road worker calls out to her 'Hello darling; how about a bit of the other, then?'. Her face is impassive as she hurries past; the camera aligned with her fast pace and disinterested progress rather than with the fixing gaze of the leering men. The second time, she is walking to a meeting with Colin, the young man who is attempting to court her. Her journey to the rendezvous point is halted when she comes upon a crack in the pavement. Bending to her knees, she remains rooted to the spot, her eyes fixed on it, with the result that she is over an hour late for her date. Thus, Deneuve's walking in the street is interrupted, first by unwanted sexual attention and second by external schisms that mirror her internal ones and that hold her fascinated. She is effectively, repeatedly immobilised by the pressure caused by the sexual imperatives that are presented as an inevitable part of the modern imaginary. Unlike Hitchcock's dyed blondes, whose hair colour signifies artificiality and duplicity (two Hitchcock heroines change the shade of their hair expressly in order to commit crimes: the eponymous Marnie and Novak's character in *Vertigo*), Deneuve's long, loose blonde hair in *Repulsion* is suggestive of the naivity and guilelessness that characterise Carol. She is a lost little girl, an Alice in Wonderland; the perverse and grotesque Wonderland in question being 1960s Britain.[2]

As we watch Carol descend into madness, it is the world as we know it that becomes increasingly unfamiliar, taking us back to our position at the opening of the film. The repulsion of the film's title is communicated effectively to the audience by the focus on several objects which gain significance as the film progresses. The first significant repulsion-object is the skinned carcass of a rabbit which Helen takes from the fridge in an early scene. She plans to cook it for supper for her lover, but he decides to take her out to dinner instead. The location in which the rabbit is found – a fridge, an example in 1960s Britain of ultra-modern 'white goods', suggests the bright optimism of the epoch, a container in which one can preserve and stave off decay. Once Carol is left alone in the apartment, she removes the rabbit from the fridge and leaves it out on display in the flat (in what we are repeatedly told are sweltering hot summer conditions). The camera will close in on the rabbit several times throughout the film, charting the progress of its putrefaction. A couple of potatoes left in the kitchen will similarly sprout increasingly elaborate growths as Carol's madness escalates. These objects are at once banal and uncanny. Their role in the film is as markers of the real, announcing the emergence of psychosis over symbolisation (though obviously they themselves are mediated symbols of the schism in sanity within a tightly constructed metaphorical filmic language).

The disruption and eruption to which they attest is occasionally violently suggestive, as in one of the most striking scenes of the film. Bridget and Carol are discussing the details of a Charlie Chaplin film which Bridget has seen the previous evening. She describes Chaplin's antics in animated fashion, and Carol, for the one and only time in the film, is moved from her internally gazing reverie to a noisy, spontaneous laughter. When Bridget suggests she should go to see the film too, Carol responds with genuinely joyous enthusiasm. A second later, Bridget mentions that she saw the film with her boyfriend and Carol's face freezes instantly into her expressionless mask at this mention of boyfriends. This reminder of the heterosexual economy works to rupture Carol's perception of their colluding female solidarity. We are reminded of Sheila Jeffreys's strongly worded assertion regarding the limited scope of the life allowed for sexually liberated 1960s woman: 'whereas the spinster in the 1950s might at least take comfort in her intelligence and her women friends, the 1960s single woman was given only one function in life, the stimulation of the male sexual appetite' (107). A second later, not having noticed the change in her friend's attitude, Bridget reaches for Carol's handbag to pass it to her, but is arrested in a moment of horror of her own. The head of the now putrescent rabbit is lying alongside the purse, cosmetics and the other feminine accoutrements in her bag.[3] Thus, an equivalence is created within the internal logic of the film between the way in which talk of heterosexual dating practices disturbs Carol's equilibrium and the sudden sighting of a rotten rabbit's head disturbs Bridget's. Crucially, neither response is privileged over the other, such that 'normality' becomes radically unstable.

This is not the only example of how the film works to make the discourses surrounding the sexual mores of the time unfamiliar. In one scene, we watch from Deneuve's viewpoint as a client in the beauty salon chats about her 'man troubles' with another beautician. The woman speaks the following words: 'there's only one way to deal with men [...] Keep them on their knees. They love it'. From where Deneuve is standing, at the head of the massage table where the client lies, the woman's face appears upside down. A close-up on the lower (which, within this frame, has become the upper) part of the woman's face shows the lips moving grotesquely, for one has the impression that a new, uncanny face has been created with a gaping mouth above which appear not a nose and eyes, but a blank, unseeing fleshy stub (the chin). In this shot, we see the world as Carol sees it and, by means of a visual trick, the discourse spoken by the upside down woman becomes as odd to us as it is to Carol. By privileging Carol's perspective throughout the film, the director encourages us to invest in her humanity, not to dismiss her as a monster. The socially constructed delimitation between sane and insane–sexually active and sexually repressed, etc., as 'types of person' that one might be, results in us having to see the assumptions and behaviours of the 'ordinary' world as alien, deformed and dehumanised *if* we are to accord humanity to Carol. This is the logical outcome of such binary thinking.

A star (text) is born (constructed)

In his seminal study *Stars* ([1979] 1992), Richard Dyer demonstrated that stars do not straightforwardly represent or reflect ideology, rather they work to show up or to occlude the ways in which ideologies are constructed according to paradoxes and contradictions. Deneuve's performance in *Repulsion* problematises assumptions about the meaning of sexual liberation for women in the 1960s and about cultural understandings of femininity that hang on polarities between frigidity and whoredom; infantilism and monstrosity. However, it would be a mistake to assume that the figure of 'Polanski's Deneuve' is a wholly redemptive one, and the processes of power and commodification at work in the creation and exchange of star images deserve consideration.

The persona that Polanski created for Deneuve in *Repulsion* made her the obvious choice for Séverine in Buñuel's *Belle de jour* (1966). Colin McArthur (1968/9: 15) has pointed out that *Repulsion* can be read as a homage to Buñuel's cinema. The film's language of symbols echoes Buñuel's lexicon, with its repeated focus on Deneuve's eye and the cut-throat razor recalling the surrealist classic, *Un chien andalou* (Buñuel and Dalí 1929). In a response to this homage, Buñuel in turn will cite Polanski by casting his icy, perverse blonde Catherine Deneuve in *Belle de jour* a year later. She effectively becomes the star commodity which links the filmic corpuses of the two male directors. It is precisely in this handing over of the actress from one director to the other in 1965–1966 that Deneuve as star-text becomes indelibly associated with iciness and a perverse sensuality.[4] So, the female star functions as a passive object of exchange between male filmmakers who are also makers of cultural meanings.

However, as Richard Dyer has suggested, the ways in which star commodities function and circulate, and the meanings they convey, are never simply reducible to the intentions of the individuals using the star commodity, nor to the individual bearing the star name. Moreover the *uses* to which a persona of stereotypical/archetypical femininity is put can undermine rather than reinforce its dominant meanings. In the case of *Repulsion*, I have been arguing in this chapter that the complex ways in which the figure of Carol is represented undercuts the politically problematic construction of the young Deneuve as the male fantasy of frigid virginity and of passivity masking pathology, even as it creates it.

At the level of her performance in this film, for example, 'passive' is simply not an adequate label for Deneuve's embodiment of Carol. The striking blankness of her facial expression – described by Claire Clouzot in *Cahiers du cinéma* as 'insipid ... empty [...] totally atonal' ('insipide ... vide [...] totalement atone') (1966: 109) – alludes, in fact, to a complex element of the performance. Clouzot goes on unflatteringly: 'it's not that she acts "well", it's rather that Polanski has been able to make full use of this actress's inexpressive qualities' ('ce n'est pas qu'elle joue "bien"; c'est que Polanski a su utiliser pleinement la force inexpressive de l'actrice'). Deneuve's tendency for understated acting has become a central part of her reputation.[5] The use made of the young Deneuve's 'inexpressiveness' or 'blankness' in *Repulsion* is highly suggestive, as is the use of silence (deployed to great effect during the imagined rape where the scream we see on her mouth is silent and only the clock is heard, or during the murders where all diegetic sound is killed). Her blank face is not a gauge of passivity or emptiness in the later scenes of *Repulsion*, so much as a marker of psychosis, insofar as psychosis stands here for a system of meaning that is unfamiliar and closed off to our ability to read. The suspended animation of Carol's face signals a suspension of her belief in the terms of the society in which she is living, a retreat from the symbolic order that would construct her in a given socio-sexual role. Deneuve's understated performance allows for an embodiment of femininity that is not obvious, decidable or fully reducible to the labels that it suggests. The trope of madness is used to significant effect in *Repulsion*, not to reinforce stigmatising female psychology, as Bisplinghoff would have it, but rather to metaphorise the condition of alienation from and within dominant social codes and mores. The use made of Carol's madness by Polanski seems to suggest at moments the figure of the 'schizophrenic position' as deployed in the theoretical work of Deleuze and Guattari (1972 and 1980). For these thinkers the 'schizo' subject is the subject of capitalism carried to the point of disjunctiveness, set adrift from both the Oedipal desire of the neurotic and the capitalist concerns of the bourgeois. When Carol stares into the cracks in the pavement rather than meeting her suitor, or carries a rotting animal carcass in her bag, her fascination with and desire for destruction and decay suggest a break from the (re)productive uses to which female sexuality is put in the heterosexual economy. The sexological label of 'frigidity' is a construct which delimits and pathologises the woman unwilling or unable to draw pleasure from the rituals of heterosexual penetrative sex. The film turns the pathologising label on its head, suggesting that 'frigidity' may be a strategic alternative to both the reproductive femininity required by heterosexual normalcy *and* the sanctioned promiscuity of the 'swinging sixties'.

However, Carol's subjectivity cannot simply or uncontroversially be elevated to a politically radical position. The final images of Deneuve in the film are as an immobile, catatonic body being lifted and carried by Helen's lover, who, in alignment with the camera, looks down at her recumbent form with a mixture of desire and repulsion. The point of view from which we have watched most of the film's action has been effectively closed down in these closing scenes, and Carol finally becomes object rather than subject. The wages of mental and sexual deviation from societal norms are revealed to be heavy in the logic of the film's denouement.

Deneuve in *Repulsion* is thus a locus of ambiguities. The resistance offered by her Polanski-created persona to dominant ideological norms is elliptical and partial, rather than straightforwardly readable. If the partial pathologisation of Deneuve in *Repulsion* led to the overwhelming association of the young Deneuve with an icy 'frigidity' or 'perversity', it is a sign of the mobility of Deneuve as star text across the decades that Benoît Jacquot could cast her as 'Princesse Marie' in his TV film of 2004, a role in which she plays the princess of psychoanalysis, Freud's female disciple Marie Bonaparte. Yet this movement from psychotic murderess in the 1960s to psychoanalytic pioneer in the new millennium is not as contradictory as it seems. Already in *Repulsion*, it is by looking through the eyes of Deneuve's character that we are offered an analytic insight into the sexual and capitalist neuroses of society, even if the analysis is filtered through a psychotic rather than therapeutic lens; more a Deleuzian 'schizoanalysis' than a classic psychoanalysis.[6] That an interpretation of *Repulsion* as challenging and contestatory to social norms and sexual stereotypes can viably exist alongside the more commonplace reading of the film as a piece of sensationalist misogyny is a testimony to the complexity and fruitful tensions of both Polanski's film and Deneuve's performance style and nascent star image.

Notes

1 See, for example, Michel Caen's account of Carol: 'she is a nympho-maniac but only alone, in dreams, can she make love to herself. Her hallucinations are peopled by rapes which, owing to their obsessional character, are the opposite of her sister's normal sexuality [...]. Because of the pleasure they can give – inflict – Carol hates men'. ('Il s'agit d'une nymphomane mais elle seule sait, en rêve, se faire l'amour. Ses hallucinations sont peuplées de viols, qui, par leur caractère obsessionnel, s'opposent totalement à la sexualité normale de sa sœur [...]. Pour [le] plaisir qu'il est capable de donner – d'infliger – Carol déteste l'homme') (1966: 73). Such accounts demonstrate that misogynistic discourse and assumptions were alive and well on the part of critics in 1965–1966, even if not they are not the message (or at least not straightforwardly the message) of Polanski's film.

2 The notion of Carol's blonde hair connoting 'naturalness' is however complicated by our knowledge that Deneuve herself is a dyed blonde. This extra-filmic knowledge adds another dimension to the play with the 'nature' and 'construction' of feminine beauty with which this film, whose protagonist is a beautician, is concerned.

3 Carol's attachment to this putrefied rabbit – and her preference for decay over preservation – is interesting in the light of recent critical perceptions of Deneuve's early star persona as inextricably linked to post-war French values of cleanliness and the 'domesticated sublime' (Henri Lefebvre's term, cited in Austin 2003). Guy Austin has argued that in 1965 'discourses of whiteness, cleanliness and timelessness reads [sic] like a definition of Deneuve-as-star' (2003: 45). An attentive reading of *Repulsion* shows a fissure in Deneuve's 'clean' early star image, suggesting the existence of a set of more ambiguous and richly textured associations than is usually acknowledged, and drawing attention to the discrepancies that often exist between an actor's on-screen and off-screen star personae. (For more on this question, see Chapter 10 of the present volume.)

4 Although she does not discuss the specific process by which Catherine Deneuve's star persona became fixed, Ginette Vincendeau points out that the 'key to her early image is the concept of coolness (terms such as 'ice', 'iceberg' and 'cool' recur in all the literature on her), which refers to her personality and especially her sexuality. As opposed to Bardot's 'hot' availability, the young Deneuve's dominant trope was that of 'cold' unavailability ...' (Vincendeau 2000: 202).

5 In a recent interview with Deneuve at the NFT in London (21 September
   2005), the interviewer Geoff Andrew commented: 'I think that if there
   is a secret to your acting it is the tendency to underplay' (Guardian
   Unlimited Film/Interviews/Catherine Deneuve 2005).
6 Significantly, Deneuve plays the role of a psychoanalyst twice in the
   same year: in *Princesse Marie* (Jacquot, 2004) and in *Rois et reine*
   (Desplechin, 2004).

Works cited

Guardian Unlimited Film/Interviews/Catherine Deneuve (2005), at: http://
   film.guardian.co.uk/interview/interviewpages/0,6737,1577158,00.
   html (accessed 6 November 2005).
Austin, Guy (2003), *Stars in Modern French Film*, London: Arnold.
Bisplinghoff, Gretchen (1982), 'Codes of feminine madness', *Film Reader*,
   5, 37–40.
Caen, Michel (1966),'Victime et bourreau', *Cahiers du cinéma*, 179, March,
   72–3.
Creed, Barbara (1993), *The Monstrous Feminine: Film Feminism, Psycho-
   analysis*, London: Routledge.
Deleuze, Gilles and Félix Guattari (1972), *Capitalisme et schizophrénie:
   L'Anti-Œdipe*, Paris: Minuit.
Deleuze, Gilles and Félix Guattari (1980), *Capitalisme et schizophrénie 2:
   Mille Plateaux*, Paris: Minuit.
Deneuve, Catherine (2004), *A l'ombre de moi-même*, Paris: Stock.
Deneuve, Catherine ([2004] 2005), *Close Up and Personal*, trans. Polly
   McLean, London: Orion.
Dyer, Peter John (1965), '*Repulsion*', *Sight & Sound*, 34(3), 146.
Dyer, Richard ([1979] 1992), *Stars*, London: BFI.
Foucault, Michel (1976), *Histoire de la sexualité, la volonté de savoir*, Paris:
   Gallimard.
Handyside, Fiona (2002),'Stardom and nationality: the strange case of Jean
   Seberg', *Studies in French Cinema*, 29(3), 165–76.
Jeffreys, Sheila (1990), *Anticlimax: a Feminist Perspective on the Sexual
   Revolution*, London: The Women's Press.
Johnson, Albert (1966),'*Repulsion*', *Film Quarterly*, 19:3, spring, 44–5.
McArthur, Colin (1968/9), 'Polanski', *Sight & Sound*, 38:1, winter, 14–17.
Vincendeau, Ginette (2000), *Stars and Stardom in French Cinema*, London
   and New York: Continuum.

2

Buñuel blonde

Peter William Evans

Belle de jour (1966)

R obert and Raymond Hakim gave Buñuel the opportunity of
working with Catherine Deneuve on Joseph Kessel's scandalous
1929 novel *Belle de jour*, a book that caused as much uproar on
publication as the first screening of *Un chien andalou* (1929).
Buñuel's previous film had been *Simón del desierto* (1965) which,
like most of those he had made in Mexico, was completed in two
weeks. The Hakim brothers offered him the luxury of a ten-week
working schedule on what was to become only by then his third film
in colour (preceded by *Robinson Crusoe*, 1952 and *La Mort en ce*
jardin, 1956). Buñuel had already admired Catherine Deneuve in
Polanski's *Repulsion*, a film exposing the darker side of the innocent
ingénue who had also made her mark in upbeat films like Demy's
Les Parapluies de Cherbourg. The two sides of the Deneuve persona
– one, exemplified by what Michael Wood has described as her
'doll-like innocence' (2000: 17), the other concealing inner turmoil
beneath outward self-possession, and repeated in later films like
Hustle (Robert Aldrich, 1975) and *The Hunger* (Tony Scott, 1983)
– play into her role as Séverine, a character of ethereal detachment,
reacting with almost spectral impassivity towards her surroundings,
as if lost in the reverie of more pressing needs and drives. Her Yves
Saint-Laurent wardrobe pins her down provisionally to the routines
of an upper middle-class milieu from which she is periodically able to
escape to a secret world of perverse desire. As 'Belle de jour', Séverine,
fleeing temporarily every day from the boredom of her marriage to
Pierre (Jean Sorel), a respectful well-to-do, or as M. Husson (Michel
Piccoli) christens him, a 'boy scout' of a doctor, is indeed trapped in
chronological time – she can only be at Mme Anais's house of shame
'from 2 to 5, but no later than 5' ('de 2 heures à 5 heures, mais
pas plus tard que 5 heures') – seemingly replaying through unconscious and conscious drives the latent meanings of her time-warped
memories of sexual abuse as an 11–year-old child, to which there is
a significant flashback before she embarks on her career as a high-
class prostitute. Séverine's frigidity is to be understood as caused
by trauma, a condition perfectly exemplified by Deneuve's glacial
expression, gilded coiffure and a body often shrouded in polar-
white costumes, photographed by Sacha Vierny in an evenly lit style
that stresses the materiality of the *haute bourgeoise mise-en-scène*.
Avoiding complex effects of contrast and shadow, the lighting style

provides the ideal environment for commentary on the comforting but to Séverine's mind limited rewards of materialism.

For all its aura of Parisian chic, and for all its indebtedness to Buñuel's many years in Mexico, the film reveals indelibly Spanish characteristics. Following its enormous success at the Venice film festival, Buñuel remarked in interview:

> I am completely rooted in Spanish culture. Moreover, even if I did not want to I would continue to be Spanish. I speak five languages but all with an Aragonese accent. The Spain to which I belong is not modern Spain, but eternal Spain. The Spain of today, or of the last forty years, is not Spain
>
> (Estoy completamente enraizado en la cultura española. Incluso, aunque no lo quisiera, continuaría siendo español. Hablo cinco idiomas pero todos con acento aragonés. España, de donde soy yo, no es la España actual, sino la España eterna [...] La España actual, o la de hace 40 años, no es España). (Lanteri n.d.)

As Buñuel observes, Spain is Janus-faced, one side turned towards religion and other forms of ideological conservatism, the other towards irreverence and iconoclastic interrogation of the assumptions and beliefs supporting the pillars of conformist society. Catherine Deneuve's Gallic, unHispanic difference, ideally suited to Séverine's disengagement from her own social world, places her formally in the tradition of the *auto sacramental*, challenging the conceptual as well as the emotional responses of the audience. The *auto sacramental* was a form of early modern mystery or miracle play performed on the feast of Corpus Christi, with representative figures who exemplified aspects of Church doctrine or history. Shorn of psychological verisimilitude, the characters forced the audience to engage with conceptual moral or theological issues. *Belle de jour*, where the brothel becomes a place allowing Séverine to reenact her refusal, at her First Communion, of the Eucharist – avoiding consumption of the body and blood of Christ, in favour of the body and blood of her mortal saviours – often seems like a surrealist anti-version of the sacred prototype. The brothel stages secular not divine sacrifices in pursuit of temporal rather than eternal salvation.

The characterisation of Séverine lends itself to psychological interpretation, but Catherine Deneuve's somewhat awkward, lifeless aura also encourages reflection on the wider meanings attached to Séverine and, through her, an understanding of the rudiments of a culture somewhat predicated on guilt and mortification. The awkwardness of Catherine Deneuve's performance, ideal for the split-persona character of Séverine/Belle de jour, was to some extent the happy result of her distress on-set: '[...] *Belle de jour* ... wasn't a terribly positive experience ... Very exposed in every sense of the word, but very exposed physically, which caused me distress; I felt they showed more of me than they'd said they were going to ... There were moments when I felt totally used. I was very unhappy' (Deneuve 2006: 128).

Buñuel explained his attraction to the novel *Belle de jour* as exclusively due to its central character, Séverine:

> the character of the protagonist is well defined and pathologically accurate. Only she interests me somewhat. The novel seemed melodramatic, but well constructed. It offered me, furthermore, the possibility of introducing through images some of Séverine's daydreams, the main character, starring Catherine Deneuve, and to carry out the portrayal of a young bourgeoise masochist.
>
> (el personaje de la protagonista está bien definido y es patológicamente riguroso y exacto. Sólo ella me interesa algo. La novela me parecía melodrámatica, pero bien construída. Ofrecía además la posibilidad de introducir en imágenes algunas de las ensoñaciones diurnas de Séverine, el personaje principal, que interpretaba Catherine Deneuve, y de precisar el retrato de una joven burguesa masoquista). (Sánchez Vidal 1984: 297).

Catherine Deneuve's distress gave an edge to Buñuel's Séverine, and led to a performance combining psychological plausibility with conceptual significance. Above all, it conveyed the sense of female alienation. Comparable in some senses to Emma Bovary's, Séverine's life leads her to the point where daydreaming so dominates her thoughts that she begins to live a fantasy life even before determining to visit Mme Anaïs. In discussing Emma Bovary, Ignês Sodré refers to a romance of the mind 'so repetitive and impoverished, so lifeless it needs to be compulsively enacted in external reality' (1999: 49). Séverine dramatises herself to such an extent that the mask becomes more agreeable than the reality beneath. Daydreaming and fantasising can of course be perfectly normal activities, but Séverine's daydreaming appears to be pathological (Buñuel's word), colonising the mind, replacing life with artifice, leading to perverse relations with self and others. Deneuve's frigid persona perfectly reflects the morbidity of Séverine, deprived through pathological daydreaming of normality, frozen into the patterns of a perverse fantasy.

The conditions of this perversity demand social as well as psycho-analytical explanations, and the underlying social determinants lie as much in Spain as in Mexico – where Buñuel had lived since the early 1940s – or France, where the film was shot. For all Buñuel's disclaimers about the vanished essence in modern times of Spain's identity, his links with the country remained throughout the Franco years: his mother retained the family home in Calanda; he was in constant touch with friends who had stayed behind after the end of the civil war; he had many admirers in the world of the arts in Spain, especially in film, one of whom, Carlos Saura, had been hugely influential in arranging for his return from exile to film *Viridiana* (1961). One of the principal actors from that film, Paco Rabal, plays the part of the older gangster Hyppolite in *Belle de jour*. Buñuel was clearly abreast of ideological currents in Spain under Franco, elements of which inform his reworking of the Kessel novel, especially in relation to the place of women. Even though *Belle de jour* is a film about 1960s France, Buñuel's references to his unchanging cultural identity mean that preoccupations with Spain and Spanishness underlie to some extent the construction of Séverine.

The few progressive psychiatrists working in Spain in the 1960s included Carlos Castilla del Pino whose work, anathema to the regime, was nevertheless allowed publication on the grounds of its minority appeal. Some of his most unorthodox publications – from the Franquist perspective – concerned the place of women in Spain. In an essay on the alienation of women, Castilla del Pino defines prostitution as the most extreme form of this condition:

> Turning a woman into a mere appetising thing represents the most brutalising form of alienation. It is, in short, a form of prostitution of her own self.

> (... convertida la mujer en mera cosa apetecible, signifique la más embru-tecedora forma de alienación. Es, para decirlo con pocas palabras, una forma prostituida de su propio ser). (1971: 26).

Séverine's visits to Mme Anaïs's house of shame are partly readable as expressions of this idea: the hyperbolised dramatisation of the reduction of women to mere gratifiers of male desire. The memory of abuse as a child points to the widely held notion that women, unlike men, direct their anger and humiliation violently towards not others but the self. And yet, beyond this negative assessment of the psychosocial status of women in late 1960s Spain, Séverine's irresistible attraction to the secret address at no. 11 Rue Jean de Saumur, also reveals, in addition to instincts for self-harm, transgressive impulses that acknowledge the alienation of her own and perhaps all similarly constrained women. The extreme 'masochistic' measures taken by Séverine to satisfy obscure desires entail challenges to class, economy, sex and religion. From the point of view of class, she exchanges the *soignée* milieux of her *haute bourgeoise* activities – luxurious apartment, tennis club, skiing resorts – for contact with salesmen, gangsters and whores. If marriage is above all a way of maintaining class barriers, prostitution is at the very least a sort of carnivalesque assertion of classlessness. In the bourgeois world Séverine is a kept woman, denied no luxury but unemployed; at the brothel she earns a wage. 'Frigid' in her marriage to Pierre, she learns to become polymorphously perverse in the company of clients. Frigidity has attracted the attention of leading Freudians like Karl Abraham and Karen Horney, both of whom identify the condition with 'the masculinity complex of woman' (Freud, 1977; Abraham [1920] 1927; Horney, 1967: 74). According to this argument, unable to express sexual desires in her own conventional and patriarchal relationship with Pierre, Séverine finds in the brothel a convenient space in which, without wishing to compromise her marriage, affection for Pierre and the comforts of a bourgeois habitus, she can freely indulge her sexual fantasies. Masochistic submission to the Japanese client, lesbian attraction to Mme Anaïs and, above all perhaps, waiving the fee for her young gold-toothed gangster, are examples of her newly discovered powers. The brothel is also readable as the site of the blasphemous parody of the mass, where only secular deities are worshipped and consumed in acts of carnal worship.

At the very least, the brothel allows Séverine to resist some of the pressures, especially infantilisation, to which she is subjected in the outside world. But, characteristically, the infantilisation of women referred to by Castilla del Pino (59), the process through which in reactionary ideologies women are made to depend on men, is given both straight and ironic expression in *Belle de jour*. Often dressed in the conventional world like a schoolgirl, drawing the comment from M. Husson that she seems like a 'collégienne précoce', Séverine also becomes one of the 'enfants' in Mme Anais's establishment. The 'collégienne précoce' is the living proof of that infantilisation to which Castilla del Pino refers:

It could be argued that the adoption of the 'woman's function' does not only bring with it her infantilization but also the need to maintain her regression and immaturity [...] A 'mature' woman appears 'less' of a woman to herself, because she identifies herself, and is identified, with the male. When the woman becomes a 'lady', fundamentally through age, she lives and is made to live out her role in a different way, less overtly sexualised than in previous stages of her life. Thus, the best way of prolonging her function as sex object lies in the preservation, usually in unreal ways, of the attributes attached to that object.

(Puede decirse que la asunción de la 'función de mujer' no sólo conlleva su infantilismo por sí, sino además la necesidad de mantener su regresión y su inmadurez [...] Una mujer 'madura' parece a sí misma ser 'menos' mujer, en la medida en que se identifica, y se la identifica, con el varón [...] Cuando la mujer deviene en 'señora', fundamentalmente por su edad, vive y se la hace vivir su función con 'otro' carácter, por decirlo así, menos directamente sexuado que en etapas precedentes. De esta forma, la mejor manera de perpetuar su función de objeto erótico estriba en la conservación, la mayor parte de las veces irreal, de los rasgos que a este objeto caracteriza). (59)

He develops the argument by claiming that this process, preserving the woman as an object of male sexual gratification, eventually leads to frigidity, a rejection of the status conferred upon her by her conventional milieu:

Frigidity, the multiple and frequent sexual difficulties, are an expression of an unconscious rejection, of a hostility towards the passive dependency expected of the woman.

(La frigidez, los múltiples y frecuentísimos trastornos de carácter sexual, son expresión de un rechazo subconsciente, de una negativa a culminar la relacion pasivodependiente a que se le impulsara). (60)

As she sits at the end of the film in front of her disabled and blinded husband Pierre, Séverine gives the impression of a woman, like Jane Eyre beside Mr Rochester, who has avenged herself on the system that would reduce her to a sexual plaything, an infantilised china-doll of a wife. Not wholly satisfied by the life of a whore either, she has at least used the brothel, in no way here treated as an alternative sexual utopia, as a space of self-discovery, an underworld from which she has attempted to rescue her inner identity. Catherine Deneuve's difficult, even unhappy, experiences on *Belle de jour* register the ambiguity of Buñuel's deeply troubled Séverine, who progresses from observer – the prostitute encouraged in her initiation by Mme Anaïs to watch through the peephole at the sexual antics of the customers – to participant in the *liaisons dangereuses* of the brothel. In the process, Catherine Deneuve becomes, as in *Tristana*, fascinating as much as for her own specularisation as for the arabesques of desire performed by the clients chez Mme Anaïs to which – through her – we are provocatively introduced.

Tristana (1970)

The darker shades of the Deneuve persona are in even greater evidence in *Tristana*. Made, in a Spain still ruled by Franco, four years after *Belle de jour*, it was a film from which although by all accounts she was still difficult on the set (Sánchez Vidal 1984: 327–8), Catherine Deneuve retained far happier memories: '*Tristana* is one of my favourite films. Personally, as an actress, I prefer *Tristana* to *Belle de jour*' (Deneuve 2005: 130).

By now accustomed to Buñuel's association with Catherine Deneuve, Spanish critics gave her performance in *Tristana* a largely positive reception. A. Martínez Tomás in *La Vanguardia* (1 April 1970) wrote: 'Perhaps she is not entirely the Iberian Tristana, but she is as close to perfect as possible' ('Tal vez no da del todo la figura de la Tristana ibérica, pero lleva a término una labor artística que se aproxima a lo perfecto'). The critic in *ABC* was equally flattering:

> Catherine Deneueve shows that her inclusion was justified. She is excellent as the protagonist: the innocent, disorientated girl who later becomes a kind of monster, obsessed with the idea of avenging herself on the guardian who stole her honour.

> (Catherine Deneuve demuestra que su inclusión estuvo justificada. Da muy bien a la protagonista: la muchacha inocente, desorientada, que luego se convierte en una especie de monstruo, obsesionada por la idea de chasquear al protector que la deshonró). (Anon, 1970).

Occasionally, the credit for Deneuve's performance is couched in exaggeratedly patriotic terms: 'finally a Spanish Buñuel film: *Tristana*' ('al fin un Buñuel español: *Tristana*') (Casado et al. 1970: n.p.); or:

> The sublime, refined, beautiful and elegant Catherine Deneuve is more expressive than on other occasions, something I imagine also down to the director. As far as she is concerned the greatest sensation she is going to create with female audiences will be related to her costumes, which are up to date and characterised by maxi skirt, given the changeableness and shifts of fashion.

(La excelsa, fina, guapa y elegante Catherine Deneuve está más expresiva que otras veces, lo que también me imagino que será debido al director. Respecto a ella, estoy seguro que lo que más sensación va a causar entre el público femenino será su vestuario, absolutamente actual y 'maxifaldoso', por aquello de la volubilidad y vueltas atrás de la moda). (Horno 1970: 7).

The references to Buñuel's handling of Deneuve are in line with many reviewers' comments about his return to a directly Spanish subject. *Tristana* was the second of Buñuel's films inspired by Spain's foremost realist novelist, Benito Pérez Galdós (1843–1920). *Nazarín* (novel: 1895; film: 1958) was an earlier stab at a Galdós novel (*Viridiana*, 1961, is also loosely based on Galdós's *Halma,* 1895). In all three cases Buñuel changes the time and place of the originals: *Nazarín* substitutes Madrid for Mexico; *Viridiana* updates the time scale to the 1960s; and *Tristana* transfers the action from Madrid to Toledo, trading the 1890s setting for the 1920s, compounding interest in provincialism with attention to the ideological premises of the Primo de Rivera dictatorship (1923–1930) and the emergence of the Second Republic (1931–1936). In *Tristana* the double-sidedness of the Deneuve persona is even more openly displayed as, in the role of Tristana, she is transformed from innocent ingénue into ice maiden *femme fatale*, the avenger of her own dishonour when she accelerates the demise of her abusive husband and former guardian (Fernando Rey) on a dark and wintry night by opening even wider his bedroom window as he struggles in bed against a fatal illness.

The metamorphosis is achieved in a number of ways: words, actions, and, above all, cosmetics and dress. As theorists like Elizabeth Wilson, Stella Bruzzi, Pamela Church Gibson, Sarah Street and others have argued, dress has come to be seen as playing a vital performative role as an extension of inner identity, potentially either camouflaging or asserting an inner self. In *Tristana*, the heroine's transformation from tainted waif into exterminating angel is measured among other ways through costume (a wardrobe created under Buñuel's supervision by Cornejo) across a time span that charts her surrender from Deneuve's girlish innocence to the Grand Guignol masquerade of Rivierian awe and dread (Riviere 1964: 35). We see her at first dressed in black, in mourning for her mother. The blackness, though, points ahead, beyond respect for a lost parent, to the sable thoughts and desires she will later harbour for her guardian whose unwelcome attentions lead to his sorry demise. Early on she is every inch the schoolgirl as she romps in her plaits with her young friends, the bell-ringer's son and Saturno (Jesús Fernández), the deaf-mute son of her guardian Don Lope's maid, Saturna (Lola Gaos). The game they play – chasing one another up the bell tower – carries a sexual innuendo, suggesting the curiosity of youngsters exploring the mysteries of the body and the urges of blossoming sexual desire. But even here, in the germination of late adolescent libido, morbid anxieties emerge. At the top of the tower, as Tristana plays with the bell clapper, her happy girlish expression gives way to a look of horror as she suddenly sees in the bell not the clapper but the severed head of her guardian. The film cuts to show Tristana in bed waking from a nightmare, being comforted by her bedside at first by Saturna and then by Don Lope, who remarks that dreaming is no bad thing, since only the dead are denied the privilege. He tells Tristana that she screamed as if she had seen the devil himself, and adds that when she was a little girl she used to scream at him in just the same way. With Saturna now out of the room looking for a *tisane* to help soothe her troubled mistress, Buñuel shoots the scene in close-up. The sombre colour of Tristana's mourning clothes have been usurped by the white of her dressing gown. She sits up in a two-shot that contrasts the fresh beauty of the vulnerable waif with the pitiful sight of the elderly guardian who ministers to her. Her auburn hair – no longer Séverine's golden helmet – released at night from its daytime plaits, tumbles over the side of her face, adding lushness and softness to her perfectly chiselled regular features. This picture of tender beauty is matched with the lined and bearded appearance of a man whose self-definition as Old Nick himself is made only partially in jest. The white of Tristana's nightgown exposes the innocence beneath the darkness of daytime mourning in a scene where darkness is now unambiguously identified with Don Lope, her eventual tormentor, here dressed in a shadowy dressing gown.

Before the scene ends, Don Lope leaves his mark. Noticing that Tristana's nightgown is unbuttoned, he covers up her bosom. As he exits, the camera remains fixed on Tristana's face, long enough to catch her lowering her lids, suddenly transfixed by foreboding, that 'inquiétude' (a favourite word of Buñuel's) so characteristic of the surrealist aesthetic. She lifts her eyes, looks in the direction of Don Lope's departure, parts her lips very slightly as if releasing an incomplete sigh of alarm, making the connection now between her guardian and the sexual demon who is about to damage irreparably her future. The moment is reminiscent of many a scene from the Gothic narratives, so admired by Buñuel, of defenceless women held captive by ruthless men.

Tristana has premonitions of seduction by her surrogate father, and while these remain unconverted into experience, her costumes, once a decent period of mourning has passed, begin to reflect her gradual loss of innocence. Her first change of costume occurs during a promenade in the streets of Toledo. Here she wears a smart ankle length 'maxi' brown outfit, with matching brown shawl and white hat. Girlish charm has been supplanted by womanly sophistication. As they pass a couple pushing a pram, Don Lope rails against marriage, exclaiming that love must remain free of ties, contracts, obligations, adding that Tristana should never marry. But these are hollow words for, like Tristana, a character undergoing metamorphosis, Don Lope will become transformed, abandoning libertarianism for convention when he later succumbs to marriage to his ward. His liberal politics and anti-clericalism forgotten, he befriends traditionalists and conservatives, a transformation most wittily portrayed in a late scene at home over chocolate and *churros* (fritters) with a group of priests. Here, though, he is still the libertine, bold enough to ask Tristana her opinion of him. When she answers that she finds him unobjectionable, he requests a kiss. Not satisfied with a peck on his cheek, he pulls her lips to his own in a gesture that leaves her at first amused, and then mildly horrified. As she smiles, she reveals minatory teeth – the one aspect of her looks over which Deneuve has expressed dissatisfaction – in a way that warns the audience of what Jo Labanyi, in a Barbara Creed-inspired piece, has referred to as her castratory power (1999: 76–92). This scene is remarkable not only for the portrayal of the easy abandonment of previously held firm principles by a man hitherto committed to radical views, but also for the power of an *amour fou* to turn an elderly man into a plaything of desire, clutching at the straws of convention, relying on those very laws of which he had once been contemptuous, to force a woman in the only way known to him to keep her from flight. Don Lope joins a list of jealous old men in classic Spanish narratives from Cervantes and Calderón down to Valle-Inclán and García Lorca who resort to the law to hold on to the women they love. Depriving them of self-determination through independent careers, these men continue in the 1920s during the dictatorships of Primo de Rivera – the setting of the film – and of Franco – the time of its making – to invoke the demands of a conservative ideology to keep their women at home, an ideology whose most grotesque meanings through reference to a well-known Spanish proverb, are later given visual expression in the amputated leg of Tristana, the emblem of all ideologised women in Spain: 'decent women should have a broken leg and stay at home' ('La mujer honrada, la pierna quebrada y en casa'). When we do see Tristana at home again, she wears a light-coloured, chequered dress, buttoned up at the front, attending to some household chores, before being whisked off to bed for the first seduction by her guardian. In public she is an object of conspicuous consumption, the valuable object possessed by Don Lope, on display for his benefit; at home, she takes charge of household duties and is expected to be ever ready for sex.

For the moment, though, in the walkabout scene, Tristana is only beginning to discover the ambiguities and restrictions of her position and that of all women in Spain. As they enter the cathedral, she dwells on the face of the statue of an archbishop, whose body lies in the tomb beneath it. As in the nightmare scene, two faces are now joined together, Tristana's and the archbishop's, the latter's recumbent beneath the former's. Both wear hats, the smooth whiteness of the brim matching the white lapels on Tristana's brown outfit, as if mirroring the marbled texture of the archbishop's mitre. Catherine Deneuve's famed expressionless pallor matches the lifeless mien of the venerable divine. Tristana's quest is perhaps the result of fascination with the identity of a figure so honoured by the church but, as in the nightmare scene, the moment portends the future. The archbishop is a flashforward to Don Lope himself, who will overthrow his diabolical aura for the pious identity he acquires from his clerical friends. Most significantly, though, Tristana occupies the superior position, leaning over a recumbent archbishop/guardian, a prophesy of the role reversal that will soon take place in relations with her guardian, as Don Lope becomes the victim, Tristana his tormentor.

The film continues to monitor Tristana's progress from girlish innocence to womanly experience through costume and cosmetics, a process that reaches its most Grand Guignol moment when, by now an amputee, Tristana displays herself to Saturno, becoming increasingly aware of her powers, a classic *femme fatale* controlling men through sex. The mixed feelings of awe and dread felt by insecure men in the presence of such fatal beauties is even sketched out through the impact of the mature Tristana on the still immature deaf-mute Saturno. The measure of the growing distance between these two characters is made through costume and cosmetics, Saturno remaining unchanged from his look at the beginning of the film, Tristana now almost unrecognisable in her appearance as a *señora de clase acomodada* (well-to-do bourgeoisie).

Following her return to Don Lope's household, after a brief fling with the painter Horacio (Franco Nero), Tristana is struck by an illness that requires the amputation of a leg. By means of this mutilation, Buñuel playfully recalls the seventeenth-century miracle by the Virgin Mary involving the restoration of the severed limb of Miguel Juan Pellicer, a labourer from Calanda in Aragón, Buñuel's native town. Tristana consents to an offer of marriage from Lope but in the scene prior to the wedding, Saturno follows her to her room, where her prosthetic leg lies discarded on the bed (recalling, as Victor Fuentes (2005) points out, the photographs of Man Ray), as she makes up at her dressing table, wearing an expensive brown nightgown. In the hallowed tradition of a certain dark tendency in Spanish art, characterised most especially perhaps by the paintings and drawings of Goya, a fellow Aragonese, Buñuel combines the sacred and the profane through his own Sadean fantasy of the cruel surrealist temptress, the Tristana of Catherine Deneuve.

Saturno pleads with her for a sexual favour, and only departs on the promise that she will display herself to him from her bedroom balcony. He leaves her room and takes up a position in the garden below. Tristana goes to the balcony, her hair tied back in a bun, eyes and lips heavily cosmeticised, ears adorned with expensive dangling pendants. Saturno gestures for her to expose herself; the camera shows Tristana in close-up unfastening her robe; a smile begins to spread across her face. Buñuel cuts to a medium shot of the boy, stunned in wonder and delight at the sight before him. The camera reverts to Tristana in close-shot, and now the smile begins to widen to reveal those minatory teeth, or *vagina dentata,* a gesture that seems to be a cross between pleasure at the effect her body has produced on the boy, and satisfaction at the extent of her powers over men. Buñuel cuts again to the boy. This time, as he forms his hand into a fist and places it against his mouth, the memory of Adam's consumption of the forbidden fruit is deliberately called to mind; the boy's expression continues to be a mixture of fascination and anxiety, as he retreats into the bushes. Furthermore, as the Madonna is also a mother, Tristana's role as the *femme fatale* is designed to provoke in Saturno's mind the contradictory feelings for his own mother, with Tristana as the screen for their projection. His deaf-muteness may be read as a sign of castration by his phallicised mother, the Saturna who like her mythical male precursor has devoured her son emotionally and ideologically, socialised by a patriarchal ideology represented by Don Lope, in the same way that Tristana herself has been partially devoured by that system, and of which the amputation of her leg is the most disturbing sign. Saturno displays the infant's delayed ambivalence towards the mother: in awe of her sexually, dreading her powers over him, attempting to distance himself from her, in need of self-sufficiency, yet unable to sever the umbilical cord. As this scene of Tristana's disrobing is followed immediately by shots of various images of the Madonna in the church where Tristana is about to become a bride in black, a contrast is made between the Edenic temptress and the virginal ideal revered by Christianity.

The fantasy of virginal innocence, of the 'collégienne précoce' prototype introduced by Catherine Deneuve in *Belle de jour*, represents Don Lope's desire for release from his rakish past as well as the pursuit through Tristana of his own lost youth, her virginity offering the additional delight of what Freud refers to as 'no memory of sexual relations with another' (1977: 265), making of his object of desire an exclusive, hitherto untouched, possession in the hope of creating 'a state of bondage in the woman which guarantees that possession of her shall continue undisturbed and make her able to resist new impressions and enticements from outside' (265). That fantasy fades as Tristana turns into a monstrous blend of biblical vamps from Eve to Judith – dreaming of Lope's severed head – and beyond.

The juxtaposition of the images of *femme fatale* and virgin mother recreates the ambivalent treatment of women in western culture: submitted on the one hand, to a process of idealisation as a defence mechanism and, on the other, to demonisation, and transformation into sirens to counter the imagined threat. Tristana submits to the socialising process, but in a way that recalls Riviere's theory of the masquerade (Riviere, 1986), exaggerating her femininity in order to conceal her true identity, all the better through immersion in the ways of the world to taste its forbidden fruits. In the process, Deneuve's Tristana contributed to what Isabel Santaolalla has described as

Buñuel's masterly account of 'female agency in a male-dominated world' (2005: n.p.).

The transformation of Tristana from innocent waif to crippled *señorona*, like the metamorphosis of Catherine Deneuve from malleable, passive ingénue into sophisticated temptress, remains intriguingly ambiguous. The choice of Deneuve, the epitome of French chic, appears to contradict the film's portrayal of Castilian provincialism. Buñuel himself recognised the disparity between the Tristanas of Deneuve and Galdós (Sánchez Vidal, 1984: 325). And yet, as with Carlos Saura's use of Geraldine Chaplin, Deneuve offered Buñuel – seduced as much by the conceptually oriented writers of Spain's Golden Age, especially Gracián, as by the Gothic and romantic progenitors of surrealism – irresistible opportunities for indulging his taste for the cool, distancing aesthetic that so characterise his films.

Catherine Deneuve, both as Tristana and as 'Belle de jour', allowed him to indulge an incurable fascination with the ice-maiden prototype, that incarnation of a fantasy of Olympian pallid aloofness so fitting for demystifying the equivocal sensibilities of the threatened male.[1]

Note

1 I am indebted to Javier Herrera and other members of staff at the Filmoteca Nacional in Madrid for allowing me to consult material in the Buñuel archive.

Works cited

Abraham, Karl ([1920] 1927), 'Manifestations of the female castration complex', in *Selected Papers on Psychoanalysis*, trans. Douglas Bryan and Alex Strachey, New York: Basic Books.

Anon. (1970), 'Catherine Deneuve demuestra que su inclusión estuvo justificada', *ABC*, 31 April: n.p.

Bruzzi, Stella and Pamela Church Gibson (2000), ed., *Fashion Cultures: Theories, Explorations and Analysis*, London: Routledge.

Casado, Francisco, J. I. García Gutiérrez and Juan Fabián Delgado (1970), 'Al fin, un Buñuel español: *Tristana*', *Correo de Andalucía*, 2 April: n.p.

Castilla del Pino, Carlos (1971), *Cuatro ensayos sobre la mujer*, Madrid: Alianza.

Deneuve, Catherine ([2004] 2005), *Close Up and Personal*, trans. Polly McLean, London: Orion.

Freud, Sigmund (1977), *On Sexuality. Three Essays on the Theory of Sexuality and Other Works*, trans. James Strachey and edited by Angela Richards, Harmondsworth: Pelican Books.

Fuentes, Victor (2005), *La mirada de Buñuel; cine, literatura y vida*, Madrid: Tabla Rasa.

Horney, Karen (1967), *Feminine Psychology*, ed. with introd. by Harold Kelman, London: Routledge & Kegan Paul.

Horno, María Luisa (1970), 'Tristana', *Aragón Express*, 30 March: 7.

Klein, Melanie and Joan Riviere (1964), *Love Hate and Reparation*, London: W.W. Norton.

Labanyi, Jo (1999), 'Fetishism and the Problem of sexual difference in Buñuel's *Tristana* (1970)', in Evans, Peter William (ed.), *Spanish Cinema: The Auteurist Tradition*, Oxford: Oxford University Press; pp. 76–92.

Lanteri, Roger [n.d.], 'Luis Buñuel. Ovaciones en Venecia al presentarse *Belle de jour*', Filmoteca Nacional, Madrid, Archive 184:19.

Martínez Tomás, A. (1970), 'Tristana', *La Vanguardia*, 1 April: n.p.

Riviere, Joan (1986), 'Womanliness as a masquerade', in V. Burgin, J. Donald and C. Kaplan (eds), *Formations of Fantasy*, London: Routledge, pp. 35–44.

Sánchez Vidal, Agustín (1984), *Luis Buñuel; obra cinematográfica*, Madrid: Ediciones J.C..

Santaolalla, Isabel (2005), 'Tristana' in *Tristana. Luis Buñuel*, sleeve notes, BFI DVD.

Sodré, Ignês (1999), 'Death and daydreaming: Madame Bovary', in Bell, David (ed.), *Psychoanalysis and Culture: A Kleinian Perspective*, London: Duckworth.

Street, Sarah (2001), *Costume and Drama; Dress Codes in Popular Film*, London: Wallflower.

Wilson, Elizabeth (1985), *Adorned in Dreams: Fashion and Modernity*, London: Virago.

Wood, Michael (2000), *Belle de jour*, London: BFI.

3

Demy and Deneuve: the princess and the post-'68 fairy tale

Susan Weiner

In the documentary *L'Univers enchanté de Jacques Demy/The World of Jacques Demy* (Agnès Varda, 1995), Catherine Deneuve paid the filmmaker an actress's greatest compliment when she described him as 'the charming prince who woke Sleeping Beauty'. It was, though, a mutual awakening. Deneuve's screen persona and Demy's cinema developed in tandem in the first decade of their careers, each a showcase for the other. Demy's first major film, *Les Parapluies de Cherbourg/The Umbrellas of Cherbourg* (1964), was also the revelation of Deneuve in her first major role. In *Les Demoiselles de Rochefort/The Young Girls of Rochefort* (1967), she and Demy revealed their capacity for comedy. In *Peau d'âne/Donkey Skin* (1970), Demy's visual rendering of Charles Perrault's classic fairy tale places Deneuve at the center of its workings of enchantment.

Deneuve's fairy-tale metaphor also pays homage to Demy's own playful description of his filmmaking style. *Cinéma en-chanté*: the pun communicates on several levels. Like the new-wave directors who were his peers, Demy favoured on-location shooting and original scripts. But in his first two 'enchanted' films, *Cherbourg* and *Rochefort*, Demy chose his locations the better to transform them. Typical provincial façades and interiors were painted over with brilliant colour, actors' costumes designed to coordinate or clash with the decor. In tandem with visual enchantment, Demy's cinema is also *en-chanté*, 'in song'. Demy took the movie musical in a direction different from Hollywood genre. He did not cast actors for their voices: all of the singing in his films is dubbed. And in *Cherbourg*, all of the dialogues are sung: Michel Legrand's score wove Demy's lyrics into the natural musicality of French language and conversation. While *Rochefort* was not, as *Cherbourg* was, an opera of the everyday, the film's dialogues and songs showcase the recognisable rhythms of social exchange, blurring the boundary between French spoken and sung. The viewer initially experiences Demy's *cinéma en-chanté* as pure exuberance – a quality that already makes it an odd entry in the annals of cinema history. French auteur cinema rarely expresses exuberance without political or social critique. The realities underlying enchantment in *Cherbourg and Rochefort* – the grey façades of the post-war provinces, the Algerian war, the discomfort of class differences, the impossibility of the heterosexual couple – pass many spectators by. Demy's cinema thus has the rare quality of appealing to adults and to children, to cinephiles and the general public alike.

In these early Demy films, enchantment communicated just as subtly the unsettling nature of the screen image that was beginning to take shape for Deneuve. In *Cherbourg* and *Rochefort*, the sexual subjectivity of Deneuve's character is synonymous with a purity her somewhat tawdry circumstances cannot entirely sully. As Geneviève in *Cherbourg*, she has sex as an expression of true love, becomes pregnant, then saves her mother from bankruptcy by marrying for money. In *Rochefort*, she is both the one-time lover of an abstract-art gallery's crass owner, and the timeless 'feminine ideal' and uncanny double of a figurative painter, who has never set eyes on her and whom she'll never meet. A darker version of this persona was drawn out in the first decade of her career by Roman Polanski and Luis Buñuel, as the previous two chapters of this volume have shown. Deneuve's projection of purity was an ideal vehicle through which to explore female perversity – primarily as a function of mind. The central yet ambiguous place accorded to fantasy in both *Repulsion* and *Belle de jour* constitutes the link between the Deneuve of *Cherbourg* and *Rochefort*, and *Donkey Skin*. In *Donkey Skin*, Deneuve plays a princess who must thwart the threat of incest, a narrative Demy considered inherently perverse (Simsolo 1971: 74). But unlike the original fairy tale, in Demy's rewriting the princess's urgent trajectory to safeguard her purity is revealed to be at the end of the film no more than the effects of fantasy – and not primarily her own. Demy's adaptation reorients fairy-tale logic in his own enchanted direction.

Perrault's 'Donkey Skin' tells the story of a princess, victim of her mother's deathbed wish that the king only remarry one wiser and more beautiful than she – a creature the queen is confident does not exist. Soon after, the king concludes that the only one in the land to satisfy and surpass so lofty an ideal is his own daughter. The troubled princess follows her fairy godmother's advice. She presents to her father a series of requests to test his desire, beginning with the fabrication of three dresses, in the colours of the weather, the moon and the sun. When the king complies with her final request for the skin of his prized possession, a donkey that excretes gold, the fairy godmother's final advice to the princess is to flee.

Disguised in the donkey skin, the once beautiful princess turns frightful, but not frightening: in the faraway land where she finds refuge, villagers who scorn her solitary filthiness derisively dub her Donkey Skin. To them she is indistinguishable from her ubiquitous donkey skin. In guise of solace, the fairy godmother has endowed the exiled princess with magical access to her dresses and jewels, limited to the privacy of her own shack. As luck would have it, a prince comes upon the shack and glimpses through a keyhole Donkey Skin dressed in her former finery. The prince falls in love on the spot, returns to his castle, and takes to his bed. There he devises a two-part strategy to make Donkey Skin his wife and future queen.

Most importantly for Demy's adaptation, Donkey Skin is no innocent, as the narrator only belatedly reveals. Well aware of the prince's admiring gaze at her keyhole, she acts with him to carry out his plan. Donkey Skin receives an order that would otherwise be puzzling: to prepare a cake for the prince. She intentionally allows a valuable ring to drop into the batter, thus enabling the prince to articulate the second part of his strategy: he'll marry the one who fits the ring. In the end, Donkey Skin's royalty is rendered. She and the prince marry with great pomp, she reconciles with her chastened father, and the fairy godmother tells the story to all present at the ceremony. In the happy ending, Donkey Skin gets her man, and the admiration she deserves.

Demy worked with Perrault's version of 'Donkey Skin', a 1694 verse narrative written for adults and published separately from his *Mother Goose Tales/Histoires ou contes du temps passé, avec des moralités: Contes de ma mère l'Oye.*[1] The narrative itself dates from the Middle Ages, but structurally it is ageless for Freudian critics. 'Donkey Skin' bears all the signs of the family romance, beginning with the ostensibly unintended rivalry of queen and princess for the king's affections. The king's decision to marry the princess, her obedience to the ill-fated strategy that would thwart his powers, and the princess's taking on of their mutual shame in the guise of his donkey's skin, are read as figures of fantasy in the evolution of female psychosexual identity (Seifert, 1996). But what has entranced generations of French-speaking children and made its heroine a cultural icon are the tale's visual elements, specifically its evocations of costumes and disguises. Fans can buy porcelain reproductions of the princess clad in her donkey skin. To the delight of neighbours young and old, a florist's recent window display in Paris's fourth arrondissement featured a life-size diorama of Donkey Skin in her shack, in the throes of kitchen preparation. Several illustrated editions of the tale are currently in print, as is a paper-doll set. In June 2005, fashion designer Jean-Charles de Castelbajac created three dream bedrooms in the indefinable colours of the moon, the sun and the weather for the Paris branch of the upscale home design shop Ligne Roset.[2] Canadian new-media artist Valérie Lamontagne also referenced the three dresses named in Perrault's tale as the point of departure for a 2005 installation and performance. Lamontagne created three mutable costumes using wireless and solar energy to chart weather patterns from different geographic locations and at different times of the day.[3] In the transformation of Donkey Skin to popular icon, dresses and donkey skin alike are imbued with a sense of play and of the mobility of identity. The threat of incest that moves the fairy-tale princess from one costume to the next is simply conjured away.[4]

Demy, on the other hand, kept incest centre stage, and playfully so. In the colour, costume, and song that had become his trademark, he refashioned Perrault's tale to appeal to adults and children alike. Demy's *Donkey Skin* is arguably an equal source of the tale's iconic status in France today, and largely because of Deneuve. As she observed in *The World of Jacques Demy*, children have looked at her open-mouthed for decades; to them she is not a star, but a fairy-tale heroine come to life. Deneuve considered *Donkey Skin* more broadly appealing than either *Cherbourg* or *Rochefort*: 'Of all Jacques's films, I think it's the one that's gone the furthest' ('Je crois que c'est le film de Jacques qui a le plus voyagé'). Demy's cinematic style transforms the tale's nightmarish qualities into a visual experience more like a dream, strange but not necessarily bad. As in the illusionistic cinema of his mentor Jean Cocteau, statues come to life, fairy-tale pastness is punctuated with twentieth-century anachronism, superimpression creates ghostly appearances, and slow motion conveys dream states. Demy added his own liberal use of jumpcuts, and fluorescent iris-outs between sequences. 'Psychedelic' is how Demy described his approach to *Donkey Skin*'s *mise-en-scène* (Simsolo 1971: 70). Sets by San Francisco designer Jim Leon quote the psychedelic artists of the late 1960s who sought to render visually the effects of hallucinogens on the mind. The kaleidoscopic patterns of the castles' stained glass windows, the placement of crumbling columns and fake flowers in lush forests and countryside shot on location, talking roses, and servants and horses coloured red and blue against the backdrop of Chambord and Le Plessis-Bourré, are among the elements that contribute to the film's oneirism. One of Leon's original posters for *Donkey Skin* is a textbook illustration of psychedelia's pop aesthetic: cartoon-like in its palette, starry purple sky, magic mushrooms, exotic birds. Deneuve with her donkey skin costume is the central image. The king in purple robes stands off to the side, as if in a corner of her mind.

Against *Donkey Skin*'s sets, Deneuve's costuming establishes the narrative trajectory of this psychedelic dream, an imposed dream that necessarily becomes her own. She dons each of the dresses in a confused state of dread and delight, finds equally confusing the fairy's decree that she cannot marry the father who has had them created for her as if by magic. The fairy's averred part in this dream of escape from incestuous desire culminates with the princess's 'change of skin', a sequence marked by the oneiric as the king lays the donkey skin on the bed where the princess pretends to sleep. His departure signals the arrival of the fairy, who finally divulges the last-resort purpose of the drastic act of skinning the donkey. Over the princess's long white nightdress, the fairy godmother drapes the skin that will disguise her head to toe, and dabs castle mud on her cheeks. Slow motion and a lateral travelling shot communicate the fluidity and long duration of the princess's dreamlike flight, through the iron gates of the castle, as she runs barefoot across the frame from right to left and off-screen. Not even the possibilities of off-screen space can alter her trajectory. Instantly she reappears on-screen, still running. She boards a horse-drawn carriage, reassuringly fairy-tale like, apparently waiting just for her. The interior is filled entirely with white feathers. The carriage begins to move; in a medium shot Deneuve's eyes flutter shut to the rhythm of carriage wheels and horses' hooves. The camera contrasts multiple times in shot–countershot of Deneuve on her featherbed with high-angle shots of the carriage moving forwards on a country road. The hovering point of view shot can be none other than the fairy's surveillance.

The princess awakens to find herself in a rickety wagon, feathers turned to hay, high-necked white nightdress now in tatters. Once again she runs across the frame in slow motion, right to left and into off-screen space, her bare feet on the forest floor and birdsong the only sounds we hear. Once again she instantly reappears on screen, and runs through a set of wooden doors that open in slow motion. A travelling shot follows her into a courtyard. Villagers absorbed in daily tasks are frozen like statues, the sole sign of life the flick of a horse's tail. It is a dream put into place by the fairy godmother; the camera establishes her point of view through travelling shots and high-angle shots, juxtaposed with medium shots of the princess as she is lulled to sleep. The insistent use of slow motion, however, communicates the princess's own experience of movement. The princess may have stepped into a dream laid out for her, but its embodied nature is hers alone. Slow motion also reminds the spectator that normal movement begins when the princess hears for the first time her new name: Donkey Skin.

The expression 'changer de peau', literally 'to change skin', idiomatically means 'to become someone else entirely'. The donkey skin makes Deneuve unrecognisable within the film's diegesis, if never to the spectator. For the most salient feature of Deneuve's disguise is its artifice. A dirty, tattered nightgown and furry animal skin could easily connote feminine nightmare, the shame of sexuality. The costume might have done just that, if Brigitte Bardot had not declined the role in 1962 when the adaptation was still just an idea (Taboulay 1996: 99). Deneuve wears the donkey skin to opposite effect. She moves about stiffly in her now humble surroundings, the animal's large head sitting on her own. Deneuve looks more like a little girl playing an uncomfortable game of dress-up with stuffed animals than a bearer of father–daughter shame. The only visual connotation for a Deneuve turned frightful but not frightening calls upon another sense: people hold their nose when she walks by.

While dressing up in a donkey skin brings no pleasure, nor does it cause suffering. The pleasures of dressing up do become hers in the privacy of her own shack, with her treasure chest of mirrors, jewels and dresses. It is easy for the spectator to forget the dresses' original meaning: they now allow Donkey Skin to play. As a sundress-clad Deneuve primps in front of a hand mirror, coiffed and bejewelled, she sings the love song without object that first enchanted the king: 'Love, love, I love you so ('Amour, amour, je t'aime tant'). In her mirror, she sees the reflection of an appreciative prince looking in through her window. Her desire, though, does not immediately mirror his own. As Perrault's Donkey Skin is no innocent, neither is Demy's. Deneuve's gaze in the mirror betrays knowing, not longing, as a strange dream turns to her own fantasy of escape. The dresses thus reveal a third meaning: they can transport her from the tawdry world to which they led.

The prince's advisers attempt to dissuade him from setting his sights on a 'scullion' ('souillon'); he insists she is a 'beauty' ('beauté'). For the prince as for the spectator, magic dress and shack are disguises under which lies beauty continuous with an essential purity. And this despite the knowing gaze we are alone to glimpse. For the princess's desire to escape is more realistic than love at first sight, and Demy infused his psychedelic fairy tale with doses of realism in *mise-en-scène* and dialogue alike. As Demy described his film in an interview in *Le Monde*, 'I think I've been true to the spirit of Perrault's tale, if not to the letter...Children are realists. They prefer truth to fantasy' ('Je crois avoir été fidèle à l'esprit (du conte de Perrault), sinon à la letter ... (L)es enfants sont réalistes. Ils préfèrent la vérité au fantastique') (Le Monde, 1970). Deneuve's gaze in the mirror doubles as a wink to the spectator, signalling the next stage of the performance. This time she will perform the role of the girl in love.

Even as she busies herself in joint strategy with the prince, Deneuve's performance of purity allows the spectator to believe she would never have dreamed extravagance, sacrifice or even escape from her donkey skin on her own. For young audiences, this is the true and human-princess nature that lies beneath Donkey Skin's story. For the rest of us, that 'nature' is always Deneuve. The star in her most outlandish roles and costumes is also always 'herself', also always her previous roles. In *Cherbourg* and *Rochefort*, Deneuve's circumstances are tawdry. That tawdriness is taken to an extreme in *Donkey Skin*: first the threat of incest, then actual dirt, as Deneuve performs her scullion chores in pigsties and barnyards. Here as well, *Donkey Skin* echoes *Belle de jour*, where dirt thrown on Séverine is fuel for her erotic fantasy. As in these earlier films, beneath the tawdry or the dirty, the projection of purity that is Deneuve's 'self' is a performance nonetheless.

That Deneuve's essence remains untouched by all forms of masquerade is highlighted in the sequence where she bakes a 'love cake' for the prince, following the recipe in song: a duet for two costumes. In shot–countershot, Deneuve sings the recipe and prepares the cake in her sun dress, while she performs *sous-chef* duties in her donkey skin. One Deneuve looks directly at the other, whether at the side of the screen or directly at the camera. Only at the last minute does she remember that her donkey-skin-disguised self should be the one to go out the door to hand the cake to the prince's messengers. Donkey Skin bakes the cake for the prince, but performs the duet in two costumes for the spectator alone. Complicity rather than voyeurism is the nature of the spectator's gaze. We know as she does that it matters little which disguise she wears. With our participation, her costume changes become inconsequential play.

Deneuve wears the costume intended to communicate her character's essential purity in a psychedelic sequence of Demy's invention,
inspired by Perrault's brief description of the sole action taken by
the neurasthenic prince. Upon finding the cake's hidden ring, he puts
it under his pillow ('Sous son chevet il le mit à l'instant'). Demy
expanded this single verse into a musical out-of-body sequence whose
costuming bears no resemblance to the rest of the film's mix of period
styles. The prince takes the ring out of his mouth, where he has been
hiding it. From the vantage point of his bed, he sees in superimpression the ghostlike figure of Donkey Skin. She wears neither donkey
skin disguise nor one of the magical dresses that first enchanted him
through the window of her shack. A flowing white gauze robe with
scattered sequins envelopes her, hippy luxe, a garment more demure
than her princess nightdress, unconstricted and yet still regal. From
the prince's sleeping body, a white-clad self rises to join her. Having
shed all signs of caste, they are equals in a shared, asexual dream.
Prince and princess tumble about on a hillside dotted with candy-
coloured fake flowers, gorge themselves on pastries and imagine an
ideal day of forbidden activities appealing to children in a late 1960s
sense of the word. 'We'll do what's forbidden/We'll smoke a pipe in
secret' ('Nous ferons ce qui est interdit/Nous fumerons la pipe en
cachette'): Demy's fantasy of liberation from royal decorum comes
straight from Haight-Ashbury in 1967, the summer of love. The
out-of-body sequence also served as Demy's return to *Rochefort* via
Deneuve – and Jacques Perrin, cast in the role of the prince. Three
years after Perrin had played the *Rochefort* sailor-artist for whom
Deneuve was the unseen ideal, in *Donkey Skin* Demy brought them
together face to face for the first time, in a fantasy encounter.

Musical sequences like the preparation of the 'love cake' and the
out-of-body encounter between prince and princess make it easy to
forget about the threat of incest. While that threat is never hidden or
denied, the psychology of father–daughter relations was not really
the issue for Demy. The facet of the family romance he sought to
explore in Perrault's tale was the mother–daughter rivalry. It is the
queen's narcissistic deathbed wish that triggers the princess's narrative trajectory in the fairy tale. Demy goes a step further: mother *is*
daughter in his *Donkey Skin*. Just as Cocteau cast Jean Marais as
both beast and prince in *La Belle et la bête/Beauty and the Beast*
(1946), Demy cast Deneuve as *Donkey Skin*'s princess and dying

queen. The embodied reality of the daughter comes to stand in for the maternal fantasy of irreplaceability, and indeed exceeds it. As the queen, Deneuve wears a dark wig, over the radiant blondeness she unmasks in her role as the daughter, 'more beautiful than the queen, and much more charming and intelligent' ('plus belle que la reine; elle la surpasse beaucoup en esprit et en agrément').

Demy takes a further cue from the original text to expand narratologically the link between mother and fairy godmother, each of whom determines in her own way the princess's fate. In Perrault's conclusion, the narrator passes on to the fairy godmother the authority to relate the story of Donkey Skin. Generous in words as in deeds, the fairy godmother fashions the princess/Donkey Skin as heroine rather than victim: 'And what she had to tell added to the final triumph for Donkey Skin' ('Et par son récit acheva/De combler Peau-d'âne de gloire'). In Demy's film, the fairy godmother offers a very different frame for the princess's tale. Her words at the end of the film completely alter the sense of all that has preceded, for princess and spectator alike. Demy's fairy appears at the wedding not as solitary storyteller, but at the king's side. In response to the princess's quizzical look, she offers a most unfairy-tale-like aside: 'Oh darling! I'm marrying your father. Try to look pleased' ('Tout est arrangé, ma fille; j'épouse votre père. Tâchez de faire bonne figure'). The silent reaction shot of Deneuve is equally unfairy-tale-like. For a moment, she is a girl annoyed with her mother; at the same time she is a woman unfairly defeated in competition for a desirable man. By putting the fairy godmother in the place she wanted to be all along – the place of the queen – Demy turns Perrault's 'happy ending' into an ambivalent one, where the cultural meaningfulness of the princess's trajectory is overturned. In the princess's silence, she sees as we do that her ordeal has served her fairy godmother first and foremost.

With godmother recast as rival rather than protectress, the lessons in exogamy of her 'incest song' and its refrain, 'children do not marry their parents, my child' ('Mon enfant, on n'épouse jamais ses parents') take on a new level of meaning. Demy's ending gestures toward another narrative that has played itself out. Like the princess, the spectator may know of the fairy's hand, but not its intention: to get her out of the picture – the picture off-screen. For the signs on-screen have been there all along. The incest song can now be heard as an oblique confession before the fact: Have no fear of getting lost, my child/I shall show you the way that I have traced without delay...

But first you must conform to the plan which I have concocted for you' ('Ne craignez pas les égarements/J'ai pour vous un chemin par mes soins tout trace .. .Il vous faut conformer au plan/Que j'ai conçu pour vous savammant'). The dresses and donkey skin that are the substance of her plan have meanings of which neither spectator nor Donkey Skin has never dreamed. Costumes and disguises for the princess, they do double duty as a series of messages sent back and forth from fairy godmother to king, tests of his power and will, strategies to deplete him. With the princess's 'monstrous' request for his 'donkey bank' ('mon âne banquier!'), the king comes to suspect the work of the fairy – a suspicion that the ending reveals to be the vestiges of their unresolved story.

More subtly, and more audaciously, Demy's ending puts a new fantasy into place by calling into question the incest taboo, at least in this fairy-tale world. In a land where roses can talk, statues come to life, a donkey excretes gold and fairies fly about, perhaps the sole reason for preventing the king's marriage to his daughter is the fairy godmother's own. Ultimately, her response as to why the princess cannot marry her father when he clearly loves her so deeply is a personal one. She concedes that at one time, the king behaved badly with her. And 'fairies, like women, do hold grudges' ('les fées, comme les femmes, ont de la rancune'). By calling into question the incest taboo, Demy's ending also reminds us that incest is, after all, what *Donkey Skin* is all about. As a prince charming comes on scene and a more familiar fairy-tale trajectory unfolds, it is all too easy to forget that the threat of incest is what triggered the narrative chain in the first place. Deneuve's performance is central to Demy's reorientation of the text of the fairy tale in his own enchanted direction. As she enters a dream not of her own making, Deneuve continues to signify purity beneath the play of costumes and disguises and their fluctuating meanings. At the same time, non-verbal moments in which Deneuve signals that purity is as much artifice as costume reinforce Demy's own brand of 'enchantment', where 'reality' can creep back in at any given moment. In the prolonged 'happily ever after' long shot that brings *Donkey Skin* to an end, Deneuve stands next to her fairy godmother and between king and prince, all of them dressed in white. The photograph-like immobility places the ambiguities of Deneuve's screen purity within the timeless image of the traditional family romance.

Notes

1 All quotations are from the tale accessible online both in French and in English: http://www.anthologie.free.fr/anthologie/perrault/conte02.htm http://www.pitt.edu/~dash/perrault11.html
2 http://www.ldbinteriortextiles.com/pdf/aug_2005/Vive-la-Difference.cfm
3 www.mobilegaze.com
4 In *Peau d'âne* (Paris: Stock, 1993), Christine Angot's recent rewriting of Perrault, her autobiographical lens of incest survivor brings to the forefront the narrative's traumatic core underneath its fanciful disguises.

Works cited

Le Monde, 17 December 1970: 'Interview with Jacques Demy'.
http://www.anthologie.free.fr/anthologie/perrault/conte02.htm
http://www.ldbinteriortextiles.com/pdf/aug_2005/Vive-la-Difference.cfm
www.mobilegaze.com
http://www.pitt.edu/~dash/perrault11.html
Angot, Christine (1993), *Peau d'âne*, Paris: Stock.
Morin, Edgar (1957), *Les Stars*, Paris: Seuil.
Seifert, Ruth (1996), 'The second front: the logic of sexual violence in wars', *Womens' Studies International Forum*, 19, 35–43.
Simsolo, Noël (1971), 'Entretien avec Jacques Demy', *La Revue du cinéma*, 247, February.
Taboulay, Camille (1996), *Le Cinéma enchanté de Jacques Demy*, Paris: Cahiers du cinéma.

4

Deneuve's Italian interludes

Pauline Small

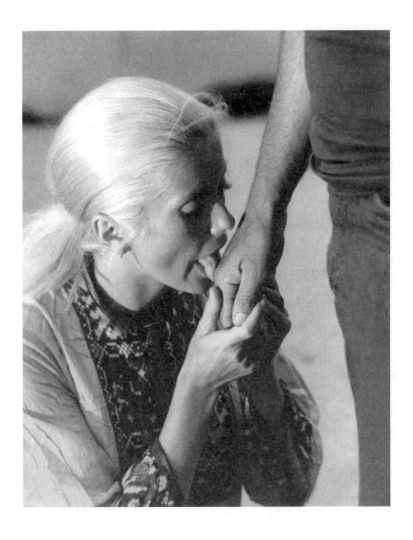

Catherine Deneuve's Italian career is relatively brief: she made three films in the early 1970s, *La cagna/Liza* (Marco Ferreri, 1971), *Fatti di gente perbene/Drama of the Rich* (Mauro Bolognini, 1973), *Non toccare la donna bianca/Don't Touch the White Woman* (Marco Ferreri, 1974), and some ten years later participated in one further production *Speriamo che sia femmina/Let's Hope it's a Girl* (Mario Monicelli, 1985).The aim of the chapter is to identify and analyse the star qualities of Catherine Deneuve as they are manifested in these films. Career profiles of Bolognini and Monicelli (Poppi 1993: 39–40 and 175–6) show that her work with them can be located exclusively within the traditions of Italian national cinema. However, Deneuve's most significant Italian films are those she made with Marco Ferreri, in particular *La cagna*; as this chapter will show, Ferreri is a filmmaker much more difficult to classify as belonging within a single national cinema. It is essential to recognise the multiplicity of meanings that accrue to the image of a star with a career as long and varied as that of Deneuve. The main period of Deneuve's 'Italian interludes' occurs in the late 1960s and early 1970s, without doubt one of the most innovative and fruitful periods of her work, evidenced also and most particularly in her collaborations with directors Roman Polanski and Luis Buñuel.

Richard Dyer (1998: 63) argues that in attempting to assess the elements that combine to forge the 'complex totality' of a star's image, one may validly make use of the notion that there exists a 'chronological dimension' to that image – pinpointing a particular facet of the star's career relevant to a particular chronological era. Referring to the career of Jane Fonda, Dyer develops the point further: 'Images have a temporal dimension [...] images develop or change over time. In the case of Fonda, the direction is for the most part in terms of change, but it may also be seen in terms of continuity' (64). Ginette Vincendeau interprets the role as Liza in *La cagna*, the film central to Deneuve's Italian work, as characterised precisely by continuity: she argues (1995: 109) that it reiterates a quality of '"perverse" sexuality' already evident in earlier roles that Deneuve enacted, as Carol in *Repulsion* (Roman Polanski, 1965), and as Séverine and Tristana in Buñuel's *Belle de jour* (1966) and *Tristana* (1970) respectively. If one considers a summary of the narrative of *La cagna*, it seems that this is indeed a valid argument. In the film Deneuve playes Liza, a middle-class society girl who lands on a desert island inhabited only by Giorgio (Marcello Mastroianni) and his dog Melampo. Jealous of the master–animal relationship, she kills the dog and dons its collar. The film narrates and resolves (in a conclusion of non-resolution) the bizarre relationship of the sexes that ensues. The evidence thus suggests that the role of Deneuve in *La cagna* displays the element of 'continuity', highlighted by Dyer, with her recently established image. Through close scrutiny of the individual film this chapter will challenge such an assumption, arguing that the discourse of the film offers a much more complex nuancing of Deneuve's star image. At the same time it will demonstrate that nevertheless, questions of continuity and difference of image inevitably inform any critical analysis of her Italian career.

La cagna: director, casting and script

Before proceeding to an analysis of *La cagna*, it is worthwhile considering the long period of the film's gestation, and the context of the film in relation to the work of Marco Ferreri. Deneuve herself saw Ferreri as a key figure in her career in the early 1970s. If there appears to be a logic to Deneuve's choosing *La cagna* as a subject that might be suited to aspects of her screen persona in the early 1970s, one can say that there is also a logic to Ferreri's involvement in the project. As we shall see, in his career prior to *La cagna* Ferreri had already established a reputation as a risk-taker who pushed at the limits of censorship in his acerbic representation of middle-class mores. It is difficult to classify Ferreri as a purely Italian auteur. His work with Deneuve is better understood within the context of a period of rich cross-fertilisation of European filmmaking, suggesting that both Ferreri and Deneuve may more properly be termed transnational cinematic artists, among the most significant of this era. Ferreri was Italian born, and served an apprenticeship in the Italian film industry (Morandini 1997: 585), but his first major successes were in Spain, where he made a number of films with the scriptwriter Rafael Azcona, with whom he formed a long and fertile partnership. Morandini (1997: 586) indicates that Ferreri was as a result termed for a time 'the Spanish Milanese', but such a classification is too restrictive. He went on to involve himself in film projects throughout Europe and the United States with a range of diverse actors and scriptwriters so that, in a summary of his career Jean Gili (1997: 21) terms him as 'un cineaste inclassable' ('a filmmaker impossible to classify'). When *La cagna* first came out, it was termed another contribution to 'Ferreri's female menagerie' ('il bestiario femminile di Ferreri') (Kezich 1972: 22), underlining that *La cagna* is the third example of a Ferreri film that explores male–female relations, where female identity is directly associated with animal qualities. In 1963 he made *L'ape regina/Queen Bee* with Marina Vlady and Ugo Tognazzi in which Vlady's role increasingly takes on the characteristic of a destructive female, the queen bee, whose tireless sexual appetite saps the energies of her husband. In the same year he made *La donna scimmia/The Ape Woman* where Maria (Annie Girardot) is discovered by Antonio (Tognazzi), a circus entertainer and charlatan, who marries and goes on tour with his trophy, an animal-wife. Both films encountered extensive censorship difficulties: the premiere of *L'ape regina* was delayed for six months by the Italian state authorities (Gili 1997: 142) and the international distributors of *La donna scimmia* forced Ferreri to make radical changes to the film's conclusion (Sanguineti 1999: 197). *La cagna* is one of his many Franco-Italian co-productions: Noël Simsolo (1995: 112) has shown that these were commonplace when Ferreri returned from Spain to work in Italy:

> In 1960s Italy collaborative film production funding often meant the imposition of a Franco-Italian cast on a particular film. These conditions were part of the logic of the film industry in this period, what might be termed the golden age of the European film industry, where France and Italy were the undisputed leaders.
>
> (Nell'epoca degli anni sessanta in Italia la produzione di un film viene spesso impostata in base a un cast franco-italiano. Siamo nella logica dell'industria cinematografica dell'epoca, nel periodo d'oro in cui l'Italia e la Francia sono le incontestabili capofila dell'industria cinematografica europea).

The collaboration between Deneuve and Ferreri cannot simply be attributed to the commercial requirements in vogue at the time. On the contrary, as this chapter's section on the film's script will show, both parties chose to work together and in so doing consciously shaped this most fertile period of their separate careers. It is notable nevertheless that Ferreri should repeatedly cast non-Italian actors in his female roles though as Simsolo shows (1995: 113) this had been common practice in the co-produced films of directors such as Fellini and Visconti in the 1960s. In the early 1970s, when Ferreri was in his most productive phase of filmmaking, the suitability of Italian actors for Ferreri's work was problematic. Stars who developed an international reputation such as Sophia Loren and Gina Lollobrigida had emerged in the 1950s and were thus associated with an earlier era. Loren now only undertook occasional roles where she often elected to 'act against type' (Nowell-Smith 1996: 73) as for example in *Una giornata particolare/A Special Day* (Ettore Scola, 1977) in which she played a dowdy middle-aged housewife. Recently emerging actors such as Monica Vitti had developed close associations with individual directors in the 1960s; however, towards the end of the decade Vitti's roles had shown a break in her association with Antonioni and art-house cinema. Instead she turned to comedy roles such as *La ragazza con la pistola/The Girl with A Pistol* (Mario Monicelli, 1968) and *Modesty Blaise* (Joseph Losey, 1966). Although in this period there existed gifted young actors such as Stefania Sandrelli and Mariangela Melato, they did not achieve the status of their Italian predecessors, nor of Deneuve herself. One must understand their fortunes in relation to the overall state of the national film industry in the early 1970s. As Chris Wagstaff shows (1996: 228), the 'vigour of the Italian authorial art cinema in the 1960s', was buoyed up by a healthy production sector that derived its strength largely for popular cinema (above all, spaghetti westerns, but also the horror films of Dario Argento and Mario Bava). With the relentless inroads that television made into leisure activities, and the advent of a reinvigorated American sector, the so-called New Hollywood cinema, the 1970s showed a sustained decline in Italian audience and film-production figures (Nowell-Smith 1996:160). Within a shrinking domain, it is thus perhaps only figures with an exceptional cinematic profile such as Deneuve, and with an exceptional commitment to producing non-mainstream cinema such as Ferreri, who could sustain an independent dimension to the film industry. From the perspective of Deneuve herself and the trajectory of her career, collaboration with Ferreri developed her work with a range of cutting-edge auteurs, thereby augmenting further her reputation beyond the confines of French filmmaking. This was also a highly significant moment in Deneuve's personal life. She had worked for the first time with Marcello Mastroianni in *Cela n'arrive qu'aux autres/It Only Happens to Others* (Nadine Trintignant, 1970) during which they began a long personal relationship that continued through the making of *La cagna* and resulted in the birth of their daughter Chiara in 1972.

There is valuable evidence of the very particular way the script
of *La cagna* and the collaboration of Deneuve and Ferreri came
about. The broad lines of the film's narrative are the work of
Ennio Flaiano, which was initially published as a novel, and then
modified by the author into a film script. Flaiano's reputation as
a scriptwriter is founded on his long and highly successful collaboration with Federico Fellini, surely one of the most productive
filmmaking liaisons in post-war Italian cinema. Flaiano submitted
the original draft of the script to the American Writers Guild in 1968
(Tassone 1978: 156). He based the subject matter on his experiences in America in the late 1960s and proposed, at this late stage
of his career, to realise the project as both scriptwriter and director.
Marcello Mastroianni, with whom Flaiano had worked on a
number of films immediately accepted the role of Giorgio, and after
some further negotiating, Deneuve agreed to take the part of Liza.
However, Flaiano was unable to secure funding or an agreement to
film his highly unusual script. Negotiations with the producer Carlo
Ponti centred on Ponti's attempts to afford it a more light-hearted
tone and eventually the entire project, which had the title *Melampo*,
completely foundered, triggering Flaiano's bitter comment that 'the
words "Ponti" and "Melampo" will be written on my grave' ('Ponti
e Melampo mi hanno condotto alla tomba') (Tassone 1978: 159).
Mastroianni and Deneuve remained committed to the film. First,
and unsuccessfully, they approached Polanski as a possible director
(Tassone 1978: 148), and then they secured the agreement of Ferreri,
as he explains: 'The impetus to make *La cagna* came from the actors
Mastroianni and Deneuve who were keen to make a film with me'
('L'occasione per fare *La cagna* sono stati gli attori Mastroianni e
la Deneuve che volevano fare un film con me') (Faldini and Fofi
1983: 121). Ferreri then secured the participation of Jean Claude
Carrière who, with Buñuel, had adapted the script of *Belle de jour*.
There is a critical consensus that together they made such radical
alterations as to refashion the script entirely, leaving only the basis
of Flaiano's original narrative premise: that it would concentrate on
a woman who takes on the role of a dog (Maleo 1986: 51; Tassone
1978: 161). Thus in this phase that preceded the shooting of the
film Deneuve exercised a choice to participate in two almost entirely
separate projects. Her original discussions with Flaiano convinced
him that 'Deneuve was without doubt the best choice for the role
of Liza' ('nessuno poteva interpretare Liza meglio della Deneuve')

(Tassone 1978: 158). When the project changed hands Deneuve's agent and Mastrioanni both had misgivings about the way Ferreri might alter the role of Liza, but the actress resolved the matter, expressing commitment to the new regime 'because she knew Marco and held him in high regard' ('perché conosceva e stimava Marco') (Tassone 1978: 160).

Female identity in *La cagna*

In 1971 when Deneuve and Ferreri worked on *La cagna* there was every indication from their respective careers that the film would explore further the quality of 'perverse' sexuality that was already emerging in the screen persona of Deneuve. In the early part of the film her role develops in a manner that appears to support this possibility. Liza arrives on the island from a yacht moored in the bay. Her companions, whom the camera does not show, are heard calling to her to return, but she refuses, wades ashore with a suitcase and dons a flowing Yves Saint-Laurent suit. The elegance of the yacht and of her costume signal a middle-class identity. This offers the prospect of a difficult encounter with Giorgio, seen garbed in a suitably rough castaway style. The opening sequences have shown him already established on the island and living in harmony with his dog Melampo as companion. The couple embark on a sexual relationship, a curious *ménage à trois* with the dog in a bunker-like dwelling that is Giorgio's island home. Liza then takes the dog swimming, far beyond the confines of the island. She returns alone and the camera cuts to a shot of Liza and Giorgio, spade in hand, burying the dog that Liza has drowned. She picks up the dog's discarded collar and puts it round her neck. Throughout the remainder of the film she regularly adopts a dog-like pose, crouching down beside Giorgio, licking his hand, and fetching the sticks he throws for her in the sea. A most fruitful approach to Deneuve's role in *La cagna* is achieved by analysing the use of camera in the film. In her role as elegant socialite she is initially shot in the manner of classical Hollywood cinema, the voyeuristic object of 'the three "looks" in the cinema' (Kaplan 1983: 14), of the male protagonist, the camera and the spectator. This is made absolutely explicit in the scene of the couple's first sexual encounter in the internal setting of the bunker. Liza has changed into a flowing satin gown, and the camera, located behind Giorgio, tracks down and objectifies her body as he prepares to embrace her. The narrative then develops to the point where she eliminates the dog, her rival for Giorgio's affections. Once she has put on the dog collar, there is a close-up of her crouching down and sensuously licking her 'master's' hand. In the following shot, a medium shot of Liza and Giorgio, she is shown biting his hand. The frontispiece is without doubt the pivotal shot of the film. It suggests a transitional moment, shifting from a liaison of conventional sexuality, filmed with shots that give a conventional representation of her sexual identity, to a relationship with a radically different basis. Through the promptings of Liza the couple, it appears, will embark on a new relationship of owner and dog, master and slave. Subsequent camerawork shows that the reverse is true. It explicitly resists the delineation of 'perverse' sexuality seemingly implicit in the film's narrative. The objectifying of the female body briefly proposed in the early sequences is discarded. It is assumed that sexual relations continue between them in conventional fashion, but this is merely implied in long shots showing them together in the 'bed' of their bunker. The nature of the camerawork gives support to Ferreri's own perceptive comment on the tenor of the couple's relationship for the remainder of the film (Gardies 1972: 82):

> I think that relations between Giorgio and Liza in the film are very human and very loving. Within the dynamic of their relationship one is never clear who is the master and who is the slave, they can both be seen as slaves of the same situation.

> (Je trouve que les relations entre Giorgio et Liza dans le film sont très humaines et très amoureuses. A l'intérieur du couple on ne sait jamais qui est le maître et qui est l'esclave, ils sont tous deux esclaves de la même situation.)

It is more accurate to argue that the film's focus is on the role of Giorgio, and that it is more usefully interpreted as a savage satire that exposes the unconvincing nature of his desire to rebel and escape. From the earliest shots of the film the props of his island existence subvert his independent stance (Accialini and Coluccelli 1979: 123):

> Everything surrounding him is a sham. He has not truly broken his ties with the world, nor is he really capable of doing so. The radio, the motorboat, the tins of food, all these details signal to us that Giorgio is acting out a pretence.

(Tutto intorno a lui è fasullo, i legami con il mondo non sono stati spezzati a sufficienza, né era possible farlo. La radio, il motoscafo, i cibi in scatola, tutto ci avverte che Giorgio sta simulando.)

Ferreri's work consistently resists a single, limiting interpretation. In *La cagna* an openness of interpretation is achieved through the use of the desert island, a location that traditionally distances the text from any specific socio-historical framework. Nevertheless, a possible critical perspective, is briefly uncovered in the film when the setting shifts to urban Paris. Giorgio's son comes to the island to plead with his father to return, and to tell him that is wife is ill. The camera cuts to Giorgio and his unnamed friend (Michel Piccoli) walking through the centre of Paris, and then to the interiors of the family home where he interacts briefly with the family he has abandoned. The family are shown watching a television report of the student street rebellions of May 1968. This invites a reading of Giorgio as a man of his time, and whose role mocks as illusory his middle-class aspirations for rebellion and change. If we accept this possible approach to the film – always recognising that Ferreri only hints at its substance – it is possible, in turn, to consider the relevance of the couple's relationship to this interpretation. Liza has followed Giorgio to Paris, and the couple then go back to the island together. They have undertaken a revolt against the conventions of society, and by now they recognise that they are no longer able to function within the conventions of that society. The animal–master relationship is constructed not for its sexual potential but to demonstrate the fruitlessness of the bizarre *modus vivendi* that they have established between them. The film may thus be read as a bitter reflection on the heady atmosphere of sexual and individual liberation in late 1960s Europe and America. The narrative now evolves to make clear that they have become 'slaves of the same situation'. Rather than achieving an existence of release or escape they are locked in their self-styled but arid relationship. The role of Liza serves as the catalyst that exposes Giorgio's illusions and the final freeze-frame of the film forces them to face this uncomfortable truth. The camera shows them about to take off in a plane to an uncertain destination: the shot suggests, not without humour, a range of possible resolutions to their fate, conveying ultimately the nihilistic conclusion that theirs is 'an escape impossible to realise' ('una fuga impossibile') (De Giusti 1995: 222).

The film is thus important evidence that Deneuve, in conjunction with Ferreri, chose a role that works against the expectations that her screen persona might generate at this time. The shot of Liza licking Giorgio's hand echoes the scene of bondage in *Belle de jour* where she presents 'the figure of the ice queen, a bait for sadistic male fantasies' (Vincendeau 1995: 109), tied up and whipped by the husband/master's servants: in both cases the female's eyes are half-closed and the instrument of bondage (the rope, the collar) is prominent. The female appears compliant in her subjection, implicitly deriving sexual gratification from this enslavement. Thereafter, as we have noted in *La cagna* the female body ceases to be presented as the object of the gaze (of the camera, and of the film's male protagonist). The film's critique of the central characters is realised through a focus on social, not sexual interaction. There is prior evidence that Ferreri was a filmmaker who liked to play with the expectations of his audience in relation to his representation of female identity. Like *La cagna* the script of *La donna scimmia* promises a potentially exploitative representation of 'perverse' female sexuality.

But rather than an account of a debased and subordinated female, once again in *La donna scimmia* we find that Ferreri uses the female role to point up the inadequacies of the male lead. The animal-like 'monkey woman' played by Girardot is in fact depicted as a highly sympathetic figure and it is her ruthless exploitation by Antonio, played by Tognazzi, that is the object of the film's satire. Above all, the possibility that the camera will explore and exploit the female body, covered in hair, is rejected. The shots of Girardot are seldom in close-up. The couple marry so that, as we discover, Antonio can control his 'trophy'. As in *La cagna*, sexual relations between this bizarre protagonist couple are understated, rendering completely unfounded the various censorship efforts and scandal of its critical reception in 1963. Rather than being the conduit that itself exploits the female body, *La donna scimmia* is a film that takes as its subject matter the exploitation of the female body. The resolution of the film comes as Maria gives birth to a child. She dies in the act of giving birth, and the child dies shortly after. The final shots of the film, excised when the film was first distributed, show a supposedly grieving Tognazzi putting on show the body of the monkey woman and her dead child. Inviting revulsion, the camera offers this ugly spectacle in a very distant aerial long shot. This conclusion suggests echoes of nineteenth-century circus shows of physical deformity – the Elephant Man, the Hottentot woman – but it also holds relevance for the contemporary era where the world of fashion and advertising continues to display and exploit the female body.

After *La cagna*, Deneuve made two further Italian films in the 1970s – a second film with Ferreri, *Non toccare la donna bianca* (1974) and one film with Mauro Bolgnini, *Fatti di gente per bene* (1974). In both films her role is a minor one, that offers little development of her screen persona. *Non toccare la donna bianca* reassembles the cast of Ferreri's *La grande bouffe/Blowout* (1973), including Mastroianni, Michel Piccoli, Ugo Tognazzi and Philippe Noiret. These actors play out a reconstructed version of the Battle of Little Bighorn, Custer's last stand, in the setting of the derelict construction site of Les Halles in central Paris. The film constitutes a more light-hearted exposure of western values than is present in *La cagna*. Deneuve plays a cameo role as Marie Hélène de Boismonfrais, the mistress of Custer (Mastroianni), who rides on horseback with him through the streets of Paris. The film is notable for marking Ferreri's definitive move to base himself in Paris, and the film's cast shows that by now he had created around him a group of European actors, including Deneuve, with whom he worked regularly to articulate his controversial perspective on western European society. In *Fatti di gente perbene* Deneuve is again in a minor role, this time in a family melodrama that takes place in late nineteenth-century Bologna and Venice. The film has an impressive international cast that includes Giancarlo Giannini and Fernando Rey. Her role as Linda Murri, an upper-class wife, is the focal point of the narrative. However, as is appropriate to the argument of the film, she remains a passive, minor figure, the centre of a struggle by her various male relations to control her fate. She is married to a brutal husband, who is murdered by her brother Paolo Murri (Giannini) to avenge the family's honour. Again Deneuve's talents are little used. Bolognini's best work can be found earlier in his career in a range of literary adaptations of works by novelists Vitaliano Brancati (*Il bell'Antonio*, 1959) and Alberto Moravia (*La giornata balorda/A Crazy Day*, 1960 and *Agostino*, 1962). In terms of her Italian career in the 1970s, *La cagna* remains the definitive film.

La cagna and Italian cinema

Categorising *La cagna* as an example of Italian cinema raises some problematic issues of definition, as this chapter has shown. However, there is one absolutely certain way in which one can understand this film as belonging within the canon of Italian national cinema. It is one of three films by major auteurs that narrates the experiences of a blonde *bourgeoise* female in an island setting. Deneuve's role is directly comparable to that of Claudia (Monica Vitti) in *L'avventura/ The Adventure* (Michelangelo Antonioni, 1960) and Raffaella (Mariangela Melato) in *Travolti da un insolito destino nell'azzurro mare d'agosto/Swept Away* (Lena Wertmüller, 1974). Antonioni's film, made in 1960, is the point of reference for the later works, a point explicitly verbalised in Wertmuller's film by Raffaella's words to Gennarino, the boatman, (Giancarlo Giannini) when they first find themselves adrift from their companions: 'What an adventure! What a great adventure this is!' ('Che avventura! Che bella avventura!'). The relationship between *L'avventura* and *La cagna* is found in a host of narrative details of the film (the elegant yacht, the island as the starting point of an intense relationship, the progressive separa-tion of the protagonist couple from their accompanying bourgeois companions). But it is elements of the *mise-en-scène* and cinematic style of Antonioni that most closely resonate with the foregoing interpretation of Ferreri's film, in particular the camerawork and use of setting. Nowell-Smith (1997: 46) describes Antonioni's technique in this way: 'In *L'avventura* camera movement and editing are in a constant process of flux. The camera pans, tracks, reframes, moves to a new position. Events unfold from a series of camera positions, all of which uncover new details of a scene'. The restless, constantly shifting camera generates a sense of instability (attributable to the narrative form, and to the characters in the narrative) that pervades the film. Seymour Chatman (1985: 199) summarises the relationship between character and landscape in this way: 'The camera manages to make the landscape at once functional to plot and the characters' moods and "irrelevantly" beautiful, worthy of aesthetic contempla-tion in its own right. It remains a positive visual force'. As Chatman shows, the alienated characters of *L'avventura* may not themselves register the beauty of the landscape within which they are framed, but the repeated use of long shot, extreme long shot and aerial shots opens up vistas for the viewer, utilising the rocky landscape to enhance the sense of mystery that the island engenders.

On the other hand, to repeat Chatman's term, in *La cagna* the camera is purely 'functional to the plot'. What is remarkable is the *difference* between the camerawork of Antonioni and of Ferreri and how it affords meaning in the separate films. Throughout *La cagna*, Ferreri naturally makes frequent use of the two-shot in the narrative of Giorgio and Liza's relationship. But his preferred framing of the figures is repeatedly in medium close-up, a choice that denies to the characters within the film and to the viewer the visual and metaphorical release that the island setting might offer. As we have seen, the conclusion of their adventure is nihilistic, underlining the film's satirical take on bourgeois aspirations for escape and release. Use of a moving camera to capture a range of vistas is an approach that by any account would seem inherent to representing the island setting. Ferreri studiously avoids such an approach, and the practice of using static, closed camerawork is a major element in creating meaning in the film's narrative. 'Difference' is also the appropriate term to apply to the relative roles of Deneuve and Monica Vitti in the two films. The sexuality and indeed the body of Deneuve becomes a lesser element in the discourse of the film once she adopts an animal-like role. Effectively her body ceases to be a focus for the camera, and a central point of reference for meaning in the film. On the other hand, in *L'avventura* (and indeed in a number of Antonioni's films in the early 1960s) the reverse is true. Nowell-Smith (1997: 43) argues that 'Vitti's role was to be the artist's model, to lend her body to the purposes of the work that he intended to create [...] She is literally an embodiment'. Vincendeau suggests that Deneuve's role as Liza may be understood in relation to that of Carol, in *Repulsion* and of Séverine in *Belle de jour*. While the argument concerning continuity with these roles has been challenged, there is no doubt that the persona developing in the earlier films informs the meaning of the role of Liza. To this we may add the meaning it derives from engagement with Vitti's role in Antonioni's film. We can conclude that the role of Liza is thus is to a degree derivative, but that the film presents already-established elements of Deneuve's persona in a challenging and innovative configuration. Above all, *La cagna* demonstrates Deneuve's (and Ferreri's) resistance to any form of typecasting, and at the same time a preparedness to push constantly at the boundaries of possibility of European cinema.

Screen persona in the 1980s

Catherine Deneuve returned briefly to Italian filmmaking in 1985 to work with Monicelli on *Speriamo che sia femmina*. The film was again a Franco-Italian co-production. Producer Giovanni Di Clemente honoured his agreement with the company Producteurs Associés of Paris by casting Deneuve, Philippe Noiret and Bernard Blier for the film. Deneuve liked the subject matter, and agreed to play the part of Claudia saying 'I am happy to take part, even if my role is very much a minor one' ('je suis contente d'y participer, même pour un rôle peu important') (Codelli 1986: 12). However, though constituting a minor role in the film the part of Claudia is important for signalling a positioning of Deneuve's screen presence very different from her work in the previous decade. In his works on star identity, Paul McDonald (2005: 11) offers an analysis that is helpful in differentiating the two phases of her Italian career:

> Stars do appear to offer an unrivalled opportunity for product differen-tiation. At one level, various individual stars appear to share common characteristics, and the system of stardom differentiates performers according to type [...] At a further level however, the star system seems to resist the classification of stars as types. Staiger suggests that from an economic point of view 'stars may be thought of as a monopoly on a personality' (1985b: 101). Monopolies emerge when there is only one supplier to a market. Star monopolies are based on a belief in unique individuality: 'there is only one Jim Carrey'.

One can paraphrase McDonald's conclusion to argue that in the 1970s 'there is only one Catherine Deneuve'. The major film of her Italian output demonstrates her capacity to work with and against the challenging persona that developed in other films in that period. On the other hand it seems that, in Monicelli's film, she works with an ensemble cast where she is allocated within the group type of 'the older woman', in conjunction with Liv Ullmann (who plays Elena, the central role) and Stefania Sandrelli as Lolli. In *Speriamo che sia femmina* female identity predominates and is realised through a range of roles, split between this 'older woman' grouping and the younger generation, their daughters.

The title refers to a moment late in the film, when Ullmann's daughter Franca announces that she is pregnant. By this point in the narrative the male characters (husbands, lovers) have been margina-lised or wholly eliminated from the text, and the group assembled at the family table consists entirely of women. The one remaining male figure, the eccentric Uncle Gugo sits separately in isolation by the hearth. Franca's news of her pregnancy elicits a response from her mother, 'Let's hope it's a girl' ('Speriamo che sia femmina'). The comment draws to a conclusion the main thrust of the film's narrative which suggests humorously that those of the male sex have served their purpose of fathering children but are henceforth superfluous to the future of the assembled women. The narrative strands that involve the grouping of the older women played by Deneuve, Ullmann and Sandrelli have a similar pattern. Each character is initially associated with a male lover whom she eventually discards. Each forms part of a couple, where she agonises and finally finds release from her failed relationship. The script sets this attitude – torn between a sense of duty and need to assert selfhood – against that of the younger generation. Franca is seen meeting and abandoning a series of lovers in the course of the film. The news that she is pregnant is preceded by the announcement, 'I've broken up with the father' ('ho rotto con il padre'). Deneuve, Ullmann and Sandrelli are presented as elegant, dignified, moving hesitantly to the point where they embrace their liberation. This contrasts sharply with the free-thinking outlook of the younger generation. These elements emphasised in the role of the diegetic older woman create interesting tensions with the extra-diegetic persona of all three actresses. All are associated with innovative European filmmaking in the 1970s, a full decade and more earlier than Monicelli's film, and all undertook innovative roles within that era of filmmaking. It remains valid to label Deneuve's persona as a 'monopoly' in that era: hers were the roles that were most diverse, most wide-ranging in the radical representation of female identity. However, Ullmann's illustrious career with Ingmar Bergman, and Sandrelli's notable roles in Italian cinema such as *Divorzio all'italiana/Divorce Italian Style* (Pietro Germi, 1971) and *Il conformista/The Conformist* (Bernardo Bertolucci, 1970) are evidence that they too made a substantial contribution to altering conventional delineation of cinematic female identity in that era.

These tensions are not fully resolved within the film; instead they create a series of contradictions that relate to the persona of the separate actresses. *Speriamo che sia femmina* achieved considerable commercial success and critics viewed it very much as a return to form for Monicelli, whose reputation as one of the great comic auteurs of Italian cinema was long established in works such as *La grande guerra/The Great War* (1959) and *L'armata Brancaleone* (1965). More significantly perhaps, it was interpreted as distinctly autobiographical in tone, 'a highly personalised film [...] set in his favourite countryside location, the place of his Tuscan childhood origins' ('une

œuvre-confession [...] au milieu de son paysage de prédilection, la
Toscane de ses origines'). The representation of setting may serve
as an ironic underpinning to the film's gentle assertion of female
independence. It is centred on a beautiful Tuscan farmhouse where,
it is argued, 'Monicelli realises in concrete form his utopian idyll'
('Monicelli concretise son utopie') (Codelli 1986: 10). Throughout
the film, the use of soft filter affords a honeyed tone to the rich
colours of the countryside location. There emerges the implicit
suggestion – intended or otherwise by the director and camera crew
– that it houses an impossibly idyllic city of women whose gender
encoding belongs only to the fictive world of the celluloid screen.
One can also speculate that there emerges from Monicelli's film a
subtext that evokes past cinematic success, of his own career and of
the golden age of European filmmaking. *Speriamo che sia femmina*
is produced in Italy in the 1980s, a period of catastrophic decline
for the industry during which it is said 'the film world was mourning
the death of Italian cinema' (Gieri 1995: 198). The steep decline in
audience figures was partially halted in 1989 with the emergence
of the loosely based group of 'new Italian cinema' signalled by the
success of *Cinema Paradiso* (Giuseppe Tornatore). The 'older women'
stars of Monicelli's film would thus seem to be consigned to holding
significance primarily in terms of their illustrious cinematic past.
Such an argument may be partially true for the career of Ullmann,
for whom the film was a brief return to filmmaking, part of the
sporadic pattern that marked her great career. It does not characterise at all the subsequent trajectory of the careers of Deneuve and
Sandrelli who consistently fashioned new dimensions to their work.
Arguably Monicelli's city of women also implies that the mature
stars of his film are marked by a declining sexuality. Contrast with
the active sexuality of the younger generation may imply that this
is a quality partially or wholly absent from the role of the older
woman. A survey of the subsequent careers of Deneuve and Sandrelli
would suggest otherwise. For Deneuve the very successful output
of her career continued in the 1990s, with films such as *Indochine*
(1992) and *Place Vendôme* (1998). Sandrelli's recent roles in *Matri-
moni/Marriages* (Cristina Comencini, 1998) and *L'ultimo bacio/
The Last Kiss* (Gabriele Muccino, 2001) are often comic, but as the
troubled mother of wayward offspring in both films, she continues
to assert the importance of her own separate, and sexual, dimension
in their narratives.

Without doubt, Deneuve retains the greater prominence, the greater international success. After *Speriamo che sia femmina* it is she who carries most powerfully the role of the mature woman in roles where she remains sexualised, assertive, unapologetic. The Italian dimension of Deneuve's career, briefly revived, may be said to conclude with her film with Monicelli. The discourse of the film proffers her as if in a kind of cul-de-sac that proves untypical of the rich and varied facets of the career that she continues to pursue beyond the confines of Italy. Dyer (1998: 63) argues that 'the possibilities of meaning [of the star image] are limited in part by what the text makes available'. Deneuve shows a most interesting capacity to negotiate and resist the limitations to her image that the Italian texts apparently make available.

Works cited

Accialini, Fulvio and Lucia Coluccelli (1979), *Marco Ferreri*, Milan: Edizioni Il Formichiere.

Chatman, Seymour (1985), *Antonioni, or the Surface of The World*, Berkeley and Los Angeles: University of California Press.

Codelli, Lorenzo (1986), 'L'utopie de Monicelli: Entretien avec Mario Monicelli', *Positif*, no. 304, June, 9–15.

De Giusti, Laura, 'La Cagna', in Parigi 1995: 220–2.

Dyer, Richard (1998), *Stars*, London: BFI.

Faldini, Franca and Goffredo Fofi (1983) (ed.), *Il cinema italiano d'oggi racccontato dai suoi protagonisti 1970–84*, Milan: Mondadori.

Flaiano, Ennio (1978), *Melampo*, Turin: Einaudi.

Gardies, René (1972), 'Entretien avec Marco Ferreri', *Image et son*, no. 262, June–July, 80–4.

Gieri, Manuela (1995), *Contemporary Italian Filmmaking: Strategies of Subversion*, Toronto: University of Toronto Press.

Gili, Jean, A. (1997), 'Hommage à Marco Ferreri', *Positif*, no. 437/438, June/July, 142–4.

Grande, Maurizio (1974), *Marco Ferreri*, Florence: La Nuova Italia.

Kaplan, E. Ann (1983), *Women and Film: Both Sides of the Camera*, London and New York: Routledge.

Kezich, Tullio (1972), 'La Cagna', *Il Giorno*, 19 August.

McDonald, Paul (2000), *The Star System: Hollywood's Production of Popular Identities*, London: Wallflower.

Maleo, Marco (1986), *Cinegrafiques: Marco Ferreri*, Paris: Edilig.

Morandini, Morando (1997), 'Italy: auteurs and after', in G. Nowell-Smith, *Oxford History of Cinema*, Oxford: Oxford University Press, 586–96.

Nowell-Smith, Geoffrey (1996), *The Companion to Italian Cinema*, London: BFI.

Nowell-Smith, Geoffrey (1997), *L'avventura*, London: BFI.

Parigi, Stefania (ed.) (1995), *Marco Ferreri: Il cinema e i film*, Venice: Marsilio.

Poppi, Roberto (ed.) (1993), *Dizionario del cinema italiano: i registi dal 1930 ai giorni nostri*, Rome: Gremese.

Sanguineti, Tatti (ed.) (1999), *Italia Taglia*, Ancona-Milan: Editori Associati.

Simsolo, Noel, 'La parte francese', in Parigi 1995: 111–20.

Tassone, Aldo, 'Nota di Aldo Tassone', in Flaiano 1978: 155–69.

Vincendeau, Ginette (ed.) (1995), *Encyclopaedia of European Cinema*, London: BFI.

Wagstaff, Christopher (1996), 'Cinema', in Forgacs, David and Robert Lumley (eds), *Italian Cultural Studies: an Introduction*, Oxford: Oxford University Press, 216–32.

5

Incongruous femininity: Catherine Deneuve and 1970s political culture

Bridget Birchall

Introduction

This chapter investigates Catherine Deneuve's films of the 1970s; their role in shaping her star persona and – via an exploration of their context – the ways in which they position Deneuve in relation to French political culture. Until recently, little attention has been paid to this period in Deneuve's career, despite the fact that the 1970s is her most prolific decade in terms of film output. This oversight is consistent with the overall lack of criticism of the French stars of the 1970s. Most analyses of Deneuve's work focus predominantly on the 1960s or the 1980s onwards, and almost all ignore her career beyond *Tristana* (Buñuel, 1970). This critical oversight ignores two issues. First, that Deneuve still experienced some commercial success during the 1970s (see for example *Le Sauvage*, Rappeneau, 1975 and *Courage fuyons*, Robert, 1979).[1] Second, it ignores her continued relevance during this decade as an icon and figure of French femininity and feminism. Deneuve is one of the few French film personnel who has willingly associated themselves with the title of 'feminist' and was active in women's movement campaigns. But, in the 1970s, due to her presence in advertising campaigns and women's magazines, Deneuve also remained an important icon of popular women's culture. These factors demonstrate that greater critical attention needs to be paid to this period.

Existing studies of Deneuve's 1970s films have focused either on her incongruity with other actresses of the decade (Vincendeau 2000: 203) or her containment through the romantic comedy (Le Gras 2005: 265–73). Le Gras's study looks at Deneuve's experimentation with comedy in the mid to late 1970s with particular reference to *Le Sauvage* and *L'Africain* (de Broca, 1985). It overlooks two key factors. First, Le Gras's is a study of genre and does not engage with the rest of Deneuve's 1970s filmography. Second, Le Gras's argument does not fully develop the reasons for Deneuve's contradictory star persona during this decade and what this might tell us about 1970s political culture. Le Gras argues that Deneuve can be associated with a new type of romantic comedy that emerged during the 1970s. In these films Deneuve tends to play young, modern women who invade the otherwise tranquil life of a solitary older male. Ultimately, the plot allows the male to contain the wayward and wild female. Le Gras argues that this is a backlash against the increasing emancipation of French women during the 1970s. According to Le Gras, on the one hand many of Deneuve's on-screen roles of the 1970s reveal a subjugated woman, while on the other hand her off-screen 'public image symbolised the rise of feminism post-May '68' (268).

The opposing significations of Deneuve's star body will allow us to understand some of the complex inconsistencies of 1970s France. Richard Dyer argues that stars can be read as polysemous texts, a term which refers to the way in which the star's image is composed of many complex layers which are constantly shifting and are often contradictory (Dyer 1998: 63). This characteristic of contradictions is particularly relevant to Deneuve in the 1970s. We shall see that her star persona constantly shifts between the feminine, exploited as object, and the feminist, as expressed in her politics. Dyer sees the contradictions inherent to star bodies such as Deneuve's as articulations of shifting ideologies: '[S]tar images function crucially in relation to contradictions within and between ideologies, which they seek variously to "manage or resolve"' (34).

Several critics have noted that Deneuve was inconsistent with new images of femininity represented by contemporaneous French stars of the 1970s, for example Miou-Miou and Annie Girardot (see Vincendeau 2000: 203 and Le Gras 2005: 268).[2] Far from being an irrelevant figure to the 1970s, however, Deneuve in fact embodies many of the decade's contradictions. It will be argued here that through a multitude of different discourses (films, advertising, reviews, interviews and spectatorship) Deneuve's star persona articulates, in the words of Dyer, the 'contradictions within and between [...] ideologies' of 1970s political culture. This chapter will argue that Deneuve's inconsistent approach to feminist issues during the 1970s can be seen as a metonymical of the wider contradictions inherent to France's political culture during this decade, specifically in terms of the conflict that existed between liberalism and conservatism.

France and its government's contradictory approach towards the condition of women's lives during the 1970s will provide a contextual background to Deneuve's own engagement with feminist discourses during this decade. This chapter will then begin to explore the diversity of Deneuve's 1970s filmography through three key films: *A nous deux* (Lelouch, 1979), *Courage fuyons* and *Zig zig* (Szabó, 1975). The analysis will consider how Deneuve's contradictory star persona manifests itself within these films, and will ask how each text might signal varying degrees of anti-feminism.

Contained liberalism: France 1970–1980

Despite the apparent revolutionary spirit of May '68 and the subsequent 'toppling' of the patriarch General de Gaulle in 1969, France remained a conservative country. The public's fear of instability in the late 1960s and early 1970s (Larkin 1988: 317, 327 and 329 and Bell 2000: 108) led to the continued reign of right-wing governments. Both Georges Pompidou (1969–1974) and Valéry Giscard-D'Estaing (1974–1981) attempted to liberalise French society, but to a certain extent both continued to emulate the political ideologies of de Gaulle. Giscard D'Estaing's political style can be described as contained liberalism. Contained liberalism is used here to describe the inherently contradictory nature of Giscard D'Estaing's employment of liberalism. In its specifically French context, the word *libéral* has two principal connotations which express the different facets of Giscard D'Estaing's political approach.[3] The first refers to a society that favours individual liberties and the liberalisation of society. Giscard D'Estaing's reform of the workplace and the electoral system clearly link his government to this meaning of *libéral*. However, contrary to this first meaning, in its second context, *libéral* refers to economies that encourage competition. This second conservative manifestation of *libéral* refers to American-style capitalism, and favours the success of individuals rather than society as a whole (Frears 1981: 128–9). Giscard D'Estaing's interpretation of the word *libéral*, combined with France and its government's continued fear of change, lead to a constant tension between liberalism and conservatism during the 1970s.

This tension is particularly clear in Giscard D'Estaing's approach to issues relating to gender. During his presidency, Giscard D'Estaing made changes to divorce and abortion law, and to the working conditions of women (Frears 1981: 151). However, despite popular support for these measures, backing within parliament for reform was inconsistent (Frears 1981: 152). Where changes to the lives of French women did occur, they did not involve 'major expenditure' (Larkin 1988: 341). Moreover, it has been argued that these changes would never have been implemented without the instigation of reformist feminists and the Minister for Health Simone Veil (Marks and de Courtivron 1981: 29). Party political resistance, and Giscard D'Estaing's own inherent conservatism, led to an inconsistent approach to feminist issues and what many contemporary feminists referred to as tokenism (Frears 1981: 151). Consequently, Giscard D'Estaing's claim that he had 'inserted the French woman into the life of our society' (Larkin 1988: 341), was not wholly representative of his position regarding women's lives.

The tensions that existed within Giscard D'Estaing's politics were inherent in his liberalisation of censorship. Before Giscard D'Estaing was elected, France had lived through a long period of extreme media censorship, largely implemented by President de Gaulle (1958 and 1969). Change to this system was demanded in May 1968 by campaigners. Film censorship was increasingly liberalised during Pompidou's presidency but it was not until Giscard D'Estaing's election that film censorship was virtually abolished. This liberalisation of censorship had a specific effect on French cinema. It led to the increase in the production of pornographic film and its subsequent distribution and consumption in mainstream viewing spaces (Jeancolas 1979: 44). On the one hand the liberalisation of pornography is testament to Giscard d'Estaing's commitment to individual liberties. On the other, pornography (as it existed in France during the 1970s) was ultimately a product that simultaneously commercialised and policed desire. As Susan Hayward argues, pornography is concomitant with 'a society that is intent on frenetic consumption', and it superficially answers to the desires of the dissatisfied (1993: 245). For women, whose sexuality was in the process of liberalisation, pornography was a way 'of policing desire, of making women conform to a specifically phallic conception of them' (Hayward 1993: 245). In her suggestion that pornography functions as a way of policing of desire, Hayward is arguing that its proliferation in Giscardien France indicates a backlash against the female agency promoted by the women's movement (245). Situated within these conflicting discourses of the 1970s, Deneuve's feminism is similarly contradictory. Her films occupy an interesting position which is in a way analogous to pornography's containment of female bodies. Arguably, Deneuve's films of the 1970s also seek to contain the star within stereotyped notions of femininity.

Deneuve and 1970s French feminism

Critics have often cited Deneuve's liberalised private life as evidence of her emancipation.[4] She refused to marry either of her partners, Marcello Mastroianni and Roger Vadim, despite the fact that she had children by both of them. However, as feminists argued during the 1970s it is dangerous to suggest that sexual liberalism necessarily leads to emancipation (Bard 1999: 309–12).[5] Crucially though, Deneuve's feminist impulses were not limited to her private life. In 1971, Deneuve joined several other public figures and signed the *Manifeste des 343 salopes*, the petition published in *Le Nouvel Observateur* which called for the legalisation of abortion and the increased availability of contraception. Each of its signatories admitted to having had an illegal abortion. The letter was unique not just in the eventual effect that it had but that it brought about a change in political process. It was the first notable public protest letter led by women in France – where the practice of writing these sorts of letters is common. Abortion would eventually be legalised in 1975, but this petition was seen as an important part of the campaign for this legislation. It acted as a catalyst for several acts of protest in the following years and has been seen as instrumental in the eventual liberalisation of abortion.[6] Deneuve thus took part in a pivotal moment in the French feminist movement.

We can find further evidence to support the 'feminist' aspect of Deneuve's star persona in her interviews. During the 1970s, when asked her thoughts regarding feminist causes, Deneuve openly declared herself a feminist and emphasised the importance and magnitude of feminist issues. Here is an example taken from an interview conducted in 1974:

> Catherine Deneuve, are you a feminist in the true sense of the word?
> *Of course. Even without campaigning, one cannot not be. It is vital to feel affected because one is implicitly.* (Germain, 1974)

Deneuve's engagement with feminist issues seemed to extend to her understanding of the cinema. She demonstrated that she was aware of questions of representation and spoke sensitively about the portrayal of women on-screen (Alion, 1978). Deneuve argued in interviews that, unlike other actresses, she specifically sought out roles that allowed her to occupy an active position. She also suggested that an increased presence of women filmmakers would perhaps create more active roles for actresses (Esposito, 1978). Contrary to this argument, Deneuve herself only worked with one female director during the 1970s (Nadine Trintignant), despite the fact that in the late 1970s there was a considerable increase in the number of women filmmakers making feature films (Hayward 1993:

244). This inconsistent approach to the politics of representation is highlighted by the following statement made by Deneuve in 1978:

> Sometimes, it's true that I accept to do things that seem to me to be contradictory with what I think or with how we should represent women today. I accept the idea that there are contradictions in what I do, in certain roles [...] I will never accept really misogynist things, but I accept certain things when it doesn't seem to me too serious, it's true. (Alion, 1978)

This quotation begins to reveal the conflict between Deneuve's opinions espoused off-screen and her own films. As I shall argue in the discussion that follows, contrary to Deneuve's claims, several of her films could be seen as misogynistic.

Deneuve and the heterosexual imperative: the case of *Courage fuyons* and *A nous deux*

In order to illustrate how Deneuve's films might represent a contained liberalism that contradicts her off-screen political positioning, this study will now focus on two films: *Courage Fuyons* and *A nous deux*. These films were produced at a key moment in French feminism. In their anti-feminist rhetoric they can be seen as symptomatic reactions to their political context. Produced in 1979, the films coincide both with the beginning of the decline of the women's movement and the rise of antifeminism in France (Allwood 1998: 30).

In *Courage fuyons* and *A nous deux*, we can trace reactions against the liberalisation of representations of the female body. I will argue here that in Deneuve's films of the 1970s attempts are made to fix the star as an object of desire, in ways that undermine her politics. In her films of this decade Deneuve manifests a hyper-femininity. Michèle Sarde described her as 'a kind of ultra-woman in whom femininity is exacerbated to the point of caricature' (quoted in Vincendeau 2000: 204). What is meant here by an 'ultra-woman' or 'hyper-femininity' is that through the *mise-en-scène* (particularly costume, hair and make-up), Deneuve displays a multitude of signs that are overdetermined in their encoding as feminine. In the case of Deneuve, as Vincendeau suggests, these signs of gender resonate reassuringly with the continuity of past femininities during a decade of immense change (Vincendeau 2000: 203). At a moment when heterosexuality was being questioned by feminism, the gay liberation movement, and new, alternative representations of femininity in the shape of actresses such as Miou-Miou and Annie Girardot, Deneuve's hyper-femininity and status as desirable object go some way towards serving as a guarantee of the heterosexual order.

In order to understand how and why Deneuve might display hyper-femininity it is instructive to consider Judith Butler's discussions of the gendered body. According to Butler (1999) our bodies are culturally encoded in order to make the heterosexual binarism pass as 'natural'. What is meant by this is that in order to ensure the perpetuation of heterosexuality, the body displays and reproduces signs which are understood culturally as either distinctly 'feminine' or 'masculine', suggesting the inherent complimentarity between male and female, and the impracticality of dispensing with the distinction. Butler explains that:

> The heterosexualisation of desire requires and institutes the production of discrete and asymmetrical oppositions between 'feminine' and 'masculine', where these are understood as expressive attributes of 'male' and 'female'. (1999: 23)

In her films of the 1970s, Deneuve's hyper-feminine body perpetuates this system and institutes culturally intelligible divisions between 'male' and 'female' bodies. We shall see that in these films Deneuve is configured as an object, and coded as feminine in order that she is ideologically positioned in a way that naturalises the heterosexual dispositions that Butler describes here.

This process of objectification and ultra-femininity is one that Deneuve actively colludes in through her off-screen discourses. Deneuve's self-conception as an actress seems to suggest a desire to be controlled and moulded by the director:

> Above all, I want to be an actress, I mean a tool, an object, the most efficient, the most malleable possible, at the service of the director. If I am a star, it's not a situation that I have particularly sought out nor prepared for – but that I do not reject: it allows me to choose my films, it gives me the time (and the capital!) to say 'yes' or 'no' to a director, according to whether his work, or the script he proposes appeals to me or not. (Abitan 1970: 69)

Arguably, this desire to be positioned as an object undermines Deneuve's independence in her career and her position as self-conceiving subject. At the moment of this interview (1970) she was, as she explains in the quotation above, able to choose her films more freely, and was even able to form her own production company, *Les films de la citrouille*, which supported projects such as her film *Zig zig*. Ironically, it was also at this point of autonomy, that Deneuve made a number of auteur films which seem to have exploited her desire to be an object at the service of the director. Deneuve frequently expressed that she preferred to work with auteur film makers and actively sought to work with these directors who were able to control her image:

> I principally believe in auteur cinema [...] From the moment I start working with him, my confidence is total. I count on him to discover one of my unseen faces, in order to reveal a new aspect of my talent. I use the director in order to know myself better. (Anon., 1970)

In her early films with Buñuel and Ferreri, Deneuve becomes an object of sadistic and sexualised abuse.[7] Her desire to work with auteurs who controlled her image to the point of objectification and denigration is in conflict with Deneuve's declaration that she had sought out active roles. Though these auteur films were largely the work of non-French directors, the centrality of Deneuve's presence in them ensures that they belong, at least partially, within a French context. With the exception of *Tristana*, the majority of these films use predominantly French actors and are set within specifically French social or geographical contexts. In this way, the work of these foreign directors can be seen to be in dialogue with Deneuve's own specifically French political positioning at the beginning of the 1970s.

Deneuve worked frequently, though not exclusively, with foreign auteurs at the beginning of the 1970s.[8] Deneuve's apparent prefer-ence for working with foreign auteurs could be indicative of her relationship with French auteur cinema. French new-wave auteurs on the whole rejected the employment of stars, unless it was to denigrate them in some way (Vincendeau 2000: 114–15). Similarly, auteurs who emerged during the 1970s either sought to undermine the status of stars within the film text (see Bernard Blier's employ-ment of Jeanne Moreau in *Les Valseuses*, 1973) or tended to focus on the experience of disenfranchised young men. Gérard Depar-dieu was, for example, particularly popular with auteur filmmakers during this period since his background and body type brought an authenticity to the naturalistic *mise-en-scène* prevalent in these films (Vincendeau 2000: 224–5). Deneuve's polished image did not work within this naturalistic *mise-en-scène*, and she was reluctant at this point to challenge her image (Tenret, 1977) in the way she would go on to do in Téchiné's post-1970s films.

From 1975 onwards, Deneuve continued to work sporadically with foreign directors and auteurs,[9] but her filmography also diversified as she sought increasingly to make comedies with directors such as Rappeneau, Santoni and Robert, or work with other French directors such as Lelouch. Although the objectification of Deneuve in these later, more mainstream, films was perhaps less explicit than that which occurred in her auteur films of the early 1970s, on-screen, Deneuve's star-body continued to be manipulated by directors. Le Gras has described the star as: 'a desirable figure often reduced to silence' (2005: 271). Contrary to this observation, critics remarked that by the time Deneuve made *A nous deux*, the star appeared more relaxed and dynamic than in her earlier work, and moved on from what Le Gras describes as 'interiorised' performances. Despite this, the film and its critical reception continued to objectify Deneuve. Reviews of *A nous deux* in *France-soir* (Chazal, 1979) and *Minute* (Anon., 1979), focused on Deneuve's image, and both make particular reference to her beauty and her natural and un-made-up look, often sidelining her actual performance.

In *A nous deux*, Deneuve plays Françoise, a bourgeois woman who is raped while working at her family's pharmacy. This attack provokes her to embark upon a campaign of revenge against men by bribing husbands who have extra-marital affairs with her. Françoise's bribery leads her into trouble with the police and she goes into hiding. At the safe house Françoise meets Simon (Jacques Dutronc), a young criminal who differs from her in social class. Against the odds, they come together in order to flee the authorities. Gradually, as she and Simon become closer, Françoise loses her hatred of men. The film ends with the couple having escaped to the United States where they work as musicians in a hotel.

Deneuve's character in this film is punished for the disruptive use of her sexuality and her desire for revenge and emancipation is actively 'policed' (to recall Hayward). Françoise's transgression beyond the boundaries of what is perceived to be an 'acceptable' form of female sexuality leads her into trouble with the police and puts her at odds with patriarchal law. In accordance with this, while hiding out, a male character launches a caustic speech at Françoise (whom he sees reading a feminist book), in which he criticises the emancipation of women. Lelouch's message, that Françoise has stepped too far out of line, is further reinforced by an incident that occurs towards the end of the film. On their way to the American–Canadian border, Françoise and Simon stop at a roadside café. Here they encounter a group of young people who begin to harass Françoise. At the height of the confrontation one of the young men brandishes a mask shaped as a penis at Françoise.[10] The incident recalls her earlier rape by a gang of youths. This time it is Simon who removes them from this potentially threatening encounter, and leads Françoise out of the café brandishing his gun in phallic fashion at the young people.[11] This incident reminds the spectator that Françoise's retaliation against men is futile and that her only possible sanctuary will be found within a heterosexual couple, a point to which I shall return.

Released in the same year as *A nous deux*, *Courage fuyons* can be similarly seen as a popular manifestation of dissent from feminist politics in its narrative of limited female agency. *Courage fuyons* follows the unlikely relationship between Martin Belhomme (Jean Rochefort) a pharmacist who lives a mundane and cowardly existence, and Eva (Deneuve), a successful and apparently independent singer. Eva is portrayed as a sophisticated and liberated woman who has multiple lovers, no familial ties and no fixed abode. Martin, by way of contrast, is conventional and conservative. Though very reluctant, Eva agrees to marry Martin. We assume her reluctance originates in her apparently liberated mores. However, we soon learn that she is in fact a mother and married to a tyrannical American who declares 'I'm the boss'. Eva pleads with Martin to negotiate with her husband her separation from him. Eva is thus ultimately depicted as a woman enslaved to both her husband and her lover. The film delimits her emancipation and safely contains her within the narrative.

In *Courage fuyons*, Deneuve is unquestionably positioned as the object of desire. Deneuve's character is a star and is positioned as such within the *mise-en-scène* and also the narrative. Eva's costumes are made of elegant, delicate fabrics that, with her flowing hair, soften her appearance. Her immaculate, coordinated and contained appearance contrasts dramatically with Martin's awkward and dowdy dress. When Martin attempts to appear more masculine or successful by changing his dress style, he becomes a point of ridicule – even to Eva, reinforcing reactionary norms of binary gender difference. Eva also stands out dramatically from the leather-jacket-wearing *soixante-huitards* who initially introduce the couple. From Eva's first appearance, the spectator is encouraged to adopt Martin's adoring gaze. When Martin first spots Eva through a window, cast in the morning sunlight, Deneuve is literally framed as the desirable object, therefore conditioning her visibility (see Mayne 1993: 169).

To summarise, by positioning and stylising Deneuve as an object of desire, she is fixed within the text by the male gaze, and her gendered identity is secured. We recall that, according to Butler, this configuration of discreet genders reproduces compulsory heterosexuality. Thus, in accordance with Butler's theory, within Deneuve's films of the 1970s, the institution of the heterosexual couple becomes central. In this decade, Deneuve's films feature heterosexual relationships which are born out of extraordinary circumstances, and yet are inevitably successful, underlining the perceived inevitability of heterosexuality. Consequently, at a time when the heterosexual couple was in a state of flux, Deneuve's films repeatedly suggest the need for the unification of man and woman.

The narrative of *A nous deux* suggests that there is no possibility of Deneuve's character achieving liberty (from either the police or violence) without a man by her side. When Françoise attempts to escape on her own she is quickly captured by the police, and subsequently rescued by Simon. In this regard, for one critic, Lelouch's film can be summarised as follows: 'All in all for Lelouch, a woman without a man is worth nothing, and an emancipated woman could only be mad' (De Montvalon, 1979). Consequently, according to Lelouch's thesis, in order to be truly free, Françoise must give up her desire for revenge against men.

As with many of Deneuve's films of this period the couple is made up of two opposites who are reconciled due to heterosexual desire rather than realistic compatibility. The following statement made by a critic underlines their contrariness and draws attention to the adventure which is key to their union: 'It really is the bringing together of opposites. But this strong union overcomes all the hurdles of the adventure, because it is only adventure that reconciles the irreconcilables' (Chazal, 1979). This is clear in the final scene of the film when the couple (who wear matching outfits) play music together in a hotel bar, quite literally in harmony with one and other. The implausible success of their relationship serves to underline Lelouch's apparent need to accentuate the hetero-sexual imperative.

In *Courage fuyons* the heterosexual couple is again central to the film. As in *A nous deux*, Martin and Eva are positioned as two opposites, a feature which critics highlighted in reviews (see Chauvet, 1979, Clouzot, 1979 and Delain, 1979). By drawing attention to Rochefort and Deneuve's opposition, these critics emphasise the rigid distinction of the two stars' gendered identities, and simultaneously highlight Deneuve's untouchable and desirable star-body.[12] Their incompatibility is not, however, the only hurdle. From the very outset, their trajectory as a couple is interrupted by series of incidents, often ridiculous in nature. On the first occasion that Eva and Martin make love, for example, they are disturbed by the sounds of a fighting couple in the neighbouring hotel room. Eva is constantly pursued by her partners, past and present, and each man has an obsessive desire for her, one of whom threatens to kill Martin. Eva is portrayed as the perfect bachelorette throughout the film, and apparently lives out of a suitcase in her bachelorette pad. However, at the end of the film, she is ultimately contained by the institution of marriage and the myth of female emancipation is debunked.

In both *Courage fuyons* and *A nous deux*, Deneuve functions to resolve the tensions that surrounded both the female body and the heterosexual couple during the 1970s. In both films, as we have seen, Deneuve embodies a seemingly emancipated woman who is ultimately objectified and contained by heterosexuality. This is consistent with the majority of Deneuve's films of the 1970s. However, one film within Deneuve's filmography of this period makes steps to challenge this pattern, albeit with limited success. In *Zig zig*, female friendship is at last foregrounded. This film provides us with an interesting contradiction to the rule and suggests the (limited) potential for alternative expressions of desire within Deneuve's films of the 1970s.[13]

In *Zig zig* Deneuve plays Marie, a cabaret singer, who dreams of a better life beyond Pigalle with her friend Pauline (Bernadette Lafont). The pair perform together at a cabaret club, where they effectively advertise their other services – prostitution. Their motivation for prostituting themselves is their desire to buy a house together in the mountains, a dream which would break the heterosexual mould. However, this dream is revealed, unlike the improbable partnerships of *Courage fuyons* and *A nous deux*, to be impossible and is ultimately thwarted. Secretly, Pauline has a relationship with one of the musicians at the club, and helps him to carry out a kidnapping. Marie eventually discovers Pauline's treachery and notifies the police of her involvement in the kidnapping. Despite this, Marie forgives Pauline and the pair declare their love for one another, exchanging their only kiss of the film. Any happy unification of the two women is, however, finally (and fatally) prevented. Throughout the film Marie is pursued by Walter, her ex-lover, who (as with Eva's ex-lover in *Courage fuyons*), has homicidal tendencies. As the two women embrace, Walter shoots Pauline and she dies in Marie's arms. Both in Pauline's treachery and her eventual murder, the film suggests that loving relationships between women are impossible. Consequently, although *Zig zig* presents the possibility of alternative desiring positions, Marie is punished for her love for Pauline, and a particularly violent version of heterosexuality cuts short the possibility of lesbian desire.

Conclusion

All three of the films analysed in this chapter delimit the possibility of alternative female desires beyond the heterosexual frame. In this way, they deny or attempt to contain the increasing visibility of gay and lesbian groups in France during the 1970s and the challenges that these groups brought to the bourgeois family structure.[14] By focusing exclusively on the success of heterosexual couples these films hide the sociological fate of the institution of marriage during the 1970s.[15] They all signal a resistance to the emancipation of women. *Zig zig*'s negative representation of female solidarity or friendship could be seen as retaliation against the women's movement, while *Courage fuyons* and *A nous deux* are perhaps symptomatic of rising antifeminism within France at the end of the 1970s.

As Deneuve's career developed in the 1980s, her roles began to explore desiring frameworks beyond a heterosexual model. In *The Hunger* (Scott, 1983) Deneuve plays a bisexual vampire,[16] and in *Hôtel des Amériques* the *impossibility* of heterosexual relationships is depicted (Forbes 1992: 255–6). In the latter film a destabilisation of Deneuve's star image also occurs. This process signals a departure from her 1970s films, which on the whole positioned her as a fixed and objectified woman. As for Deneuve's political positioning she remained sporadically engaged in feminist issues,[17] despite the wane of the French women's movement during the 1980s and her own proclamation in 1978 that she would no longer participate actively in feminist campaigns (Alion, 1978). Indeed, as Vincendeau has argued, through Deneuve's sophistication and non-radical politicisation, she may be seen as an example of what feminism would become during the 1980s (2000: 206).

In the introduction of this chapter, Dyer was invoked in order to explain the function of Deneuve's star persona during the 1970s. According to Dyer the star functions in order to resolve contradictions 'within and between ideologies'. As a polysemous text, and one with both on-screen and off-screen dimensions that remain in tension, Deneuve reveals rather than resolves the contradictions of this decade. On the one hand (like Giscard D'Estaing and his government) Deneuve was actively involved with feminist campaigns and refused what she perceived as the imprisoning constraints of marriage. On the other hand, she can be seen as an actress who has played roles that are undoubtedly, in the words of Hayward, 'specifically phallic conception[s]', and which rely on stereotypes of the subjugated and fetishised woman. Moreover, on-screen, her hyper-femininity seems to guarantee heterosexual desire, and to prevent the development of alternative desiring frameworks. Consequently, the multiple texts that make up Deneuve's star persona during the 1970s embody the inconsistent political culture of the decade.

Notes

1 *Le Sauvage* and *Courage fuyons* rank in Deneuve's top ten box-office successes of all time (Le Gras 2005: 267).

2 Austin (2003) also dissociates Deneuve from the 1970s and sees her instead as embodying the period between 1955 and 1965 (45–6).

3 Jean-Pierre Jeancolas makes this distinction in order to pinpoint the contradictory nature of Giscardien France (1979: 240).

4 See for example Dehée, 2004:135 and Chelminski's article, 'Catherine Deneuve on her loves, her career, her liberated life' (Chelminski 1974: 29–33).

5 See also Lisa Downing's chapter on Polanski's Deneuve in this book, which discusses in more detail the lures of a rhetoric of sexual emancipation for women (Chapter 1).

6 See *L'Avortement* (1974) (Bernard George, 1996). In this documentary, key figures (including the former Minister for Justice, Jean Foyer and

Catherine Deneuve herself) attest to the importance of this political moment in the liberalisation of abortion.

7 For a discussion of the potential misogyny of *Liza*, see Pauline Small's chapter in this volume (Chapter 4). Released in the same year of the *Manifeste des 343 salopes*, *Liza* might appear to contradict Deneuve's political actions with her role as a willing, dog-collar-wearing female masochist.

8 Deneuve's tendency at the beginning of the 1970s to work in French–Italian co-productions with foreign directors is reflective of contemporaneous trends within the French film industry. As Susan Hayward points out in her study of Simone Signoret, by the mid-1970s the long production partnership between Italy and France was coming to an end. Hayward explains that deprived of this previously fruitful relationship, France was forced to find finance elsewhere, which it did by maintaining three mainstays of its national cinema: the *policier*, the comedy and films which evoked the *tradition de qualité* of the 1950s (44–5). Mirroring wider patterns within the French film industry, out of the twelve films made by Deneuve between 1970 and 1974, eleven were French/ Italian co-productions. From 1975 onwards (the point at which co-productions between the two countries began to decline) Deneuve made fewer auteur films with foreign directors (between 1975 and 1980 Deneuve made thirteen films, eight of which had French finance).

9 For example, Deneuve capitalised on her Amercian Chanel advertising campaign by featuring in *March or Die* (Richards, 1976). Deneuve also worked with two Italian directors (*Cassotto* (Citti, 1977) and *Anima persa/ Lost Soul* (Risi, 1977)), which was the sole France–Italy co-production she made in the latter part of this decade.

10 Through their interaction with each other, we observe that the group is bisexual. Thus, Lelouch casts alternative sexualities as dangerous and further reifies the heterosexual model.

11 Simon's use of the gun in this scene highlights Françoise's powerlessness, since she repeatedly refuses the use of a gun.

12 Rochefort's role as the 'poltron' (wimp) in this film contrasts interestingly with his role a year earlier in *Le Cavaleur* (de Broca, 1978). In the latter film Rochefort is cast as a man who is the object of numerous women's desires. Such is the status of Deneuve that, next to her, it is perhaps impossible for Rochefort to reoccupy the position of a credible object of desire. For a sustained discussion of Rochefort as a star embodying a fallible heterosexual masculinity, see Downing 2004: 54–81.

13 *Ecoute voir...* (Santiago, 1979) is the only other example of a 1970s Deneuve vehicle in which lesbian desire appears. In the film Deneuve kisses Anne Parillaud. Unfortunately, this film is unavailable both in France and the UK and I have therefore not been able to include it within this study. Interestingly, however, it appears to have been recuperated

by certain French websites from where it has been suggested that, while Deneuve does not actually play a lesbian in the film, *Ecoute voir...* offers potential spectatorial pleasure to lesbian audiences. See 'Deneuve et nous', http://degel.asso.fr/culture/people/people101.php (Dégel is an organisation that represents gay and lesbian students).

14 The FHAR was set up in 1971. This organisation sought to 'struggle against patriarchy and bourgeois family morality' and modelled itself on the American Gay Liberation Front (Copley 1989: 225). Additionally, in 1978 the Pétain-De Gaulle law on homosexuality was challenged, and eventually rescinded in 1982 (Copley 1989: 226).

15 During the 1970s the divorce rate rose from 37,447 in 1970 to 79,689 in 1980 (Segalen 2000:138).

16 See Andrew Asibong's chapter in this book (Chapter 9). Vincendeau also discusses this film in relation to lesbian culture (2000: 206–7).

17 In 1985 she signed the *Manifesto des 85* which called for gender equality, particularly in the workplace (Sarde 1988: 939).

Works cited

Anon. (1970), 'Confidences d'onze heures', *Le nouveau cinémonde*, http://toutsurdeneuve.free.fr/Francais/Pages/Interviews_Presse6079/Cinemonde70.html (accessed 23 July 2005).

Anon. (1979), '*A nous deux*', *Minute*, 6 June.

Anon. (2004), 'Deneuve et nous', http://degel.asso.fr/culture/people/people 101.php (accessed 5 December 2005).

Abitan, Guy (1970), 'Catherine tout en charme', *Mademoiselle tendre age*, http://toutsurdeneuve.free.fr/Francais/Pages/Interviews_Presse6079/MlleAgeTendre70.html (accessed 23 July 2005).

Alion, Yves (1978), 'Catherine Deneuve ou le triomphe de l'ambiguïté', *Ecran*, 73, 11–25.

Allwood, Gill (1998), *French Feminisms: gender and violence in contemporary theory*, London: UCL Press.

Austin, Guy (2003), *Stars in Modern French Film*, London: Arnold.

Bard, Christine (1999), 'Les antiféminismes de la deuxième vague', *Un siècle d'antifeminisme*, Paris: Fayard, 301–28.

Bell, David S. (2000), *Presidential Power in Fifth Republic France*, Oxford: Berg.

Butler, Judith (1999), *Gender Trouble: Feminism and the Subversion of Identity*, 2nd edn, London and New York: Routledge.

Chauvet, Louis (1979), 'La belle et le poltron', *Figaro*, 19 October.

Chazal, Robert (1979), '*A nous deux*', *France-soir*, 26 May.

Chelminski, Rudi (1974), 'Catherine Deneuve on her loves, her career, her liberated life', *People*, September 2, 29–33.

Clouzot, Claire (1979), 'Dans *Courage fuyons*, d'Yves Robert, le sexe faible c'est les hommes', *Le Matin*, 3 July.

Copley, Antony (1989), *Sexual Moralities in France 1780–1980: New Ideas on the Family, Divorce and Homosexuality: An Essay on Moral Change*, London: Routledge.

Dehée, Yannick (2000), *Mythologies politiques du cinéma français, 1960–2000*, Paris: PUF.

De Montvalon, Christine (1979), '*A nous deux*', *Télérama*, 6 June.

Delain, Michel (1979), 'Le dégonflé amoureux', *L'Express*, 22 October.

Downing, Lisa (2004), 'Modes of masculinity', in *Patrice Leconte*, Manchester: Manchester University Press, 54–81.

Dyer, Richard (1998), *Stars*, 2nd edn, London: BFI.

Esposito, Marc (1978), 'Entretien avec Catherine Deneuve', *Première*, http://toutsurdeneuve.free.fr/Francais/Pages/Interviews_Presse6079/Premiere78.htm (last accessed 31 October 2005).

Forbes, Jill (1992), *The Cinema in France After the New Wave*, Basingstoke and London: Macmillan.

Frears, John R. (1981), *France in the Giscard Presidency*, London: Allen & Unwin.

Germain, Anne (1974), 'Etes-vous féministe? Bien entendu!', *Le Soir illustré*, http://toutsurdeneuve.free.fr/Francais/Pages/Interviews_Presses6079/Cinemonde70.html (accessed 23 July 2005).

Hayward, Susan (1993), *French National Cinema*, London and New York: Routledge.

Hayward, Susan (2004), *Simone Signoret: The Star as Cultural Sign*, London and New York: Continuum.

Jeancolas, Jean-Pierre (1979), *Le cinema des Français: La Ve République*, Paris, Stock.

Kuhn, Annette (1994), *Women's Pictures: Feminism and Cinema*, 2nd edn, London and New York: Verso.

Larkin, Maurice (1988), *France since the Popular Front: Government and People 1936–1986*, Oxford: Clarendon Press.

Le Gras, Gwénaëlle (2005), 'Résurgence de la comédie à la française dans les années 1970–1980: Les apports de la persona Deneuve au genre dans *Le Sauvage* (Rappeneau, 1975) et *L'Africain* (de Broca, 1983), in Moine, Raphaëlle (ed.), *Le Cinéma français face aux genres*, Paris: Association Française de Recherche sur l'Histoire du Cinéma, 265–73.

Marks, Elaine and Isabelle de Courtivron (1981), 'Introduction III: contexts of the new French feminisms', in Marks and de Courtivron (eds), *New French Feminisms: An Anthology*, New York: Schocken Books, 28–38.

Mayne, Judith (1993), *Cinema and spectatorship*, London and New York: Routledge.

Sarde, Michéle (1988), 'L'Action du ministère des droits de la femme, 1981–86: un bilan', *The French Review*, 61(6), 931–41.

Segalen, Martine (2000), *Sociologie de la famille*, Paris: Armand Colin.

Tenret, Jacqueline (1977), 'Deneuve, toujours Deneuve', *Elle*, http://toutsur-deneuve.free.fr/Francais/Pages/Interviews_Presse6079/Elle77.htm (last accessed 5 December 2005).

Vincendeau, Ginette (2000), *Stars and Stardom in French Cinema*, London: Continuum.

6

'Madame La France': Deneuve as heritage icon

Sue Harris

For all the risks that the young Catherine Deneuve took with her star image, her roles from the early 1980s constructed a new kind of maturity and coherence that chimed with both her age and her screen longevity. The itinerary of this transition can be best traced through her modish incursion into the 1980s heritage film culture, and more specifically into a series of historical roles written for the actress.[1] The heritage genre has been identified as a genre of filmmaking that uses 'the national – or at least, one version of the national past – as their prime selling point' (Higson 1993: 109), and it has been perceived as operating within what Thomas Elsaesser has termed a 'cultural mode of production' as opposed to Hollywood's industrial mode of production (1989: 3). Heritage-style cinema typically offers a lavish recreation of historical texts, events and characters, and invites viewers to bask in the 'nostalgic pleasures of period reconstruction' (Tarr 2001: 252). This is enabled by an attention to display, decoration and pictorial composition, in which the potential for critical perspective is threatened, if not overwhelmed, by a visually splendid pastiche of national iconography. The past, its artefacts, and its conventionally conservative values are mythologised as desirable signifiers of a vanished authenticity, while its characters are the vehicles for constructing the itineraries of modern citizenship and identity. This type of filmmaking made a significant mark on the French industry in the 1980s and 1990s (Powrie 1999: 1–21), and marked something of a renaissance in matters of studio production and investment. It also facilitated a renewal of the star system in France, creating opportunities for young talents, as well as more established actors such as Yves Montand and Philippe Noiret.

The success of these French 'super-productions', which often boasted lavish sets, huge budgets and production values to rival those of Hollywood, was founded on what has been termed their careful display of a 'museum aesthetic' (Vincendeau 2001: xviii). Their investigation of the national past tended to favour a representation of popular French history that is stories of 'great men', the founding events of the French nation and the adaptation of classic literary texts by canonical authors. Films such as *Le Retour de Martin Guerre* (Daniel Vigne, 1982), *Danton* (Andrzej Wajda, 1983) and *Jean de Florette* (Claude Berri, 1986) were invested with a dazzling wealth of historical detail, and found receptive audiences both in France and on the international art-house circuit. The importance of stars to the success of the genre can be gauged by the example of Gérard Depardieu, the eponymous lead in the three films cited above, who by the mid-1980s had already established himself as the leading heritage talent of his generation. Conversely, the genre was not an obvious outlet for imaginative or experienced female performance; youthful beauty and innocence, as represented by young performers such as Nastassja Kinski (*Tess*; Roman Polanski, 1979), Sophie Marceau (*Fort Saganne*; Alain Corneau, 1984; *Chouans!*; Philippe de Broca, 1988) and Emmanuelle Béart (*Manon des sources*; Claude Berri, 1986) were inevitably deployed as secondary to the performance by older male leads, and were better suited to the inherent gender imbalances of the narrative mode. Nevertheless, Deneuve's age (she was 40 in 1983), range and complex performance profile made her a realistic choice for the rarer mature female parts that demanded physical elegance, bourgeois sophistication, intellectual strength and the suggestion of sexual desire held in check by social and historical circumstances. Although her incursions into the heritage mode were few, her engagement with it was significant both in terms of her own career and the project of French cultural production in the Mitterrand years.

The principal heritage roles taken by Deneuve in this twelve-year period were as Marion Steiner with Depardieu in François Truffaut's occupation drama *Le Dernier Métro* (1980); a reappearance alongside Depardieu as Parisian blue-stocking journalist Louise Tissot in Alain Corneau's epic military adventure *Fort Saganne* (1984); and as the colonial landowner Eliane Devries, the lead part in Régis Wargnier's ambitious saga of Asian decolonisation *Indochine* (1992). These film projects all feature fictional narratives and characters played out against the historical realities of twentieth-century French history: the colonisation of Saharan Africa in 1911 and the outbreak of the Great War of 1914 (*Fort Saganne*); political insurgency and revolution in French-colonised Indochina in the 1930s, and the subsequent dismantling of French colonial authority (*Indochine*); the survival of French identity, traditions and citizens under the German occupation 1940–1944 (*Le Dernier Métro*). These films served to reconfigure the nature of Deneuve's screen image, and created the circumstances by which more immediately accessible and readily exportable notions of 'Frenchness' were projected by the actress and the French cinema industry. By carefully acknowledging the screen characteristics established over the previous two decades, and channelling them into conventional, didactic narrative forms, these films elided Deneuve's more controversial filmic personae in favour of representations that positioned the mature actress as an icon of compassionate French identity, accessed through her established cinematic femininity, but whose symbolic function lay primarily in the realm of the national.

As the twin poles of mature heritage performance in the 1980s, Deneuve and Depardieu show interesting differences in the nature of their stardom. On the one hand, his incarnation of literary and historical figures such as Balzac's Le Colonel Chabert, Pagnol's Jean de Florette, Rostand's Cyrano de Bergerac and Auguste Rodin in *Camille Claudel* (Nuytten, 1988) has been read by Ginette Vincendeau in terms of 'roles which are explicitly about fame, display and acting – in short, about stardom' (Vincendeau 2000: 231). Indeed, key to Depardieu's success has been his ability to compel the French public with plausible imitations of the 'starry' men – fictional and real – of French cultural life. Deneuve, on the other hand, has tended to play entirely fictional figures, with no connection to identifiable historical or literary sources. Her performances have thus expressed more the abstract qualities of French national identity than embodied specific examples of its manifestations. This is not unusual for women in the heritage genre: while critics such as Dyer, Pidduck and Monk have argued that the heritage genre provides a space to 'challenge mainstream representations of gender and sexuality' and 'to widen the gender and sexual cinematic horizon' (Vincendeau 2002: xx), the gendering of popular history on film, particularly in French film, is nevertheless heavily reliant on common narrative patterns 'whereby male identity is (however fancifully) historical, and female identity sexual' (2002: 30). Vincendeau's analysis of the character of Marguerite de Valois, played by Isabelle Adjani in Patrice Chéreau's *La Reine Margot* (1994), reveals how a conventional sexual stereotyping operates to give prominence to a historically significant female figure through a concentration on 'her (vastly exaggerated) romantic and sexual life over her actual political ambitions and literary achievements' (Vincendeau 2002: 30). Thus, female performance in the heritage mode presupposes a presence based on performance characteristics and sexual identity rather than predetermined historical value.

The filmic project with which Deneuve engages is thus ostensibly one of uneasy complicity with conservative screen discourses that privilege male action and agency in the historical sweep of French national history, while rendering female characters as passive secondary players, even when placed at the centre of the story. What is significant, however, is that Deneuve's own fame somehow exceeds the constraints of narrative conditioning, featuring her as a central focus in ways that are aesthetically and thematically compelling. While she cannot fully escape the constraints imposed by the conventions of the genre, the 'traces' of Deneuve's career to date act as a referential model, allowing her to bring a wide range of seemingly incompatible performance characteristics to the parts offered. Her heritage roles, both individually and together, thus translate the multifaceted and sometimes bewildering screen traits of Catherine Deneuve into something more coherent and conservative, something that synthesises and 'explains' the various aspects of the actress in a context that evokes pride and affection rather than the confusion of her earlier career. This is then the genre in which the scattered elements of Deneuve's career are brought under narrative control, and in which the continuities of her career first outweigh the discontinuities. The containment of the previously unclassifiable Deneuve by heritage propriety works to mythologise the screen icon as much as it does French national history. This coincidence of agendas, and their translation into a repeated narrative framework of desired and desirable maternity, are key to understanding the public embrace of Deneuve as a contemporary symbol of, and subsequent ambassador for, Frenchness.

Furthermore, in 1985 Deneuve was elected by the committee of French mayors as the contemporary model for the bust of the republican symbol Marianne. This identification of the actress with the public face of France, replicated in Mireille Polska's statue and on national postage stamps, underscored her status as vehicle for accessing the emotions of French nationhood in these various dramas of French national identity. As we shall see, the reading of Deneuve as national heroine that the above films promote is inseparable from the actress's extra-cinematic public image in France. The 1980s thus constituted the moment in which Deneuve's iconic status as a key site of French femininity was enhanced and significantly extended, and its more problematic aspects recalibrated for a mass audience. Evidence of this is apparent in the awards and accolades that frame the period in question: she and Depardieu both received the first Césars of their careers for their roles in *Le Dernier Métro* (best actress and best actor respectively); *Indochine* won the 1993 César for best film, and the Golden Globe and Academy Awards for best foreign film. Deneuve won the second best-actress César of her career for this film, and was nominated for the Academy Award in the same category. These films and their rewards are confirmation of the gravitas of reputation that the industry, the international public and the French nation confer on Deneuve as her career moves into its mature phase.

Le Dernier Métro (Truffaut, 1980)

Truffaut's Occupation drama *Le Dernier Métro* launches this period in Deneuve's career. Here, she plays Marion Steiner, a gentile bourgeois actress, theatre director and owner who is sheltering her Jewish husband, Lucas. Deneuve plays to her established filmic strengths: the implied austerity of the Occupation years somehow eludes her, as the camera delights in her elegant tailored ensembles, dramatic fur coats, polished high heels and tight coiffure. Her body is adorned with a wealth of luxurious accessories – capes, gloves, veils, rings – while her height and the long lines of her frame exaggerate her centrality and command within the ensemble cast. The storyline and *mise-en-scène* both set Marion apart from the other women in the film in terms of perceived availability: while Bernard Granger (Depardieu) flirts with all-comers from the opening shot, his banal chat-up line an unconvincing 'I see two women in you' ('il y a deux femmes en vous'), the genuinely multilayered Marion remains an aloof and remote figure, consistent with her social standing in the world of the Parisian arts. As aspects of the character are revealed by dialogue, we learn that she has both a background in fashion and golden-age screen stardom: references to pre-war work at the Chanel couture house echo Deneuve's off-screen association with Yves Saint-Laurent,[2] while a reference to 'the infamous photo' ('la fameuse photo') of her in '*La Maison du Péché*' (*The House of Sin*) hints at a degree of sexual notoriety at the heart of the fictitious screen career. These subtle narrative details do more than simply build the historical character of Marion; more specifically, they inscribe Marion as an emblematic figure of on-screen and off-screen convergences, as a character who exists as product, consequence and extension of Deneuve's star persona. That Truffaut should also have been revisiting his on and off-screen relationship with his former lover established in his film *La Sirène du Mississippi* (*Mississippi Mermaid*, 1969) only adds a further layer of complexity to this intriguing construction. Truffaut's adoration of the actress was a prime motivation for him in making the film: 'Catherine Deneuve is so beautiful that any film she stars in could almost dispense with telling a story. I am convinced that the spectator will find happiness in just looking at Catherine and that this contemplation is worth the price of admission!' (de Baeque and Toubiana 1999: 256)

The implied sexual repression which has become such a trope of Deneuve's screen presence is here given a topographical twist in line with historical circumstances. Marion has only limited emotional and physical access to her husband hidden in the theatre cellar, and the communication system that Lucas sets up in order to direct the rehearsals from below poses a threat to both her professional management but also the possibility of sexual autonomy. This tension between affection for the hidden husband and powerful desire for Bernard Granger, her handsome young lead, is the romantic foundation of the narrative. The historically improbable sartorial extravagance that prevails in the theatre scenes serves a range of functions: to mark her distance from the impoverishment of Lucas's existence; to highlight her desirability to those who operate in her world (Bernard, Daxiat, Arlette); and to contain her desiring body with strictly tailored lines. Significantly, the moment at which Marion's estrangement from Lucas coincides with an acknowledgement of her passion for Bernard is marked by an on-stage appearance in a torn red dress and loose, dishevelled wig. As elsewhere in Deneuve's career, repressed desire comes to the fore in the shape of degradation of the codes of socially constructed femininity.

So far, so conventional. Deneuve's screen presence in this film is however complicated by a third function that was something of a departure for the actress: that of parental figure to her community of actors. From the outset, Marion Steiner functions as an efficient and concerned protector and nurturer, whose class, gender and beauty are deployed to place the subversive community beyond suspicion. While Bernard, the would-be resistance hero suspects her motivations, Marion is in fact a Marianne *avant la lettre*, actively heroic in her acts, and morally heroic in her repression of her instincts and desires. Her maternal tenacity and stoic self-effacement result in the survival of the troupe and her husband, his incarceration ending after 813 days with the Liberation of Paris. Marion/-ianne's victory

is ultimately a victory for Frenchness: for republican French identity
hidden in the form of her husband Lucas like treasure beneath the
theatre floorboards, and for the French values of 'Liberty, Equality
and Fraternity' as performed and demonstrated by the theatre
troupe. As Holmes and Ingram in their monograph on Truffaut have
suggested:

> As defender of the integrity of the theatre against the collaborating
> Daxiat, she saves her husband's life and symbolically preserves French
> honour: as a woman in love with both Lucas and Bernard, she represents
> the film's central enigma (who will she end up with?) and in a happy
> ending that befits the scenario of the Liberation, concludes the film at the
> centre of a triumphant triangle, one hand in her husband's, the other in
> Bernard's. (1998: 138)

Bernard and Marion's passion, built up cautiously and incremen-
tally over the duration of the film thus comes to stand as a metaphor
for the triumph of resistance, and the deliverance of France from
oppression. Marion, narratively overdetermined by Deneuve's screen
history, is the focus and embodiment of this national celebration.

Fort Saganne (Corneau, 1984)

Only a few years later, Catherine Deneuve lent her *'participation exceptionnelle'* to another heritage project, this time a more
substantial vehicle for the young Gerard Depardieu as ambitious
young officer Charles Saganne. Set in the late *belle époque* (1911),
the hugely expensive film (50 million francs) recounts the epic career
of Charles Saganne in colonial Africa and First World War Europe.
Deneuve's screen presence in this film is in fact unusually limited for
an actress of her stature, amounting to little more than 25 minutes in
a film lasting almost three hours.[3] Her secondary role as the George
Sand-like writer and journalist Louise Tissot, is nevertheless, significant – she is the 'bad' catalyst for Charles to change his destiny, and
seek out a life with the 'good' innocent young woman (Madeleine,
played by Sophie Marceau) who is in love with him from the outset,
and from whom he is distanced by consideration of class and rank.

Given the very limited screen time accorded to Deneuve, her
presentation on-screen is remarkably dense, and amounts to an
extreme compression of a range of previously established screen
characteristics. She is seen in three different incarnations: twice
publicly and once in the privacy of her apartment. On both public

occasions, her introduction is preceded by a view of a map of the African continent, a place associated with Charles (who in both cases reads the map) and with connotations of the untamed and undiscovered. In both views, Louise is dressed in black and white, in the first case formally, like the professional men around her, with a high buttoned white collar and necktie garment, and second as a nurse, her black cape and starched white cap consistent with those worn by the nuns evacuating survivors from a war-blasted town. These appearances frame a much longer interlude in which Louise is either naked or clad in loose bedroom robes, engaged in lovemaking with Charles in a softly lit boudoir. Her deep-red, chaotically assembled apartment is the site of Charles' seduction and of the moral crisis that will determine his future actions and his return to military and social order.

Louise's opening remark to Charles: 'I was staging the scene for you' ('Je vous préparais une mise-en-scène') hints at the ways in which her 'exceptional participation' is self-consciously exploited by the narrative. Her quiet admonition at the urgency of his passion – 'You are a young man in a hurry' ('Vous êtes un jeune homme pressé') – confirms her conventional positioning as the sophisticated and sexually experienced 'older' woman who is in control of her desires and is the agent of her own sexual encounters. Here Deneuve steps briefly out of the more elaborate narrative framework of her heritage performance as the 'tragic *grande bourgeoise*, often a heroic mother, whose sedate – if glamorous – life is disturbed by sexual passion, usually initiated by a younger man' (Vincendeau 2002: 205). In this case she is unmaternal, unheroic and the initiator of the sexual exchange. Her independence and absence of moral code are key factors in the appeal to Charles, to whom the younger Madeleine has been denied. She is nevertheless glamorous – her alabaster skin and flowing strawberry-blond hair are compellingly luminous in the otherwise dark tones of the room; and, as the narrative will reveal, she displays affinities with the conventional 'tragic *grande bourgeoise*', whose impulse to control results in a distance that will destroy her: her inability to master fully her inherent emotional instabilities – expressed in a hysterical outburst when she falls at Charles's feet – ultimately leads to the loss of the love she so desperately craves, but cannot admit until it is too late.

Deneuve's Louise is, as in *Le Dernier Métro*, a fascinating amalgam of the actress's previous screen incarnations. The facets of femininity that she expresses are constructed as 'timeless' – the dominant woman competing in a man's world; the whore-like temptress behind closed doors; the repentant sinner who dedicates her life to nurturing damaged men – and reveal Louise as a classic female cinematic construction masquerading rather superficially as something more complex. Nevertheless, the compression of the entire range of facets of Deneuve's screen femininity into one single character (whose only contrast is the equally problematic but less complex Madeleine, the ideal of female 'perfection') is set against the wide variety of male characters who are tested by the narrative events and revealed as a spectrum of 'flawed' masculinity. The tiny red cross of the international aid organisation on the starched white cap in Louise's final appearance in the film recalls the dangerous red of the boudoir. While heralding her redemption by the narrative, it is also an indelible mark of the imperfections, transgressions and paradoxes that are the building blocks of the character.

The threat posed by Louise to the male enterprise of military endeavour and conquest (both Africa and the 'good' woman who can bear Charles's good French citizens to continue his line) is contained by the narrative which transforms her into a 'heroic mother', albeit a barren one. Louise's capitulation in the face of the inevitabilities of warfare and the news that Charles has married and fathered a child with Madeleine, and her decision to release the hero when she could compel his attention and possible desertion is rewarded by the acquisition of moral strength and dignity in the face of catastrophic loss. In her final screen moment she watches stoically as Charles walks away to his death on the front line. Her emblematic status as bereft French woman, clad in the apparel of the nun/nurse, confirms her role as one prepared to make the ultimate sacrifice for her country. She is a martyr, a screen Magdelene, whose actions command respect and whose redemption is complete. She is also another variant on the symbolic Marianne, sending her sons off to defend the greater good of French national enterprise.

Indochine (Wargnier, 1992)

Indochine was a huge critical and commercial success, both in France and abroad and it stands as a climactic film in the French vogue for heritage films generally, and colonialist heritage films in particular. The 1980s and early 1990s had seen a series of such films (*Chocolat*,

Claire Denis, 1988; *Outremer*, Brigitte Roüan, 1990; *Fort Saganne*, Alain Corneau, 1984; *Diên Biên Phu*, Pierre Schoendoerffer, 1992; *L'Amant*, Jean Annaud, 1992), variously militaristic or intimist. *Indochine*, unusually, puts a female figure centre stage, in this case Deneuve as Eliane Devries, a proud, ultimately tragic heroine living out familial and romantic dramas against a backdrop of French colonial history. Her role in the film is a plural one: she is mother to an adopted Indochinese girl, the lover of a young French military officer, benevolent imperialist employer and eye witness to the process of decolonialisation. She is also crucially an 'Asiate', born and raised in the colonies. Deneuve's Eliane is thus central to the narrative and thematic frameworks of the film, and is uniquely positioned by age, nationality and gender in relation to the unfolding events of French national history.

Like *Le Dernier Métro*, the film positions Deneuve somewhat conventionally as a sexually repressed woman torn between two distinct and incompatible passions: love for her adopted daughter Camille, and love for her younger lover Jean-Baptiste (played by Vincent Perez) who will ultimately become Camille's lover. Once again, the film and Deneuve's role in it are forcefully constructed around questions of the parental, and the broad sweep of colonial history in particular is reflected though a prism of parental action and responsibilities: Eliane teaches Camille French customs and skills; she disciplines her workers to whom she is 'both mother and father'; she is a visibly older lover to the young Jean-Baptiste, whom she is eventually forced to accept as a son, and whose son she in turn adopts after his father's death and his mother's incarceration for revolutionary insurgency. Eliane is not a mother and she actively resists attempts by Guy (Jean Yanne) to persuade her into the marital framework that would facilitate such a role. And yet she is a multiple surrogate mother – an 'eternal' (if not biological) mother (Blum-Reid 2003: 34) – and as such functions as the symbolic centre for the familial rejection of old, elegant, traditional France by youthful, idealistic Indo-China. She has been described as 'the colonial Marianne [...] the embodiment of the French colony in symbol and image' (Norindr 1996: 124).

As befits a film of *Indochine*'s ambitions, it is a lavish vehicle for the expression of Deneuve's star persona. An Asiate she may be, but there is little in the film to detract from our prior identification of Deneuve with French identity. The film offers surprisingly little actual historical detail or enactment, but there are at least thirty-two magnificent costume changes, and repeated framing shots that privilege Deneuve's screen presence in relation to both environment and community: time and again we see her look proprietorially over her house, her rubber plantation, her guests, her workers, her land. Her consistency with historical models of colonial women is at least superficially intact: 'Her role was to be a "super colonizer", to introduce elegance into colonial life and to inject enthusiasm into the colonial enterprise but within the accepted norms of femininity prescribed by the existing patriarchal framework' (Ravi 2002: 76). And yet this is complicated by a number of factors including her unmarried status, and her consequent failure to sustain the family as a site of French imperial development (childless herself, her estates will pass on to Camille and the descendants of her Indochinese family). But Eliane's undoing operates more significantly at the level of her sexuality, and her failure to conform to the role of 'custodian of morality' expected of French colonial women of the era. Deneuve's beauty and feminine sophistication respond to a form of 'national duty' consistent with her gender ('French women were meant to introduce feminine values of dignity, grace and charm in the lives of vulnerable French men who were leading wild and indecent lives by taking native lovers in the colonies' (Ravi 2002: 75)). But her affair with a handsome young officer, young enough to be her son, places her outside the parameters of colonial discourses on family and femininity, and returns us to the screen persona of Catherine Deneuve, in which moral and sexual ambiguity are all the more acute for being located in images of feminine 'purity'.

The final sequence of the film further problematises, rather than resolves, the positioning of Eliane as mother and daughter of France. The final shots show her standing by Lake Geneva in politically neutral Switzerland, while she waits for Etienne to return from seeing his real mother, Camille, visiting Geneva as part of a political delegation to agree the 1954 Accords. Etienne rejects the opportunity to meet Camille, and confirms instead that Eliane is 'the only mother I ever had'. Eliane, now the mother of a young male French citizen, looks wistfully across the water to France, that country with which she has been associated throughout the colonial drama, the country to which she has given her life, her energy, her family and now her history. It is the motherland to which she now returns as a dutiful daughter, her blond hair and exotic passions once again tamed by costume, narrative closure and the swell of French history. She is an errant Marianne, who has been brought back into the fold of family and *patrie*. Interestingly, Deneuve has described her attraction to the role thus: 'The role of a woman-woman, a woman who is no longer a young girl, but who might never be completely adult. Someone quite like the woman I seem to be, both in my life and in my films' (Fache 2004: 314). ('Un rôle d'une femme-femme, d'une femme qui n'est plus une jeune fille mais qui ne sera peut-être jamais tout à fait une adulte. Un personnage en harmonie avec le genre de personne que j'ai l'air de l'être, aussi bien dans la vie que dans les films').

'La Marianne'

The choice of whose features should be used at any time as the official model for Marianne, the symbolic representation of the French Republic, is a highly controversial matter, and it is perhaps difficult for those unschooled in French history and culture to appreciate quite why the choice of the model should be such a matter of national comment and concern. Although the representation of Democracy as a woman dates from ancient times, the Marianne figure first emerged during the French Revolution of 1789 as a symbolic embodiment of the founding republican values of liberty, equality and fraternity. The image or bust of the figure is displayed on stamps, and at the 36,000 French town halls up and down the country; it is a symbolic presence in French official life, and any attempts to identify the figure with a high-profile celebrity are likely to be fraught. The fall from political grace of Brigitte Bardot, the unofficial 1969 model, is a case in point: what does one do with one's Marianne when her outspoken political views are at variance with those of republican consensus? More recently, the election by the Association of French Mayors of the Marianne of the Millennium, was the subject of enormous debate in France: the first Marianne of the twenty-first century was modelled on the face of supermodel Laetitia Casta, who was only in her early twenties at the time of the election. At the time she was famous only for roles in the comedy *Astérix et Obélix contre César/Asterix and Obelix Take on Caesar* (Claude Zidi, 1999), and for appearing in a Guess Jeans advertising campaign, and she caused a storm by immediately announcing she was moving to London to escape high French taxes.

The Marianne figure is a fusion of two distinct historical concepts: on the one hand she is depicted as fiery and militaristic, a bare-breasted warrior as evoked in the Delacroix painting *Liberty Leading the People* (1830); she wears the Phrygian bonnet of the people – the symbol of former slaves emancipated into citizenship in the Roman Empire – for whom she is a beloved and inspirational leader. Her other mode of being is that of the pacific and nurturing mother, more demure in appearance, and protective of her children, the citizens. Her function therefore moves between aggressive defence of the nation, and that of sheltering the weak and powerless for whom she is responsible. In both cases, the evocation of the mother figure is key: Marianne is an extraordinary, but ordinary woman, a fighter, a leader, but also a comforter and a familiar presence. She is someone who both embodies and upholds concepts of French republicanism, and who is close to the people while looked up to as a symbol. She is mother and motherland all at once.

Deneuve was identified as the new face of Marianne in 1985, and was a popular choice for both politicians and the public. Her selection as the image of a newly socialist, culturally dynamic France was perceived very positively, especially in the light of vigorous attempts on the part of the French government to reinvent the French cinema industry as a prestige vehicle for displaying concepts of national history, art and literary heritage (Powrie, 1999). For Deneuve, her extra-cinematic association with an enduring narrative of national maternal authority intensified the aura and appeal of her screen incarnations, and inevitably augmented the affection in which she was held in French cultural life. This has arguably remained intact in spite of subversive forays into roles such as the alcoholic Marianne in Nicole Garcia's stylish contemporary drama *Place Vendôme* (1999). Thanks to her work in the heritage film, and its impact on her film profile, by the beginning of the 1990s Deneuve was the highest paid female star in the French industry with 'a status so inalienable that it enabled her in the rest of the decade to play anything she wanted, including, paradoxically, the demolition of her own image and beauty' (Vincendeau 2000: 208). While in the UK honours system she might well be Dame Catherine by now,[4] in contemporary republican France Citizen Deneuve wears the elegant mantle of '*grande dame*': elder stateswoman of French cinema, and a heritage institution in her own right.

Notes

1 This was the case for both *Le Dernier Métro* (Truffaut, 1980) and *Indochine* (Wargnier, 1992). In Truffaut's film, Deneuve is again given the name of Marion, the character she played in their earlier collaboration *La Sirène du Mississippi/Mississippi Mermaid* (1969).

2 From 1969 to 1977 Deneuve was under contract to Chanel in the USA to promote its No. 5 perfume. In these eight years, the brand sold more than in the previous twenty (Fache 2004: 231). See Fiona Handyside's essay in this volume for a full discussion of this aspect of Deneuve's career (Chapter 10).

3 Alexandre Fache suggests the screen time is closer to 10 minutes, probably because it is shared with Depardieu (2004: 267–8).

4 The honour of Dame Commander of the British Empire has been given to a series of UK actresses of Deneuve's generation who have had particular screen success in heritage films. These include Judi Dench, Maggie Smith and Helen Mirren.

Works cited

Agulhon, Maurice and Pierre Bonte (1992), *Marianne: Les Visages de la République*, Paris: Gallimard.

Austin, Guy (1996), *Contemporary French Cinema*, Manchester and New York: Manchester University Press.

Blum-Reid, Sylvie (2003), *East–West Encounters: Franco-Asian Cinema and Literature*, London: Wallflower.

de Baeque, Antoine and Serge Toubiana (1999), *Truffaut: a Biography*, New York and London: Random House.

Deneuve, Catherine (2004), *A l'ombre de moi-même*, Paris: Stock.

Elsaesser, Thomas (1989), *New German Cinema: a History*, London: BFI/Macmillan

Fache, Alexandre (2004), *Catherine Deneuve: une biographie*, Paris: Presses de la Cité.

Higson, Andrew (1993), 'Re-presenting the national past: nostalgia and pastiche in the heritage film', in Friedman, Lester (ed.), *British Cinema and Thatcherism: Fires were Started*, London: University College London Press, pp. 109–29.

Holmes, Diana and Robert Ingram (1998), *François Truffaut*, Manchester: Manchester University Press.

Norindr, Panivong (1996), 'Filmic memorial and colonial blues: Indochina in contemporary French cinema', in Sherzer, Dina (ed.), *Cinema, Colonialism, Postcolonialism: Perspectives from the French and Francophone Worlds*, Austin: University of Texas Press.

Powrie, Phil (1999), *French Cinema in the 1990s: Continuity and Difference*, Oxford: Oxford University Press.

Ravi, Srilata (2002), 'Women, family and empire-building: Régis Wargnier's Indochine', *Studies in French Cinema*, 2(2): 74–82.

Tarr, Carrie (2001), *Cinema and the Second Sex: Women's Filmmaking in France in the 1980s and 1990s*, London and New York: Continuum.

Vincendeau, Ginette (2000), *Stars and Stardom in French Cinema*, London and New York: Continuum.

Vincendeau, Ginette (2001), *Film/Literature/Heritage: A Sight & Sound Reader*, London: BFI.

7

Of faces and roles: Deneuve–Téchiné

Bill Marshall

Catherine Deneuve has made five films with André Téchiné, more than with any other director she has worked with in her long career: *Hôtel des Amériques* (1981), *Le Lieu du crime/Scene of the Crime* (1986), *Ma saison préférée/My Favourite Season* (1993), *Les Voleurs/Thieves* (1996) and *Les Temps qui changent* (2004). (Jacques Demy, another filmmaker of movement in social and mental worlds, is the only other director with whom she has made more than two films.) Born in the same year (1943), Téchiné had for long hoped to work with Deneuve before they were brought together by their mutual agent Gérard Lebovici. Secondary texts and interviews frequently emphasise the 'complicity' between actress and director:

> André helped me a lot to move in another direction that I thought I had in me but which I would not necessarily have taken without him. He saved me time. He encouraged me in a certain form of nakedness and truth, something at once simpler and more complex in my performance.
>
> (André m'a beaucoup aidée à aller dans une direction que je pressentais en moi mais où, sans lui, je ne serais pas forcément allée aussi rapidement. Il m'a fait gagner du temps. Il m'a beaucoup poussée vers une certaine forme de nudité, de vérité, quelque chose qui, dans mon jeu, est à la fois plus simple et plus complexe.) (From a 1998 interview with Deneuve in *Studio magazine*, quoted in Fache 2004: 257)

Indeed, that complicity seems to extend to Deneuve taking an active role in the creative process of Téchiné's films. Martine Giordano, Téchiné's regular editor, has recounted that Deneuve convinced him to retain a scene in *Le Lieu du crime* in which the 13–year-old son meets the killer of his mother's lover just after he has seen the couple having sex (Philippon 1988: 141). And Julien Hirsch, Téchiné's cinematographer on *Les Temps qui changent*, tells how Deneuve would view all the dailies, and was 'much more than the main actress: a tremendous creative partner for André' ('bien plus que l'interprète principale: une formidable partenaire de création pour André'; Frodon 2004: 21).

In the 1970s, Téchiné's films were to an extent stylistic exercises, although he used stars: the Brechtian family saga *Souvenirs d'en France/French Provincial* (1975, with Jeanne Moreau), the cinephile *Barocco* (1976, with Isabelle Adjani and Gérard Depardieu) and the costume drama *Les Sœurs Brontë/The Brontë Sisters* (1979, with Adjani and Isabelle Huppert). However, after 1981 the orientation of his films changed somewhat, and became in some ways more mainstream, or at least more audience-friendly, with a greater emphasis on identification, emotion and narrative. The films of the 1980s and 1990s are characterised by a novelistic, even Balzacian sense of social inclusion, the interpenetration of social discourses with characters shifting from foreground to background and vice versa within the narrative, a strong sense of time and place, and a representation of same-sex relations and ethnic-minority cultures which permits a sometimes radical purchase on contemporary French cultural identities in their shifting, minor modes. The new realisms inaugurated by *Hôtel des Amériques* can best be described as productive of modernist melodramas, in which how people live and love in the current phase of capitalism is dissected via explorations of bodies and characters as they relate to space(s), time and also the virtual. Intriguingly, Deneuve's association with Téchiné coincides with this turning point, and she appears in a high proportion of his twelve feature films in this period.

In order to investigate the meanings of this connection, the obvious starting point is the established literature in film studies on Deneuve's star persona. Deneuve as star is a cluster of connotations that embody bourgeois glamour (her connections with the cosmetics and fashion industries), distance and emotional coolness ('blonde, lisse et distante', 'hautaine et glacée': *Le Nouvel Observateur* 1983: 60), and at the same time a heightened feminine sexuality. This well established 'fire and ice' dichotomy is encapsulated by the youthful innocence of her character Geneviève in Demy's *Les Parapluies de Cherbourg/The Umbrellas of Cherbourg* (1964) and the middle-class wife who moonlights as a prostitute in Buñuel's *Belle de jour* of 1966, and Téchiné himself has summarised Deneuve's 'smooth, well-behaved side' ('côté lisse, sage'), and 'side of her which hides depths of madness, a supremely Hitchcockian woman' ('côté cachant des abîmes de folie; femme hitchcockienne par excellence': *Nouvelle revue française* 1996: 49). Her 'feminist' engagements in favour of abortion, for example, and the unconventionality of her love life in the 1960s and 1970s, have coded her as the archetypal 'emancipated' and autonomous woman, but one who because of her 'right-bank' origins and association with conservative campaigns such as the Chirac government's privatisation of the Suez group in 1987, is sufficiently federating on a national level to be chosen as the model for the republican symbol Marianne in 1985, and to act as a bridge between commercial and auteur cinema. Her star persona is also eminently exportable (Austin 2003: 34–46; Marshall 1987: 234–51; Vincendeau 2000: 196–214).

However, while these approaches are important, they also carry risks, in, most notably, the removal of agency from both actress and director, and the imposition of one interpretative position for both spectator and audience. The diverse and proliferating output of a star such as Deneuve may become 'flattened out' in favour of a master reading or decoding which reads off her presence in terms of a pre-existing, publicly created persona. The 'star reading', while essential, is just one of a range of meanings circulating in the film text, is always articulated with that host of others, and is always itself contradictory, not in the way it encloses simple binaries like 'fire and ice', but in its existence as a cluster of possibilities which may take lines of flight in new and surprising directions. The viewing of stars on-screen can be understood not only in terms of *remembering* the accreted material of their previous roles and publicity, but also – and at the same time – momentarily *forgetting* or *suspending* that knowledge.

The relationship between art and popular cinema in Deneuve's output can also be expressed in terms of the distinction between 'star' and what I would call *acteur fétiche*. I understand by the latter term (and we are here very much in an auteurist logic) a performer who has forged a particular relationship with a director and who repeatedly appears in that director's *œuvre*, or in a particular period of it. That relationship, and its associated meanings, may emerge from one or more of the following: shared aesthetic priorities, a shared cultural or generational habitus, projection or identification on to the performer, a 'fit' between performance style–appearance and film projects, personal or sexual involvement. Examples might include Anna Karina and Jean-Luc Godard, Jean-Pierre Léaud and François Truffaut, Carmen Maura and Pedro Almodóvar, Gena Rowlands and John Cassavetes, Liv Ullmann and Ingmar Bergman. One of the ways I shall look at Catherine Deneuve in Téchiné's films is as *acteur fétiche* (an assemblage of performance, 'fit' with a film's project, and resemblances across the five films concerned), but the readings that this approach generates are not of course 'innocent' of the accretions of the star persona. That interaction can be summarised across the five films in turn, in relation to narrative, sexual politics, virtuality, cultural capital and ageing.

Aspects of the pre-existing Deneuve persona (autonomous,

empowered) happily encounter Téchiné's narratives of change, transformation, plurality, and becoming. In most of their films together,
there is what we might term a 'cardigan narrative'. In *Le Lieu du
crime*, Deneuve plays Lili, a 40–something divorcee and mother to
13–year-old Thomas (Nicolas Giraudi), who chances upon Martin
(Wadeck Stanczak), an escaped convict hiding out in a cemetery near
his home in rural south-west France. Martin demands money but later
saves his life, stabbing his fellow-escapee when he tries to strangle
Thomas. Martin then falls in with Lili at the nightclub she runs by
the river, and he offers her an escape from her stifling Catholic milieu
and mother (Danielle Darrieux), and unhelpful ex-husband Maurice
(Victor Lanoux). But their sexual escapade – its final consummation
witnessed by Thomas who has run away from his Catholic boarding
school – comes to an end one stormy night when Martin is shot and
mortally wounded by the two convicts' aggrieved accomplice. Lili
tells the police the truth, that Martin did not threaten her, and she is
carted off in a police van, finally leaving the village.

Deneuve's first scene takes place at her house, as she is observed
by Thomas as he hides while the priest from his school complains to
her about his behaviour. Lili's dress is sober, a pale-blue cardigan in
particular signifying a de-glamorisation of her star persona which
continues through this sequence (she discards it only in order to iron).
Narrative expectation is aroused – when, if at all, will she 'become
Deneuve', that is autonomous and empowered socially and sexually?
At the nightclub, she already cuts a more business-like figure than
in the scenes with Thomas or her ex-husband. Her emancipation is
conducted via a disengagement from the mother, and moreover an
exchange of fantasies with Thomas, as events and shots associated
with him in the first half of the film are associated with her. Téchiné
is interested in the persistence of the child in the adult, so that Lili
regresses to adolescence as Thomas matures to adulthood. Her final
'sacrifice' is not at all a punishment for social and sexual transgression. As Lili herself puts it, 'se sauver ou se perdre c'est la même
chose' ('it's the same thing to save or lose yourself'). *Se sauver* in
French also means to flee, and the itineraries of both Thomas and Lili
can be seen, to use a Deleuzean term, as lines of flight. If Lili becomes
at the end 'Deneuve', it is as a figure, bedraggled and rain-soaked,
that is as ambiguous as the smile that comes over her as the police
van leaves the village. Rather than the classic narrative teleology of
the discovery of a true or authentic 'self', the emphasis here is on a

process of becoming something else, and in fact 'becoming-Martin', as she takes on his guilt. As Deleuze and Guattari suggest, there is no final persona or identity which one eventually 'becomes'. This is why the ending is so provisional, hinting at other stories to come. Téchiné's procedure differs from that of other films which de-glamorise the star (a not uncommon phenomenon in her mature years), as he eschews a straightforward teleology. In Jean-Pierre Mocky's *Agent Trouble/The Man Who Loved Zoos* (Mocky, 1987), Deneuve wears a curly red wig and glasses in her role as a librarian, but her empowerment develops a linear detective narrative in which she uncovers a 'truth' concerning the murder of her nephew; in Nicole Garcia's *Place Vendôme* (1998), the first sight of her is as a broken alcoholic, but in the end she regains control of her life.

Ma saison préférée offers a similar *mise-en-scène* in terms of Deneuve's costume and persona. Here she plays Emilie, who shares a legal practice in the south-west with her husband Bruno (Jean-Pierre Bouvier), with whom she has two adult children, including Anne, played by her own daughter Chiara Mastroianni. Emilie re-establishes contact with her estranged unmarried younger brother Antoine (Daniel Auteuil), a neurosurgeon in Toulouse. A family Christmas dinner ends in a punch-up between Bruno and Antoine, who leaves with Berthe (Marthe Villalonga), their elderly mother who had just moved in with Emilie and Bruno. As a result, the latter separate, and Emilie and Antoine renegotiate their relationship. Berthe's deteriorating condition leads to her moving into an old folks' home, and then her death. The process of 'becoming-Deneuve' that is here offered is also fragile, ambiguous and open. After the funeral the family sit around discussing what is their favourite season, and this prompts her, surprisingly to the others, to perform, as she stands up, at a little distance from them. In close-up, she recites the poem 'Où est donc l'ami que je cherche?'('Where Is the Friend?'), which becomes a love poem for Antoine as she explains that she recited it to herself as she was waiting to rejoin him in the summer after boarding school. It is one of the most memorable moments, instants, of the mature Deneuve cinematic persona. Emilie, as throughout the film, continues to be dressed very soberly, here in white blouse and light-brown cardigan, and sports a short hairstyle. The camera moves past Antoine's shoulder to frame her head in the evening light, and then profiles her from her left. It then silently pans back to Antoine's reaction shot, holding him in frame for seven seconds.

The film is also about Emilie/Deneuve becoming a Bergman heroine: the poem she recites is the same used in the lunch scene in *Wild Strawberries* (1957), in a discussion about religion (it is in fact a nineteenth-century Swedish hymn). More concretely, she is able to express her love for her brother, over and beyond their difficult relationship, the frustrations and responsibilities of adulthood and middle age, and the social instabilities and ruptures of modernity. Deneuve's performance is an expression of the constant assessment and negotiation, in modernity, of what has determined the self from the past, and a future-directed freedom. Téchiné has summarised thus his approach to characterisation:

> From the moment a character is created, it seems to me necessary that at a certain point they no longer know who they are... The character must find him or herself as lacking with regard to their imaginary constructions... They must not be classified psychologically without another dimension. That would be irrelevant, for life is not like that. They must become strangers to themselves and learn from themselves through successive corrections. I do not believe in human apprenticeship. That would assume a form of human adaptation, which seems false to me. However, we can correct ourselves endlessly, without there being a last word leading to a perfect adaptation.
>
> (A partir du moment où l'on crée un personnage, il me paraît nécessaire qu'à un moment, il ne sache plus qui il est... Le personnage doit se trouver en défaut par rapport à toutes ses constructions imaginaires... Il ne doit pas être casé dans un registre psychologique sans dimension d'altérité. Cela n'aurait aucune pertinence car, dans la vie, les choses ne se passent pas ainsi. Il doit devenir étranger à lui-même et apprendre de lui-même par corrections successives. Je ne crois pas en l'apprentissage humain. Cela supposerait une forme d'adaptation humaine, ce qui me semble faux. Cependant, on peut sans cesse se corriger, sans qu'il y ait de dernier mot ou de dernière parole débouchant sur une parfaite adaptation.) (*Cahiers du cinéma* 1994: 13)

Ma saison préférée is important not only for how the Deneuve persona is narrativised in Téchiné, but also for the specificities of his take on gender and sexuality. Contrast the film's ending with that of Truffaut's *Le Dernier Métro/The Last Metro* (1980). Both films end with a close-up of a now radiant Deneuve, isolated from the other characters, looked at by a diegetic audience. The scene in *Le Dernier Métro* comes at the end of a narrative of marriage, adultery and secrecy, as Deneuve's character Marion Steiner has been concealing her Jewish husband in the bowels of their theatre during the occupation. Through most of the film, she is filmed as the object of the voyeuristic gaze of the young actor Bernard (Gérard Depardieu), via looks that are both desiring and which place her as an enigma to be investigated. Her only point-of-view shots on Bernard displace desire onto jealousy, as she sees him with other women. Antitheses between masculine authority and feminine sexuality are maintained by changes in her coiffure, worn up for most of the film, but down when she has made love. In any case, her actions are for the man, the hidden Lucas. At the Liberation, the contradictions of the film and her persona (she cannot choose between the two men, as one choice implicates sexuality and the other implicates 'France'), are 'resolved' when she becomes the object of a would-be transcendent fetishistic gaze, isolated in a medallion shot. Deneuve's other film with Truffaut, *La Sirène du Mississippi/Mississippi Mermaid* (1969), made when she was his lover, also has it both ways, as she is both a mysterious and deceiving *femme fatale* in relation to the male hero, and in the end the forgiven bearer of a transcendent love. In both cases, of course, binary oppositions associated with regimes of heterosexuality, and of femininity, however valorised, as other to masculinity, are maintained and reinforced.

In contrast, in *Le Lieu du crime* the regime of looking circulates between Lili and Thomas, and the object of desire is Martin. One of the characteristics of Téchiné's films is a pluralisation of the gaze, and a tendency towards homoeroticism. His famously relaxed portrayal of same-sex relations involves, not a hyperbolic assertion of 'gay' identity, but rather homosexuality in minor mode, on borders between a multitude of ambivalent sexualities, all the more challenging for being present within a seemingly heterosexual context. The adult brother–sister relationship, so rarely portrayed in heterosexually biased commercial or art cinema, is at the heart of *Ma saison préférée*, and offers clues to the Téchiné and Deneuve relationship as a whole.[1] Even Deneuve's name here, 'Emilie', is possibly a reference to *Les Sœurs Brontë*, with its depiction of a 'sororal' rather than Oedipal family. The brother–sister relationship, unlike friendships, sexual relationships or marriages, is indissoluble, in the literal sense that even estranged siblings do not cease to be siblings. It also brings childhood back into the frame of adult identities and relationships which Freud's Oedipal narrative would have us leave behind (a fantasy sequence, as in *Wild Strawberries*, has Emilie learning as a child from her parents that a little brother is on the way), relativises the link with parental figures, and moreover suggests alternative destinies. Emilie is afraid of Antoine for that very reason. Téchiné thus is able to play with Deneuve's star persona and to harness her subtle acting style to draw on ambivalences of emotion and restraint, to explore identification, and to establish equivalences between the male and female siblings. The 'becoming-Deneuve' of these stories of frustrated and unhappy cardigan-wearing women is, then, part of Téchiné's interest in the relationship between the actual and the virtual.

His first film with Deneuve, *Hôtel des Amériques*, was set in Biarritz, in the far south-west of France near the Spanish border, with many scenes taking place beside or overlooking the ocean, or at the railway station. The troubled love story between anaesthetist Hélène (Deneuve) and a drifter, Gilles (Patrick Dewaere), whose mother runs the eponymous hotel, is dominated by this notion of liminality, of a frontier between situation and freedom, place and (an aspiration to) somewhere else, past and future, actual and virtual. Thus for Hélène the love affair is caught between a haunting – the memory of her architect lover, who died in a drowning accident a year earlier, and the large, empty house he bequeathed to her -and a life in Paris, for which she finally leaves Gilles. Gilles is equally adrift between past and future but rendered equally vulnerable by being trapped in masculinity and the homosocial relationship with his friend Bernard (Etienne Chicot). The virtual in Téchiné is often rendered not only by hauntings and ghosts but also by doubles and doubling, as characters swap roles or develop relations of interchangeability. This is precisely what happens with Gilles, who by the end has become as fragile as Hélène in the opening scene: sitting on a railway platform, moved to tears, rehearsing the conversation he hopes to have with her in Paris. The contrast between the character she plays and the Deneuve star persona is not as pronounced as in *Le Lieu du crime* and *Ma saison préférée*, as her spectrum of development is more muted, and a 'class' contrast is played on in her relationship with Gilles/Dewaere. Throughout, her hair is tinted in a slightly less blonde and more brunette shade than usual, although at one point she eschews her ubiquitous green raincoat and reappears from a visit to Paris, radiant and with her hair down, at a high point of her relationship with Gilles. But what Téchiné exploits in this film, consistent with its general emphasis, are those 'virtual' aspects to the Deneuve persona, notably melancholy (less often mentioned in star studies of her are the connotations of the tragic and public loss of her sister Françoise Dorléac in a car accident in 1967, which colour perceptions of her 'distance'), and also the understatement of her performance. Téchiné has stated his preference in directing actors for 'those who base their performance on what they hide' ('ceux qui jouent sur ce qu'ils cachent') to 'those who base it on what they show' ('ceux qui jouent sur ce qu'ils montrent'). This 'denuding of performance which allows an inner potential to emerge' ('ce dénuement du jeu ... où l'on dégage un potentiel intérieur') is what he admires in Deneuve: 'Catherine is rather reserved, it seems there is always something to be revealed in her, that she has never reached her ceiling' ('Catherine serait plutôt sur la réserve, il semble qu'elle a toujours des choses à dévoiler, qu'elle n'a jamais atteint un plafond', *Nouvelle revue française* 1996: 42–3).[2] This emphasis on virtuality chimes with Téchiné's tendency to create multiple, decentred narratives:

> What I feel instinctively is the idea that one story can hide another within it, and that one never gets to the end of this process; not because a story never has a conclusion, but because one story is part of another, ad infinitum.
>
> (Ce qui correspond à mon instinct, c'est l'idée qu'une histoire peut en cacher une autre, et qu'on n'en vient jamais à bout, non pas parce qu'une histoire n'a jamais de fin, mais parce qu'une histoire entre dans une autre histoire, à l'infini.) (Philippon 1988: 122)

With the possible exception of *Le Lieu du crime*, all the films he has made with Deneuve place her within a plurality of stories and other characters. Even *Hôtel des Amériques*, apparently a star vehicle for the Deneuve–Dewaere pairing, features a host of other characters whose stories are summarised in a memorable final dance scene. This procedure contributes to a defamiliarisation of the Deneuve persona, as she is often thrown in with far lesser-known and even non-professional actors, and sometimes yields her place to them. This differs, therefore, from the ensemble casting of Ozon's *8 femmes* (2002), in which she shares the spotlight with female stars of (almost) equal lustre, and also from those films in which her presence is brief, contributing to the financial viability of the enterprise but generating rather static and inert readings of her persona: the dream love object for Jack Lemmon in Stuart Rosenberg's *The April Fools* (1969), the lost ideal love object to Yves Montand in Alain Corneau's *Le Choix des armes* (1981), the supportive factory worker in Lars von Trier's *Dancer in the Dark* (2000), interestingly cast against type but more than anything referenced for her contribution to the history of the musical in *Les Parapluies de Cherbourg*.

The procedure is best illustrated in *Les Voleurs*, Téchiné's most decentred film, with four different narrators and seven a-chronological chapters. Here Deneuve plays Marie, a university philosophy professor in Lyons who is involved emotionally and sexually with one of her students, Juliette (Laurence Côte), who in turn is also involved with a neurotic cop from a criminal family, Alex (Daniel Auteuil), who is investigating a failed heist in which his own brother Ivan (Didier Bezace) was killed and in which Juliette had participated. Alex and Marie develop a kind of friendship as they bid, from a distance, to protect her. Marie commits suicide (supposedly, according to Téchiné, but not altogether convincingly, out of 'exaltation', *Les Voleurs* DVD 2004), and Alex returns to his thankless job. The specificity of Deneuve/Marie in the film is twofold. The lesbian relationship with Juliette represents a world of women, a capsule of femininity, which offers an alternative space to the world of men and guns represented by Alex: there is a glaring contrast between the two sets of love scenes, between the intimacy of Marie and Juliette in the bath and the brutal couplings between Alex and Juliette in anonymous hotel rooms, and in the quasi-friendship which develops between Marie and Alex, the latter undergoes, in part, an apprenticeship of emotional literacy. Deneuve's status as 'lesbian icon' which emerged at the time of Tony Scott's *The Hunger* (1983) is developed further – the film has been shown at lesbian and gay film festivals – but altered. Instead of the chic glamour which characterised her (vampiric) coupling with Susan Sarandon in the latter movie, and which was shot and lit like a television commercial or soft-porn film (for straight men; Alex tells Marie he fantasised about her and Juliette together), Deneuve is here de-glamorised in now familiar fashion, with loose-fitting clothes, browns, greys and beiges (although she is stunning when first glimpsed dancing with Juliette). However, as in *Ma saison préférée*, in which Emile/Deneuve has silent and anonymous sex with a handsome doctor on a riverbank, de-glamorisation does not mean desexualisation, and moreover Marie is the most empowered character in the film, already 'Deneuve', even though she is as emotionally damaged in modernity as everyone else (translated, as for other characters, into physical damage, as the film takes advantage of a foot injury Deneuve suffered during shooting). The cultural capital associated with the Deneuve persona is here transmuted, using elements of her established glamorous femininity, 'class' and 'fire–ice' persona and turning them into emotion, intellect, and social authority. These constitute the 'distance' to which Alex is initially so hostile – he goes to hear one of her lectures; she at first dodges his questions about Juliette.

The fact that Téchiné's films are about the juxtaposition of heterogeneous elements produces a memorable scene when she tries to find Juliette at the flat she shares with her criminal brother Jimmy (Benoît Magimel). The task of driving Marie home through a dangerous area is entrusted to his accomplice Nabil (Naguime Bendidi), and the resulting car ride is one of the film's rare moments of humour. An aspiration to movement runs throughout the film; cars play a role in the film's narrative transitions, bringing people together, marking passages from one level of the story to another.

Nabil takes a long way round, and, after Marie's initial protests, asks for a 'philosophy lesson'. The philosophy professor, the embodiment of cultural capital, thus shares a few moments with the *beur* gang member. The conversation is shot through the windscreen, the camera sometimes framing the two, sometimes one, but always establishing a relationship of equivalence. Initially nonplussed, Marie says she needs a subject that interests him: the response is, of course, money. Marie then launches herself into a disquisition on money, pointing out its negative connotations in philosophy, its political association with capitalism and the Freudian metaphor of money = shit. Nabil not only disagrees with this negativity, needless to say, he counters Marie's high cultural discourse ('the representation you have of money'/'la représentation que vous avez de l'argent', a youthful stealing of a book as 'anything but intoxicating'/'le contraire de l'ivresse') with his own popular language ('they're crazy these blokes'/'les mecs ils sont givrés'). He then turns on the radio and sings along to the raï performer Cheb Mami's 'Douha Alia', which then becomes a recurrent theme in the film, emerging again at the fairground and over the closing credits. However, this is not so much a confrontation as a juxtaposition. Marie and Nabil's linguistic terrains at least coincided on the use of the word 'merde'. And although the final musical moments represent his attempt to regain control of the situation, to shut her up in fact, he had of course provoked the clash of syllogisms here, and in their parallel, different ways the pair share an aesthetic moment thanks to the music, the abandonment of language, and the picturesque shots of Lyons by night that close the two-minute scene. He sings, she seems momentarily at peace (her smoking – as in *Hôtel des Amériques* – underlines the interiority denoted by her serene, reflective facial expressions, but this nonetheless falls short of her tearful ecstasy when she takes Alex to see *The Magic Flute*), the car is poised between her home/territory and his.[3]

A long association between a director and an *acteur-fétiche* can also become a tracking of the latter's ageing, and the issues faced at different stages in life. This is clearly true for Truffaut and Léaud, and also to an extent for Bergman and Ullmann. Coincidentally, Bergman's television film *Saraband* was released on screens in Paris in the same month as Téchiné's *Les Temps qui changent*. Bergman's film directly references *Scenes from a Marriage* (1975), returning to the same characters, including Liv Ullmann as the former wife, thirty years later, although in somewhat darker mode. In *Les Temps qui changent*, Antoine, a French engineer (Gérard Depardieu), travels to Tangiers to supervise the construction of buildings for a new television station in the 'free zone'. His real motivation, however, is to seek out his first love from thirty years before, Cécile (Catherine Deneuve), who works at a radio station and is married to a Moroccan-Jewish doctor, Natan (Gilbert Melki). Cécile's marriage has been increasingly loveless and she eventually succumbs to Antoine's advances, initially proposing a 'brief stop' ('une halte') on life's road rather than his preference for them to end their days together, and they make love. But Antoine is left in a coma after a landslide on the building site. Cécile and Natan separate. Months later, after she has visited him in hospital seemingly every day, Cécile sees Antoine wake up, and their hands join.

This central narrative, as ever in Téchiné of course, co-exists with many others, notably that of Cécile/Deneuve's bisexual half-French, half-Moroccan son Sami (Malik Zidi). However, the main event is clearly the reunion of these two *monstres sacrés* of French cinema. Deneuve and Depardieu first appeared together in *Le Dernier Métro*, and then in Corneau's *Le Choix des armes* and *Fort Saganne* (1984), and François Dupeyron's *Drôle d'endroit pour une rencontre* (1988). Téchiné's one film with Depardieu was *Barocco*. The preoccupation with passing time dominates *Les Temps qui changent*, and is rendered in various ways. Spatially, there is a reprise of a shot from

Ma saison préférée when the central pair are filmed in a car, moving forwards but with the countryside moving backwards through and in the reflections of the windows, in a manner analogous to the cinema apparatus. And there is the crucial role of still photographs. Just as Téchiné, at 61 the same age here as Deneuve, revisits in the film actors, motifs and settings (his 2000 *Loin* was shot in Tangiers), so does the use of photographs in the romance narrative carry implications for the image of the two stars, their itineraries and place in film history.

In the film, still photographs are the index for the process of ageing, and for recapturing but also overcoming lost time. In an attempt to 'envoûter' ('cast a spell on') Cécile, Antoine sneaks into her bedroom to place a photograph of their young selves under the mattress. It is only when Cécile discovers and burns it that he wakes up from his coma. These images foreground of course issues concerning the two actors and their star personae: *Les Temps qui changent* is also about stardom, the history of cinema, the history of audiences watching Deneuve and Depardieu, and even the itinerary of the director himself. Notably, the still photograph hidden then burned in the film is a well-known publicity still from the late 1970s, with François Truffaut – cropped out here of course – standing on their right.

In many of Téchiné's films, still photographs have connotations of death. His approach is very close to that outlined by his friend Roland Barthes in *La Chambre claire/Camera Lucida* (1980). For Barthes, the dominant aspect of the still photograph is temporal: the capturing and reproduction of 'that which was' ('le ça-a-été'). This 'magic' and 'spectral' aspect to photography, which in the past expressed itself in an obsession with doubles, is repressed by the generalisation and banalisation of the photographic image. Barthes is at times ambivalent about the relation between still photography and cinema, arguing that the two are very different, as in photos there is no 'off-screen' space, and that the spectral poses of past time are in cinema recuperated by the continuous movement of the images, but also noting that 'the melancholy of photography' reasserts itself when in a film he sees actors who are now dead (Barthes 1980/1984: 124/179). The use of still photos in *Les Temps qui changent* creates a dynamic relationship between still and moving image, and between the twin poses that cinema fleetingly captures of the 'actor' and that of his or her 'role'. As Barthes pointed out, the age of photography coincided with 'the explosion of the private into the public, or rather the creation of a new social value, which is the publicity of the private; the private is consumed as such – publicly' ('l'irruption du privé dans le public, ou plutôt à la création d'une nouvelle valeur sociale, qui est la publicité du privé; le privé est consommé comme tel, publiquement'; Barthes 1980/1984: 153/98). When Cécile burns the photograph at the end of *Les Temps qui changent*, she destroys Antoine's fixation on a lost youth and past that cannot be recaptured, but she is also giving him what he wants, that she be at his side; so the 'pose of the role' is subsumed, literally consumed, in fire, by the future-directed moving images. At the same time, the 'pose of the actor' is also being burned, in a way which signals the reality and inevitability of death (as fire accelerates time), but which moreover comments on and integrates the previous star images of the now 56-year-old Gérard Depardieu and 61–year-old Catherine Deneuve, delivering for them, at the same time as they publicly age, an open future typical of Téchiné. The 'becoming-Deneuve' at the end of *Les Temps qui changent* is the fact that Cécile, now sporting a very 'un-Deneuve' short hairstyle, is now open to change and transformation.

We have seen how Deneuve's understated acting style chimes with Téchiné's interest in the virtual shadowing the real. We can broadly categorise western acting traditions into five fundamental approaches: observational and technical associated with Diderot; declamatory associated with nineteenth-century melodrama; a balanced relationship between 'the individuality of the actor' and the 'unified image of the role' (Vsevolod Pudovkin quoted in Lovell and Krämer 199: 81) associated with Stanislavsky; substitutions of personal experience for the facts of the text associated with the Method, and a self-conscious, even fragmented 'showing' of the character associated with Brechtian epic theatre. Of these, it is clearly the Stanislavskian approach that Deneuve embodies, in that her performances tend to trace the singular logic of her character, its origins and development. However, the specificity of Deneuve and Téchiné lies in a surprisingly Brechtian dimension, and in the supremely cinematic, as opposed to theatrical, nature of her performance.

Téchiné was greatly influenced by Brecht and Barthes in his passage through May 1968 and his entry into regular filmmaking in the 1970s. His most Brechtian film is *Souvenirs d'en France*, in which for example Jeanne Moreau is filmed by a static camera preparing a plain meal, a scene whose materiality makes visible the historical construction of events, practices and desires. Deneuve is used in a similar way in *Le Lieu du crime*, particularly in the early domestic scenes: when the narrative is interrupted to include a close shot of her hand wielding an iron, a *gestus* is created which opens up a world of social contradiction, of roles rather than 'psychology'. Similarly, Téchiné's self-conscious articulation of Deneuve's star persona and of her previous roles in film history could be described as Brechtian, if we recall the oscillation between remembering and forgetting that characterise the viewing of actor and role. The journal's editors said as much in the heyday of *Screen* theory, writing of 'the star system as a space within cinema where the contradictions of naturalistic presentation are both manifested and contained, and where a dislocation analogous to epic acting, separating actor and role, is manifested' (Kuhn and Nash 1978). Watching Deneuve on-screen is to watch (at least) two bodies, and the audience must work to understand the social and other determinants that construct the gap between her iconicity and her role: the ironing scene in *Le Lieu du crime*, with its whole implied history of female domestic labour, along with its echo of her mother's body, is an example of this procedure, the displacement of attention on to the construction of masculinity in *Hôtel des Amériques* is another.

Contrary to some opinion, Deneuve deploys quite a wide variety of gestures in her performance, which is sometimes marked by explosions of emotion, such as the melodramatic roll in the surf with Patrick Dewaere in *Hôtel des Amériques*, the tearful despair at the family dinner in *Ma saison préférée*, the anger when she throws Antoine out of the radio studio in *Les Temps qui changent*. However, it is above all her face, in close-up or in mid-shot, which is at the centre of her performance and of Téchiné's direction, and in particular the movement of her eyes, which always seem relatively large for her face. In *Hôtel des Amériques*, a conversation with Gilles/ Dewaere's sister Elise (Sabine Haudepin) reminds her character of her dead lover; the shot–reverse shot sequence between them shows Hélène/Deneuve's face now looking away from the girl, eyes downcast to her left, her mouth opening slightly. Later, as Hélène waits at a restaurant for Gilles, her eyes move from looking at the entrance, to looking ahead and slightly downcast, and then her head moves to her left where there is a telephone, from which she calls Gilles. Her assertive reaction to his no-show ends with him hanging up, her emotion is shown through eye and head movements that dart from left to right in a more unstable manner. In *Ma saison préférée*, in the confrontation between her character and her husband after the Christmas meal, shot in close-up partly as she is doing house-work, partly in the wardrobe mirror, and ending in a profile shot, the overall composure of Deneuve's face changes little (unlike when she sobbed in the previous scene), but she suggests much through the direction of her glances and the raising, lowering or tilting of the head, the acceleration, or the slowing to a stare, of the rate of blinking, slight movements of the eyebrows, and movements of the mouth in pauses between speaking. In *Les Temps qui changent*, her character throws Antoine/Depardieu out of her radio studio, and then her face in close-up is seen registering and pondering the event, through a range of rapid head movements, raised eyes and downcast mouth, sideways and downside glances.

Finally, and to take a distance from questions of stardom and acting technique, it is possible to see in the supremely cinematic Deneuve face one of the best examples of what Deleuze and Guattari call *visagéité*, or facialisation. In *Mille plateaux*, the face is seen as the origin of western – the face of Christ propels this historical process – regimes of signification, a system of classification and readability organised round the 'black hole' of consciousness and a 'white wall' of meaning that is produced by power structures that need 'face', such as motherhood, politics, and the audio-visual media. Deneuve's whole body, in fact, is thus facialised. One of the ways in which the face signifies is in the relation between the reflective and intensive face, between the face as outline and unity bearing an emotional state or 'quality', and the face as multiplicity of features, expressions and 'micro-movements', a force or potential tending towards a limit or a threshold ('Année zéro – Visagéité'/'Year Zero – Faciality', in Deleuze and Guattari 1980/1988: 205–34/167–91). In his cinema books, Deleuze sees Bergman's use of close-ups as a moment when that regime of individuation breaks down, as in the famous merging of the faces of Bibi Andersson and Liv Ullmann in *Persona* (1966).

In Téchiné, or rather Téchiné–Deneuve, there are Bergmanesque elements of phantoms and doublings as the Deneuve characters are placed in narratives of exchange and transformation. But as we have seen in the examples above, she is always placed in a very social cinematic universe, so that the system of unity and intensities of the face constantly reacts to socially motivated events and stimuli: in these three scenes, reaction shots, and reflective shots drawing the spectator into the 'black hole' of interiority, are part of a series which out of virtuality (the mirror in *Ma saison préférée*), leads to choice, action and further stories. In Téchiné, Deneuve's heroines, and the star herself, enter a world of second chances and future lives.

Notes

1 Deneuve on Téchiné in *Télérama* (1997): 'I haven't had a brother in my life either. So I chose one, André'('Je n'ai pas eu de frère dans la vie non plus. Alors, je m'en suis choisi un: c'est André'). http://toutsurdeneuve. free.fr/Francais/Pages/Carriere_Partenaires/Techine.htm. See also a joint interview, in which Deneuve declares: 'A brother is a man to whom one can say anything, knowing there won't be any silly sexual consequences/ Un frère, c'est un homme à qui on peut tout dire en sachant que ça n'aura sûrement pas de conséquences bêtement sexuelles'; *Libération* 1993: 32–3.

2 Geoffrey Nowell-Smith made the case for Deneuve's acting ability in similar terms: 'To seem to be doing nothing while in fact doing precisely what it takes to attract and hold an audience's attention is no doubt partly a gift, but is also a prized quality which many schools of acting have set out to develop', adding: 'To express one meaning can be to exclude others; not to express leaves meaning open' (2005: 36–40).

3 'If there is a utopia in Téchiné's cinema, it's that which consists in putting worst enemies or the most incompatible individuals together' ('S'il y a une utopie dans le cinéma de Téchiné, c'est bien celle qui consiste à mettre face à face les pires ennemis ou les individus les plus incompatibles') (Lalanne 1996: 28).

Works cited

'Deux heures dans la vie de Catherine Deneuve', *Le Nouvel Observateur*, 25 February 1983, 60.

'Deneuve/Téchiné, l'amour à deux', *Liberation*, 14 May 1993, 32–3.

Cahiers du cinéma, 481 (June 1994), 13.

'Le Dépaysement humain', *Nouvelle revue française*, 520 (May 1996), 41–57.

Interview on DVD of *Les Voleurs* (StudioCanal Video, 2004).

http://toutsurdeneuve.free.fr/Francais/Pages/Carriere_Partenaires/Techine. htm.

Austin, Guy (2003), 'Red woman/white woman: Jeanne Moreau and Catherine Deneuve', in Austin, *Stars in Modern French Film*, London: Arnold, pp. 34–46.

Barthes, Roland (1980), *La Chambre claire: note sur la photographie*, Paris: Cahiers du cinéma/Seuil.

Barthes, Roland (1984), *Camera Lucida: Reflections on Photography*, trans. Richard Howard, London: Fontana.

Deleuze, Gilles and Félix Guattari (1980), '1730: Devenir-intense, devenir-animal, devenir-imperceptible', and 'Année zéro – Visagéité' in *Mille plateaux: capitalisme et schizophrénie 2*, Paris: Minuit, pp. 284–380 and pp. 205–34.

Deleuze, Gilles and Félix Guattari (1988), 'Becoming-intense, becoming-animal, becoming imperceptible', and 'Year Zero – Faciality', in *A Thousand Plateaus: Capitalism and Schizophrenia 2*, trans. Brian Massumi, London: Athlone Press, pp. 232–309 and pp. 167–91.

Fache, Alexandre (2004), *Catherine Deneuve: une biographie*, Paris: Presses de la cité.

Frodon, Jean-Michel (2004), 'Rencontre: Julien Hirsch, chef opérateur, Eloge de la méthode et de la matière', *Cahiers du cinéma*, 596 (December), 20–1.

Kuhn, Annette and Marc Nash (1978), Editorial, *Screen*, 19, no. 2 (summer), 5–7.

Lalanne, Jean-Marc (1996) 'Comme une effraction', *Cahiers du cinéma*, 505 (September), 28.

Lovell, Alan and Peter Krämer (ed.) (1999), *Screen Acting*, London: Routledge.

Marshall, Bill (1987), 'Stars: Deneuve and Depardieu. Aspects of class and gender', in Bridgford, J., *France: Image and Identity*, Newcastle upon Tyne: Newcastle Polytechnic Products, pp. 234–51.

Nowell-Smith, Geoffrey (2005), 'Theatre of complicity', *Sight & Sound* (April), 36–40.

Philippon, A. (1988), *André Téchiné*, Paris: Cahiers du cinéma.

Vincendeau, Ginette (2000), 'Catherine Deneuve: from ice maiden to living divinity', in Vincendeau, *Stars and Stardom in French Cinema*, London: Cassell, pp. 196–214.

8

Deneuve in the 1990s

Cristina Johnston

In a recent interview with the American gay and lesbian magazine *The Advocate*, Catherine Deneuve was asked whether she had any plans to return to Hollywood. Her disdainful response highlights the rare position that she inhabits in contemporary cinema, on both sides of the Atlantic: 'There is such a taste in America for girls. But for women? *Hmmp*' (2002). In the same interview, Deneuve spoke about the difficulties faced by actresses like Meryl Streep[1] who struggle 'to find interesting parts because there is such an appeal in America for youth' (Duralde, 2002). Such comments have, by no means, been limited to observations regarding Hollywood's cinematic output.[2] And yet, her age notwithstanding, progress of Deneuve's trajectory seems to be unhindered.[3] She has appeared in at least one major film every year since turning 50 in 1993, often starring in several works in the same season[4] in a career which has encompassed, and continues to encompass, work with leading French auteurs (François Ozon, André Téchiné, Philippe Garrel, Léos Carax), mainstream box-office successes (Gabriel Aghion's *Belle Maman* and *Absolument fabuleux*, for example), and a series of films with iconic world-cinema directors (Manoel de Oliveira, Lars von Trier, Raúl Ruiz).

The focus here will be placed on three of Deneuve's recent films – the aforementioned *Belle Maman, Dancer in the Dark* (von Trier, 2000) and *Le Vent de la nuit/Night Wind* (Garrel, 1999) and will offer an examination of the varied portraits of older women and of the processes of ageing offered by (and indeed *to*) Deneuve. Through an examination of Deneuve's roles in these three very different films – Aghion's farcical game of 'happy families', von Trier's melancholic tragic musical, and Garrel's meandering musings on age, sex and loneliness – there will emerge a vision of her portrayal of gendered ageing as multilayered and complex. Deneuve's roles in these three works engage at once with established on-screen images of both maternity and sexuality while posing a series of challenges to the perceived status of '50 plus' actresses on the international screen.

Le Vent de la nuit (Garrel, 1999)

The ambiguities inherent in Deneuve's status as 'older' actress are perhaps at their most visible in the least successful – critically and indeed commercially[5] – of the three films focused on here, Philippe Garrel's *Le Vent de la nuit*. The film begins with Hélène (Deneuve) climbing the spiralling staircase towards the top floor of a Parisian apartment block. There is a moment of awkwardness as she encounters a (much) younger blonde woman who turns back, deliberately, to stare at the older visitor but no words are exchanged and the younger woman has no further participatory role to play within the narrative. Hélène rings the doorbell of the flat and, when there is no response from within, reaches up to find the spare key hidden above the door. Once inside, she goes to the bedroom, looks at the unmade bed and begins to tidy, smoothing the sheets, and then taking a small bottle of perfume from her handbag and spraying some first on the pillows, then on herself.

At no point during these opening shots is the audience told whose apartment we have entered, nor indeed what relationship might connect Hélène with the flat's habitual occupant. There is clearly a familiarity between her and the absent inhabitant. But still, the audience is uncertain of the woman's status as mother or as lover. Her age, combined with her decision to rearrange the crumpled sheets, initially guide us towards a reading of her as maternal figure, if not as mother. Yet the inclusion of that instant of intimacy, of sensuality, with her decision to perfume the pillows, brings into the frame, at the very least, an Oedipal reading of this maternal relationship. It is only when Deneuve's voice enters the narrative, through voice-over, that the ambiguities begin to be lifted: 'When we met, when you declared your feelings, I said to myself "this guy is mad", I didn't believe it...' ('Quand on s'est rencontré, quand tu t'es déclaré, je me suis dit, "ce type-là, il est fou", j'y croyais pas...'). Clearly, these are not the words of a mother to a child. Yet also this is not a description of a successful relationship, since Hélène goes on to accuse her absent interlocutor of pulling back from their union: 'Now you're the one taking a step back' ('Maintenant c'est toi qui recule').

It is only a few seconds before Hélène's younger lover, Paul (Xavier Beauvois), arrives home. His first comments to Hélène make reference neither to his absence, nor to any surprise at her presence in his flat, but rather to her physical appearance and his demands upon it: 'Pull your hair back, I like it when you're strict, with your glasses' ('Relève tes cheveux, je t'aime sévère, avec tes lunettes'). Hélène's dependence on her relationship with Paul is clear throughout the film, but particularly so in this opening sequence, in which her eagerness to please and her unquestioning submission to her younger lover are both evident as she obediently follows his instructions.

Hélène recounts her encounter on the stairs to Paul, making

reference to the stranger's physicality – describing her as having been 'very sensual' ('très sensuelle') – and thus offering the audience an explanation for her own momentary hesitation: 'I thought about her age, all of that, I was hurt by it' ('J'ai pensé à son âge, tout ça, ça m'a fait mal'). Not only have we, as viewers, spent this opening sequence first trying to position Hélène as either mother or lover and, second, critically observing the power dynamic at work within the relationship, but we now learn of Hélène's own uncertainty caused by her age.

While the Deneuve constructed through the dialogue with interviewers on both sides of the Atlantic, particularly over the past fifteen years, seems happy to discuss age and, more importantly, her own ageing,[6] the screen persona constructed here in Garrel's work is one for whom age becomes a potential point of weakness, a source of anxiety. The fleeting encounter with the younger woman in the staircase is enough for Hélène to question the attraction Paul feels for her and to doubt her own beauty, but more importantly for both to be undermined through Hélène's interpretation of herself as the object of a younger gaze: the young woman who turns back to stare, Paul who observes her from the doorway of the bedroom.

Vincendeau has commented that Deneuve's 1990s cinematic output 'to some extent trade[s] on the degradation of her once-perfect image' (2000: 203) and yet here the dialogue between on-screen and off-screen personae and individual film text seems more multilayered. Physically, in the early sequences of *Le Vent de la nuit*, there is no 'degradation' – Deneuve is impeccably dressed and coiffured – but there may, perhaps, be psychological and emotional 'degradation'. Hélène's doubts are in stark contrast to Deneuve's self-declared status as 'free woman' ('femme libre') *(L'Est Républicain*, 2004), her confident reappropriation of her own ageing, and her explicit declarations that, in fact, she feels she has grown stronger, more reckless, more grown-up as she has aged:

> It takes a long time before we let fall everything we have constructed between ourselves and the world in order to give ourselves the illusion that we are adults. In any case, today, I feel much more carefree than when I was 18. More carefree and more audacious.

> (On met longtemps à laisser tomber tout ce que l'on dresse entre soi et le monde pour se donner l'illusion d'être adulte. Aujourd'hui, en tout cas, je me sens plus insouciante que quand j'avais 18 ans. Plus insouciante et plus audacieuse). *(Paris Match*, 2004)

Particularly interesting to note in *Le Vent de la nuit* is that it is not age per se that brings with it such doubts and anxieties, but specifically the phenomenon of *female* ageing. Shortly after the opening sequences described above, Paul leaves for Naples where he meets Serge (Daniel Duval), a lonely, despondent figure, of roughly the same age as Hélène, with whom he forms a somewhat one-sided father–son relationship. Much of Paul's fascination with, and almost childlike adulation for, Serge stems, ironically, from the latter's age and his involvement in the events of May 1968 about which Paul is keen to question him at length. And yet, despite the fact that Serge and Hélène are constructed as contemporaries[7] and despite the clear implication that Paul is interested in a first-hand account of this particular period of French social history, he makes no attempt to question Hélène about any involvement she might have had in the events, nor about her views on, or place in, any of the political movements which followed in the wake of May '68.

Certainly, the off-screen Deneuve is not associated, in the popular imagination, with the student protests – in 1968, the year after the death of her sister Françoise Dorléac, Deneuve in fact left France to make a series of films in Hollywood, becoming such a recognisable star of the American screen that the magazine *Look* declared her 'the most beautiful woman in the world'. However, there is a clear association drawn between the off-screen Deneuve and, in particular, the feminist movement which began to take root in the years following May '68, not least because she was a signatory of the *Manifeste des 343 salopes*.[8] Yet, the on-screen Deneuve, in the 1999 instalment of the 'cinematographic adventure' of a director so closely connected with that troubled period of French history,[9] makes no contribution to the construction of the historical narrative.[10] While age affords Serge a privileged position within the diegesis, and, perhaps more importantly, is valorised through the younger gaze of Paul, for Hélène it is a reason for her to doubt her own beauty and her own status. The division here is not simply between youth and maturity, but rather between youth – as represented by Paul, his mobility, his confidence and his curiosity – and gendered processes of ageing, with the ultimate affirmation of the voice of the 'older' male characters at the expense of Hélène's.

Indeed, this sacrifice of an 'older' female contribution to historical narrative-building is further heightened in a sequence during which Hélène insists on Paul coming to her apartment and meeting her husband. Although the act itself can be read as provocative, daring and decisive, in fact we see Paul and Hélène's husband becoming involved in a conversation about philosophy, youth and athleticism, while Hélène remains a silent observer on the periphery. It is at this point that the psychological 'degradation' transforms most clearly into physical degradation as Paul announces he should leave and Hélène smashes a glass on the table in front of her, using one of the shards to gouge her wrist. Husband and lover both move to help her, bandaging her wrists and calling for assistance, but, in the space of a few minutes of narrative, we have seen Hélène shift from apparently courageous central female figure – enacting almost a will to conflict by bringing her younger lover to her marital home – first to silenced, then to mutilated, older woman dependent on the help of two reluctant male figures.

Dancer in the Dark (Von Trier, 2000)

The following year, in Lars von Trier's *Dancer in the Dark*, Deneuve strayed from any established pattern of usually immaculate – if latterly degraded – image, with her role as Cathy, dowdy maternal guardian angel to the film's tragic central figure, Selma (Björk). The notion of a star image dependent on forms of 'degradation' suggests a permanence of the screen persona created by a *younger* Deneuve – the order and control of her hair, the well-tailored suits – in the sense that this earlier persona must remain present in order for it now to be damaged. However, in *Dancer in the Dark*, there is no respite from the mundanity of Deneuve's Cathy – no Saint Laurent outfits to tear or to stain, no sculpted coiffure to tousle – and, as such, no 'degradation'. Rather von Trier creates a work in which Deneuve, although central to the narrative, is not required to be beautiful in order to retain that centrality and, significantly, it is a role which Deneuve actively sought to obtain, writing to von Trier after seeing his 1996 work *Breaking the Waves*.

Cathy is a maternal figure who wishes, at all costs, to protect her younger friend. She looks after Selma, scolding her for wanting to work a night shift in the factory which employs the pair, for example, but then turning up herself, in her own time off, to be there to look after her younger friend. As Selma's sight weakens, Cathy traces out dance steps on the palm of her hand so Selma knows where to place her feet. And yet she is not a mother to Selma and, ultimately, cannot save her. Similarly, although clearly the elder of the two women, her status as 'older woman' is in no way a source of either sexual tension or of dissatisfaction.

Deneuve has spoken, in interviews, of the importance she placed upon the role in terms of her own cinematic output:

> Taking a secondary role, playing the tired, un-made-up worker in Lars von Trier's latest film, *Dancer in the Dark*, [Deneuve] intends to maintain this taste for risk, this impression that she is very much alive, 'that the fact that you have good films behind you guarantees nothing'.

> (Second rôle, jouant l'ouvrière pas maquillée et fatiguée dans le dernier film de Lars von Trier, *Dancer in the dark*, [Deneuve] compte bien garder encore ce goût du risque, cette impression d'être vivante, 'que tout n'est pas assuré parce qu'on a de beaux films derrière soi'.) (Le Guilledoux, 2001)

And yet, despite the fact that her character wears no make-up, is shabbily dressed in drab colours and bears little resemblance, if indeed any at all, to the smart and striking Deneuve in most of the other films she has made since turning 50, Deneuve's physical appearance still found its way into media coverage of the film:

> We would prefer not to discuss [the start of the film], in order to preserve the all-too-rare feeling that we are entering an unknown world, the exhausting pleasure of these long moments during which we wander startled (what if it were a trap?) and marvelling (Catherine Deneuve is so beautiful; Björk, pauper with thick glasses, breaks your heart with her smile).

> (On préférerait ne pas parler [du début du film], pour préserver cette sensation si rare de pénétrer dans un monde inconnu, le plaisir épuisant de ces longs instants pendant lesquels on chemine effrayé (et si c'était un piège?) et émerveillé (Catherine Deneuve est si belle; Björk, pauvresse à grosses lunettes, fend le cœur rien qu'en souriant). (Sotinel, 2000)

Later, in the same article, Sotinel criticises von Trier's film on one ground, and on one ground alone, namely for not having shown more of Deneuve:

> The film leaves only one regret: it does not show us enough of the *demoiselle de Rochefort*, a fairy reduced to powerlessness and a woman of ineffable generosity and beauty.

> ([Ce film] ne laisse qu'un seul regret: celui de ne pas montrer assez la demoiselle de Rochefort, fée réduite à l'impuissance et femme d'une

générosité, d'une beauté indicibles).

Sotinel's remarks at once draw attention to Deneuve's part in the narrative of modern French cinema history, while contributing to the popular image of her as almost mystical figure; unknown, untouchable and, for Sotinel at the very least, 'ineffable' ['*indicible*']. Within the narrative of *Dancer in the Dark*, however, such adulation seems unwarranted or, at best, appears in opposition to the approach adopted by von Trier. Indeed, a brief examination of the film's opening sequence demonstrates that, while it perhaps offers something of an ironic nod to Deneuve's status as ex-*demoiselle de Rochefort*, it serves equally to undermine any image the audience may have clung to of Deneuve as glamorous star.

These opening minutes find Selma on-stage rehearsing a rendition of 'My Favourite Things', best-known for the Julie Andrews version in *The Sound of Music* (Wise, 1965). Selma's interpretation is to form part of an amateur theatre production and our first glimpse of Deneuve's Cathy sees her in the wings during the rehearsal, trying – and failing – to pass out the appropriate 'favourite-things' props, as Selma performs. Far from the brusque confidence to be found in many of Deneuve's other recent roles, Cathy is clumsy and unsuccessful, and the first words addressed towards her seek only to underline her shortcomings, as the director of the play criticises her for not passing objects quickly enough and for dropping props. Physically, she appears awkward and unsure of her footing as she joins in with the dance routine and, when we first hear her voice, she sings haltingly in a heavily French-accented English, a world away from the polished musicality of Demy's work. This linguistic awkwardness is maintained throughout the film, with its frequent improvised passages, and ensures that, despite Cathy's dignity, she neither strives for, nor achieves, the sophisticated confidence associated with Deneuve's 'older' screen persona. Indeed, as this opening sequence draws to a close, the on-screen director suggests that the cast attempt one final version of the song, this time including not only the visual props, but also the necessary sound effects, and the film's audience watches a despondent Deneuve sitting on the stage and barking as the song lyrics require.

Deneuve is not, here, constructed as on-screen enchantress because of the almost mythical permanence of her beauty, despite the effects of age. Rather, she is, physically, at her most ordinary, her least remarkable. Whereas *Le Vent de la nuit* can, arguably, be said to contribute to a construction of Deneuve as the object of a diegetic gaze (that of Paul and of the woman on the staircase) the opposite seems to hold true in *Dancer in the Dark*, where the character Cathy attempts, but ultimately fails, to protect is quite literally losing her gaze. Cathy gains her narrative coherence from her relationship with Selma, from her maternal love for her, and, because the plot centres on Selma's ever-worsening blindness, we know that Cathy's interpretation of Selma's gaze upon her cannot impact upon this love and this solidarity, neither to validate nor indeed to undermine.

A consideration of Deneuve's casting in these two films, released only a year apart, may initially lead us to conclude that the type of role offered to her has become limited to that of disempowered older woman. Despite the prolific nature of Deneuve's cinematic output as she grows older, she may seem condemned to play motherly figures offering protection to lost souls or mature ladies dissatisfied with life, with love or with marriage. However, if we read the characters of Hélène in *Le Vent de la nuit* and Cathy in *Dancer in the Dark* alongside, for instance, Deneuve's central role as Léa in Gabriel Aghion's comedy *Belle Maman*, released in the same year as Garrel's work, it becomes clear that there is far greater variety to be found across her roles, a diversity that is rendered more complex still by the ongoing dialogue between the on-screen and off-screen 'Deneuves' of the last decade or so.

Belle Maman (Aghion, 1999)

To return, however, to Deneuve's role in Aghion's box-office smash, here we see Deneuve playing Léa, the 'belle maman' (mother-in-law) of the title who arrives (late) at her daughter's wedding, only to have the soon-to-be bridegroom (Antoine, played by Vincent Lindon) fall head over heels in love with her. Again, on the surface, this reads as a rather unimaginative Mrs Robinson-esque older female seducer, a striking blonde woman bringing chaos and destruction to what could have been the perfect marital home. This aspect of Deneuve's on-screen persona is certainly one that Aghion manipulates here. The whole congregation is shown seated when Léa arrives in the church and all turn to watch her as she enters; as she catches her breath in the pews, we see a close-up of her feet as she removes her shoes and sensually rubs her foot against the back of her leg. Antoine, at the altar, is mesmerised by her appearance and has to be brought back to the ritual of the ceremony somewhat abruptly. Again, as in *Le Vent de la nuit*, Deneuve becomes a physical part of the narrative before we are given a definite indication of her status or, indeed, relationship with any of the other characters, and again, here, within the first few moments of this opening sequence, we have another older-female character constructed, at least in part, through the deliberate gaze of her fellow characters. And yet, the gaze is clearly affirming here and, perhaps more crucially, it is not one which Léa seems to fear, nor to covet.

However, it is not only through the nature of this constructing gaze that Léa represents an unusual character and certainly one who is far more complex than the initial interpretation as older-female predator might lead us to believe. Rather, there are a series of other aspects of Léa's character which we learn through the opening sequences of the film and which, when brought together, make for a far more challenging 'older' female character than we might be used to seeing in classical comedy narratives such as *Belle Maman*. For instance, as well as being the 'belle maman' of the film's title, Léa is also, throughout the narrative, mother, grandmother and, perhaps most interestingly, daughter. She is not consigned and confined to a single familial position, on the basis of audience expectations of 'a woman of a certain age'. Rather she is allowed to move from one role to another, without being forced to make choices between them, but also accepting criticism (from her ex-husband or from her daughter) that she has failed in her accomplishment of one or more of the roles.

There is no attempt to construct Léa as some kind of wonder-woman who has succeeded in maintaining career, family life and personal life, and her multiple positionings within a largely matriarchal family network do not attempt to represent her as the ultimate role model to be followed. We know that her marriage to Paul (Jean Yanne), the father of the bride, failed and that their relationship is now extremely acrimonious and fuelled, on the rare occasions when they do meet, by bitter recriminations about their previous life together. And we know that she has (at best) a fraught relationship with Séverine (Mathilde Seigner), the daughter whose wedding she interrupts and with whose husband she will eventually begin a relationship.[11] Yet the narrative does not shy away from presenting Léa within each of these family relationships, nor from indicating that we are dealing here with a character who *does* have a past, who *is* 'older', and who has had time to grow into the various family roles that she now inhabits.

Of these different family relationships, the one that perhaps has most to contribute in terms of its impact on the depiction of ageing offered through *Belle Maman* is her role as daughter, and, specifically, daughter to a lesbian mother, Nicou, played by Line Renaud. Given the film's status as a clearly mainstream production, it is interesting to note in passing that the relationship between straight daughter and gay mother is in no way problematised here, but rather it is taken for granted as part of the narrative.[12] Nicou and Léa's relationship appears to be one which has been wholeheartedly accepted by each party and both have key roles to play throughout *Belle Maman*, ultimately emerging as strong, vocal, positive female characters.

The first half of *Belle Maman* is set in Paris where the various family members gather first for Séverine and Antoine's wedding, and then for the birth of their daughter, Pauline. However, the setting then shifts to the Caribbean island which is home to Léa and Nicou, and their respective partners Grégoire and Brigitte, and where they have organised a party to celebrate Nicou's seventieth birthday. Léa's gift to her mother comes in the form of a song which she has written and which she sings during the celebrations. The lyrics of the song provide a clear and positive analysis of gay parenting, from the child's point of view.

They are particularly interesting in the current context, first, because of their affirmation of the mother–daughter relationship between Nicou and Léa, but also, in specific relation to questions of on-screen depictions of ageing, because they present the audience with a 50–something actress who is allowed, not only to play the maternal figure, but also allowed to adopt the position of the child, thus emphasising simultaneously her youth and her maturity. Furthermore, while so much is made of the rarity of the position of Deneuve as 'ageing actress', her own on-screen emphasis here on her role as *daughter* of a very active, and very much present, mother inevitably serves as a perfect illustration that there *is* life beyond 50, confirming so many affirmations to be found in post-1993 articles about and interviews with Deneuve. For all the 'Deneuve at 50', 'Deneuve at 53' headlines,[13] and for all that she is presented as an 'older' central female figure, she is not the oldest female character presented, and those older than her are not confined to passive contributions to the narrative either, but have an active role to play.

The song that Léa offers her mother for her birthday begins with a direct reference to Nicou's youth, and thus, inevitably, to processes of ageing:

> It's a funny old life, you were once young, you were pretty
> You even wore skirts and suspender belts.

> (Drôle de vie autre temps t'étais jeune, t'étais belle; Tu portais même des jupes et des porte-jarretelles.)

While criticism may be levelled at the film by some for its depiction of Nicou as a butch, cigar-smoking, vulgar-joke-telling dyke, this particular couplet, sung by daughter to mother, situates this particular expression of her sexuality as a development of her later life. In this way, again, they allow the character of Léa to construct a life history for another, older, female character, and to do so in a way that does not infantilise or disempower the older woman, but rather emphasises her sensuality, physicality and sexuality. Particularly interesting in terms of the lines' reflection on the parent–child relationship is that Léa recognises her mother, through this couplet, first as having had an existence prior to motherhood and second as a sexual being.

Other lines taken from the birthday song strengthen the argument in favour of Nicou's lesbian parenthood having been the result of a deliberate and proactive decision-making process, and contain implicit recognition from Léa that her mother chose her father on the basis of a number of criteria:

> You chose one who was tall, blonde,
> In short, the perfect stallion.
> You didn't lie to this poor guy
> You told him straight up, I prefer girls.

> (Tu l'as choisi bien grand, bien blond,
> En somme, le parfait étalon.
> Tu ne lui as pas menti à ce pauvre garçon
> Tu lui as dit franchement moi je préfère les gazons)

Critics of gay parenting would doubtless seize on the apparent small-scale genetic engineering involved in the selection of a tall, blond father. However, the daughter voicing this vision of her own conception seems to transmit no such judgement, but rather compliments her mother's honesty and frankness in making clear to him that his role was to father a child to a lesbian mother. Clearly, this is a somewhat idyllic and idealised impression of the decisions involved – it should be borne in mind, for instance, that the celebrations which prompt the song are for Nicou's seventieth and that, since Léa is supposed to be around 50, this progressive approach to gay parenting would have taken place in the immediate post-war years, well before the *Pacs* debates and the like brought the issue to the social fore. Nevertheless, Léa is presented as a sympathetic, strong central character, she is allowed to present her mother in equally positive terms. The implication is thus that Léa has not emerged as such a strong personality *despite* an 'alternative' conception and, presumably, childhood, but rather *because* of it.

Overall, then, what emerges through Deneuve's roles in these three very different, and yet complementary, films, is a vision of ageing that is complex and multifaceted, reliant as much upon stereotypes of maternal or sexual relationships involving 'older women' as upon challenges to those same stereotypes. From the silencing of Hélène and her pained existence through the gaze of youth, to the guardianship offered, with no reward, by Cathy in von Trier's *Dancer in the Dark*, to the unpredictable, confident, strong mother, daughter and grandmother that is Léa in *Belle Maman*. This is not only an active illustration that there exists a diversity of roles which could be played by 'older' actresses on-screen, nor simply the sum total of a prolific cinematic trajectory. Rather, it signals an ongoing dialogue between the on-screen and off-screen personae of a woman for whom age has always played a role – at times through her own volition and at times because of the media obsession with her – in constructing her star image.

Notes

1 Deneuve was born in 1943, Streep in 1949.
2 In an interview with the French weekly magazine *Télérama*, Deneuve declared: 'Ageing is difficult for any woman, for an actress, it's a pain. A real pain!' ('Vieillir, c'est difficile pour n'importe quelle femme, pour une actrice, c'est emmerdant. Très, très emmerdant!') (Frodon, 1997).
3 Deneuve herself, according to an article published in *Le Monde* on 1 January 2001, prefers to think of her cinematic output in terms of a trajectory she follows, rather than as something as solidified as a 'career': 'Catherine Deneuve still refuses to allow people to talk about a career, preferring the notion of a trajectory which has encompassed

every aspect of cinema: "We're entitled to any path, any detour, any stop".' ('Catherine Deneuve ne veut toujours pas entendre parler de carrière, plutôt une trajectoire qui a épousé tous les courants du cinéma: "On a droit à tous les chemins, tous les détours, tous les arrets"') (Le Guilledoux, 2001).

4 In 1999, for instance, she could be seen on-screen in *Est–Ouest* (Wargnier, 1999), *Belle Maman* (Aghion, 1999), *Le Vent de la nuit* (Garrel, 1999), *Le Temps retrouvé/Time Regained* (Ruiz, 1999) and *Pola X* (Carax, 1999), while 2004 saw the release of André Téchiné's *Les Temps qui changent* and Arnaud Desplechin's *Rois et reine/Kings and Queen*, as well as her prominent, prime-time television role as Marie Bonaparte in *Princesse Marie*, directed by Benoît Jacquot.

5 Around 65,000 entrées according to www.lefilmfrancais.fr, compared to over 1 million for *Belle Maman*, for instance (figures accessed online on 2 December 2004).

6 Whether commenting, in relation to her role in Téchiné's *Les Temps qui changent*, 'I'm not interested in pretending to be ageless' ('ça ne m'intéresse pas de faire semblant de ne pas avoir d'âge') in the pages of *Elle* in 2004, or claiming, in *Paris Match*, in the same year, 'I don't have the impression that I'm that different from the person I was thirty years ago' ('je n'ai pas l'impression d'être une personne très différente de celle que j'étais il y a trente ans') (both quotes taken from www.toutsurdeneuve.fr).

7 Not only are they constructed as such within the narrative but the two actors involved, Deneuve and Duval were born a year apart, in 1943 and 1944 respectively.

8 Deneuve's political engagements have also seen her, for example, demonstrating for the rights of imprisoned reporters in Cuba, or, more recently, campaigning against the death penalty.

9 Jean-Luc Douin, writing in *Le Monde*, made explicit reference to the close ties between Garrel's work and a visual narrative of May '68 in an article published in 2004 on the occasion of a retrospective of Garrel's films: 'Philippe Garrel's cinematographic adventure bears witness to a specific period [that of May 1968]. Traces of enthusiasm, despondency, rebellion. The imprint of a generation which grew up under Mendès France, sat their exams with Dylan, went to university with Mao'. ('L'aventure cinématographique de Philippe Garrel porte témoignage d'une époque [celle de mai '68]. Des traces de fougue, spleens, rébellions. Empreinte d'une génération qui a grandi sous Mendès France, passé le bac avec Dylan, fréquenté la fac avec Mao') (Douin, 2004).

10 It is perhaps worth noting, in passing, the intertextual irony inherent in this absence from the historical narrative, given Deneuve's modelling for Marianne, arch symbol of the French Republic. (For more on this, see Chapter 6 of the present volume.)

11 Antoine and Séverine, at the end of the film, have separated and both

have found new partners, Antoine with Léa and Séverine with a delivery man working for one of the many take-away food and ready-made meal companies that she uses throughout the film.

12 This unproblematic straight daughter–lesbian mother relationship can be contrasted, for instance, with the straight daughter–gay father relationship in *Le Derrière* (Lemercier, 1999).

13 'As cool, as blond and as unlined as ever, the 60–year-old Parisienne [...] dismisses the current coolness between [the US and France]', according to the *Chicago Tribune* in 2004. *Paris Match* headlined 'A 60 ans je vis une adolescence tardive' in 2003, the aforementioned article in *The Advocate* gushes about 'the radiant beauty, who turns 59 in October' and the *Standard Times* ran a story in 1996 under the headline 'Deneuve: 53, and acting her age' (all references taken from www.toutsurdeneuve. fr, accessed online at various dates in 2004).

Works cited

L'Est Républicain (2004), 'Je suis une femme libre' (www.toutsurdeneuve. fr)

Paris Match (2004), 'Je suis une femme virile' (www.toutsurdeneuve.fr)

www.lefilmfrancais.fr

www.toutsurdeneuve.fr

Douin, Jean-Luc (2004), 'Retrospective Philippe Garrel dans la douleur du temps,' *Le Monde*, 2 June.

Duralde, Alonso (2002), 'Belle toujours', *The Advocate*, October 29 (accessed online at www.advocate.com on 4 September 2004).

Frodon, Jean-Michel (1997), 'Catherine Deneuve: une icône en liberté', *Le Monde*, 24 March (accessed online at www.lemonde.fr on 2 April 2005).

Le Guilledoux, Dominique (2001), 'Deneuve dévoile Dorléac', *Le Monde*, 1 January.

Lefort, Gérard (1999), Review of *Belle Maman*, *Libération*, 10 March (accessed online at www.liberation.fr on 23 August 2005).

Sotinel, Thomas (2000), 'Le pouvoir de transformer le monde à la seule force de la voix,' *Le Monde*, 19 May.

Vincendeau, Ginette (2000), *Stars and Stardom in French Cinema*, London and New York: Continuum.

9

The killing of sister Catherine: Deneuve's lesbian transformations

Andrew Asibong

Deneuve's cinematic queerness has often emerged from on-screen evocations of a wide range of 'perverse', paradoxical or somehow *blank* heterosexualities.[1] But that queerness has also derived from an unabashed association with a perhaps more obviously non-normative tendency: female homosexuality.[2] Deneuve's screen personae have been frequently queer in a specifically lesbian sense, and to a far greater degree than mainstream audiences and journalists tend to acknowledge. As early as Luis Buñuel's *Belle de jour* (1966), we witness Deneuve's timid Séverine initially fighting off brothel-keeper Mme Anaïs (Geneviève Page)'s sexual advances; later in the film it is Séverine who attempts (unsuccessfully) to kiss her mistress's lips. In László Szabó's *Zig zig* (1975) Deneuve and Bernadette Lafont (herself fresh from the bisexual experimentations of *La Maman et la putain/The Mother and the Whore*) perform a girl-on-girl routine in the strip-joint where they are employed as dancers. In Hugo Santiago's little-seen *Ecoute voir…/See Here My Love* (1979), an offbeat mixture of Chandler and Feuillade, Deneuve's private investigator Claude (complete with Marlowe-esque hat and trench coat) enjoys an on-screen kiss with the missing girl whose disappearance she has been hired to solve, Chloé (Anne Parillaud).

In 1983 Deneuve's lesbian moments on film reach their peak of exposure with Tony Scott's contemporary vampire film *The Hunger* (French title: *Les Prédateurs*), in which she plays Miriam, last in an ancient race of apparently immortal vampires, able to bestow the gift of several centuries of youth to her chosen partners. When the time of her lover John (David Bowie) is finally up, Miriam, having packed away his murmuring cadaver in her attic of defunct paramours, seduces the woman scientist Dr Sarah Roberts (Susan Sarandon) whom John had fruitlessly consulted prior to his accelerated ageing. The protracted bedroom scene between Deneuve and Sarandon is the most celebrated in the entire film. In 1996, in André Téchiné's *Les Voleurs/Thieves*, she plays philosophy lecturer Marie Leblanc, a woman whose sexual relationship in middle-age with a young female student Juliette (Laurence Côte) emerges as the single most important event of her life. Deneuve's love scenes with Côte are, like the erotic sequence with Sarandon in *The Hunger*, played partially nude, Deneuve in the 1990s seeming to remain utterly indifferent to an ongoing association with lesbian situations on film. Her performance as 1950s *grande bourgeoise* Gaby in François Ozon's *8 femmes/8 Women* (2002) plays on lesbian motifs already accrued in the course of her career, from Gaby's bristling (though unconsummated) relationship with her lasciviously worshipful maid Louise (Emmanuelle Béart) to her celebrated sexual tussle with her sister-in-law Pierrette (Fanny Ardant). Even Deneuve's literary turns as Odette Swann in Raúl Ruiz's *Le Temps retrouvé/Time Regained* (1999) and as Madame de Merteuil in Josée Dayan's television adaptation of *Les Liaisons dangereuses/Dangerous Liaisons* (2003) are soaked in the associations of a barely suppressed feminine bisexuality, if Proust's and Laclos's original characterisations of Odette and Merteuil in their respective novels carry any weight for the viewer.[3]

If we are looking for lesbians in Deneuve's film closet, then, we do not have to look very hard: they are legion, and they do not hide particularly carefully. When critics (e.g. Vincendeau, 2000, Austin, 2003) have drawn attention to the gay dimensions of certain of Deneuve's chosen roles, or have noted that she has become (for certain lesbians) something of a heroine, they have limited their analysis to brief mentions of the sex scene with Sarandon in *The Hunger* or the kiss with Ardant in *8 femmes/8 Women*. Their point – that Deneuve has, despite a weirdly straight cultural image in France, dared to kiss other women on film and has consequently become, particularly outside France, a 'lesbian icon' – is interesting but could be taken much further.[4] One might expect consciously gay publications to probe the phenomenon with greater profundity. And yet the vast majority of 'lesbian' articles and interviews explicitly devoted to the question of Deneuve's on-screen queerness seem fixated on remarkably superficial questions: is Deneuve herself a closet lesbian or bisexual? Did she feel bad about suing the lesbian magazine *Deneuve*?[5] And did she and Susan Sarandon *really* use body doubles in *The Hunger*?[6] My intention here is to go beyond the necessarily limited material hitherto published on the question of Catherine Deneuve's relation, as film star and cultural sign, to lesbian representation. To state simply that Deneuve has played a great number of (homosexually) queer situations on film is not especially illuminating, even if it remains fascinating that this fact seems to impinge not one whit on the general French perception of Deneuve as establishment figure and incarnation of traditional French values.[7] And to strive endlessly to prove some lesbian connection in Deneuve's private life would seem to be an exercise in (at worst) voyeuristic frustration or (at best) masturbatory fantasy.[8] We need to establish some kind of methodology in our reading of Deneuve's on-screen lesbianisms. We need to consider exactly *why* directors might gravitate towards Deneuve when trying to evoke or represent forms of female homosexual activity on film, and to consider exactly *what* such directors actually make Deneuve do and mean once they have her performing these particular forms of lesbian relation. Once we get beyond the two main dangers in the relatively virgin territory of Deneuvian lesbian studies – myopic underestimation or lubricious trivialisation – it becomes apparent that lesbian behaviour is, quite indisputably, a solidly recurrent dimension of Deneuve's star persona that has often been made to function in a singular and highly *politicised* fashion.

Certain of Deneuve's on-screen lesbian moments are indeed relatively trivial. The nightclub sequences with Bernadette Lafont in *Zig zig*, for example, are innocuous titillation, worthy of comment, perhaps, only for the way in which they provide the means whereby two very different French female cinematic icons literally caress each other's image. This operation is repeated nearly twenty years later in *8 femmes/8 Women* when Gaby/Deneuve and Pierrette/Fanny Ardant roll around divinely together on the floor towards the film's climax: two beautiful, ageing goddesses of post-new-wave French cinema, two of 'Truffaut's women', two prototypes of 'French femininity', two parodies of the Franco-American *femme fatale* come together for one simultaneously erotic, ironic, comic – and, of course, highly marketable – instant, on a lushly kitsch, red-velvet surface. Aesthetically and cinematically satisfying though Deneuve's clinches with Lafont and Ardant may be, they hold little interest from a philosophical perspective. Of more socio-political importance, perhaps, are Deneuve's characterisations of the private detective in *Ecoute voir.../See Here My Love* and as the middle-aged academic in *Les Voleurs/Thieves*. In these roles Deneuve renders lesbian potential in a 'normal' woman utterly unremarkable: it is just one more aspect of the strong, self-determining, independent nature that Deneuve has often insisted that she embodies.[9] The lesbian dimension in Claude and Marie is far from the most noteworthy characteristic of either of these Deneuvian roles: its relative insignificance is, in a way, precisely what makes these films 'progressive'. I am not, however, going to linger on these performances either. The cinematic normalisation of homosexuality and bisexuality is (arguably) an important cultural process, but it is not my desire to theorise it here. It does not depend on the star persona of Catherine Deneuve for its efficacy.

Deneuve's stardom is at its queerest, at its most provocative – and at its most radically *political* – when it is simultaneously lesbian and sadomasochistic. When Deneuve is involved with another woman on screen in a systematic and ritualised dynamic of dominance and submission – as she is with astonishing frequency for a star of mainstream cinema – something remarkable occurs. All the invisible – yet profoundly ideological – processes that are constantly in motion for the construction of Deneuve as a specific type of star and as a specific type of woman are, in her scenarios of lesbian sadomasochism, suddenly revealed as just that: pure construction. The hallmarks of Deneuvian stardom, femininity and social identity itself are rendered, when Deneuve enacts lesbian ritualised power play, suddenly contingent, artificial and theatrical. In such situations Deneuve is able to deliver performances that comment directly on her status as cinematic, sexual and social subject. Why should this occur via the enactment of a female homosexual sadomasochistic dynamic? In interviews on the ethico-political implications of apparently new forms of relation, Michel Foucault expresses his enthusiasm for the potential of contemporary lesbian sadomasochistic practice to expose, diffuse and disperse otherwise largely reified forms of contemporary social and sexual power (1997: 168–9). According to Foucault, and echoed by more recent theorists of lesbian sadomasochistic practice such as Marie-Hélène Bourcier, there are various potential outcomes of women indulging in consensual bondage together. Forms of power hitherto considered immutable and non-negotiable may become unglued (via sadomasochism's relentless parody, artifice and deconstruction) from their 'permanent' owners – unchanging, 'essentialised' heterosexual males – and relocated to alternative, constantly shifting, always provisional subjects: 'women', say, who, for the duration of the sadomasochistic ritual, cease to function solely as female, or even as human subjects. More transformational than a mere reproduction and wholesale transference of power from one set of subjects to another, or from one sexual group to another, the theatre of lesbian sadomasochism might, according to its most fervent apologists, dent the historical and ideological links between sex, power and subjectivity, pointing the way towards radically impermanent, fissured and utterly revisable forms of relation between humans emptied of anything like preordained identity, beings no longer classifiable – outside the temporary and artificial theatre of the sadomasochistic ritual – as this or that type, rank, sex or class.[10]

Such a theorisation might be applied to a reading of the construction and deconstruction, via key lesbian sadomasochistic cinematic representations, of Catherine Deneuve's ideologically loaded 'power' in the course of her film career. Deneuve retains an almost magically tenacious star image in the popular (especially French) consciousness, one unshakably attached to qualities of 'natural' purity, conservatism and privilege. She has maintained this image over four decades despite constant experimentation with roles of transgression and 'perversion', and despite the queerly blank quality she so often brings to her characterisations, a blankness which might allow, theoretically at least, for a persona of limitless potentiality. That hallucination of Deneuve as eternal, inevitable, superior lady cannot be chased away, it would appear, by cinematic transgression, perversion or blankness. To crumble effectively, it must instead have the 'naturalness' sucked violently out of it. Certain simultaneously lesbian and sadomasochistic aspects of the films I want to analyse in the remainder of this chapter are, I suggest, the only cinematic tools that have hitherto proven equal to that violent task. Only in her ritualistic same-sex dealings of eroticised power with Geneviève Page in *Belle de jour* and, in a more thorough fashion, with Susan Sarandon in *The Hunger* and with Emmanuelle Béart in *8 femmes/8 Women*, is Catherine Deneuve used effectively to prick her own (potentially fascistic) myth. These three cinematic situations, forms of lesbian sadomasochist representation all, inaugurate a simultaneous theorisation, denaturalisation and *explosion* of Deneuve's putatively 'natural' superiority.

Cinema can very easily render one woman's domination and humiliation of another entertaining, casual – a mere 'naturalistic' detail of the apparently more important spectacle we are there to see. When, for example, Joan Crawford, in an early scene of Cukor's *The Women* (1939), and in her quintessential, 'sexily' aggressive shop-girl persona, barks a string of threatening commands at the 'comically' terrified black shop-maid Butterfly McQueen (uncredited in this film), nothing in the scene asks the viewer to *think* about this representation of, in fact, quite upsettingly violent domination of one woman by another. The interaction is merely part of the order of things in the film's particular ideological universe, and is matter-of-factly presented as such. The film as a whole, while often hugely enjoyable, is permeated with a discourse of naturalised roles and fixed identities: married men *will* stray from their sweet-tempered wives at some point, shop-girl mistresses *will* show their vulgar, working-class, 'real' selves sooner or later, black maids *will* talk in screeching tones and roll their eyes constantly, wronged women *will* return joyfully to their repentant husbands in the end. Power structures and modes of behaviour in this film are taken, directed and played as *given*: far more important are the laughs, tears, fights and fabulous fashion shows to be glimpsed along the way. But if *The Women* smoothes over the violence of Joan Crawford's on-screen dynamic with Butterfly McQueen as innocuously quotidian detail, a startling lesbian sadomasochist aesthetic injects Crawford's violent on-screen relations with Mercedes McCambridge fifteen years later in Nicholas Ray's western *Johnny Guitar* (1954) with the hallucinatory fire of a truly *critical* intervention. The lustfully whispered promise from Emma (McCambridge) to Vienna (Crawford) in the film's first half hour that she will – for no clearly expressed reason – kill her sustains the action of the rest of the entire narrative, initiating a bewilderingly eroticised 'contract of pain' between the two women. This contract and its consequences dramatically defamiliarise the dynamics we expect to find in a western. After its utterance, the film's (initially male- and state-governed) distribution of power and violence can never be the same again. No longer channelled through inflexible generic convention or through an inevitably penile phallus, but instead via the excessive, theatrical and ritualised desire of two enigmatically passionate women, alternately in tight trousers and long, flowing dresses, power is 'outed', in the course of this bloody female court-ship, as an irreducibly violent process dependent on costume, rhetoric and an abundance of (once disavowed but now clearly exposed) *desire*. Between Cukor and Ray's two Joan Crawfords, then, and thanks to the spoken incursion of the lesbian sadomasochist contract in *Johnny Guitar*, unspoken, taken-for-granted modes of authority and humiliation undergo a drastic cinematic dismantling. Something similar occurs to Catherine Deneuve's 'aristocratic' screen persona via the lesbian sadomasochist theatrics of *Belle de jour* (1966), *The Hunger* (1983) and *8 femmes/8 Women* (2002). In these films the Deneuvian persona and the ideology that sustains it both become thoroughly denaturalised.

Belle de jour provides a useful point of entry into understanding lesbian sadomasochist cinema's potential for the demystification of the Deneuvian persona. The film appears, at first, to be utterly complicit with the cementing of Deneuve into a sexual and social model of immutable class, power and privilege. As Séverine, Deneuve lends herself spectacularly well to the mythologisation of a certain type of phantasmatic, neo-aristocratic, white, blonde French femininity, and in *Belle de jour* one might be mistaken for thinking that Buñuel, lazily, does no more than reproduce Deneuve, statue-like, as quasi-fascistic Aryan icon. The numerous transgressions around which the film's narrative gravitates – Séverine whipped and raped by her working-class coachmen; Séverine spattered with cow-dung by the sinister Husson (Michel Piccoli) while husband Pierre (Jean Sorel) looks on; Séverine unspeakably acted upon by a monstrous Asian and his horrifyingly buzzing box; Séverine placed in a coffin, masturbated over and violently ejected by a duke claiming to be her father – all function simply to strengthen the idea that Deneuve cannot *help* but incarnate a naturally occurring nobility-cum-purity that others (and she herself) take pleasure in seeing momentarily defiled.

The only relation into which Séverine enters whose corollary is an effective undermining of her aura of 'natural class' is the explicitly contractual one she has with Mme Anaïs, her employer at the brothel. From the moment the short-haired, authoritative and gravel-voiced Anaïs lays her acquisitive eyes and mouth on Séverine – pale, blonde, hyper-feminine and resplendent in expensive black and sunglasses, 'a real aristocrat!' ('une vraie aristocrate!'), as Anaïs ironically puts it – she asserts the 'reality' of Séverine's/Deneuve's carefully packaged persona as fiction, fetish, the fantasy material of a contract to be presided over by her between the hours of 2 and 5. It is under Anaïs's tight rein that Séverine (renamed – by Anaïs – 'Belle de jour') starts to undergo her radical dissolution of 'real' identity, and that the strictly dichotomising 'reality v. fantasy' structure of the early part of the film begins steadily to unravel. Anaïs, in explicitly declaring there to be an eroticised contract of power between the two of them, creates a space whereby the persona of Séverine/Deneuve as woman, princess, object of beauty and defilement can be revealed as just another brothel costume – and can thus begin to crumble. Anaïs is, later in the film, mirrored in this function by Marcel (Pierre Clémenti), the pretty young thug whose combination of girlishness and aggressive authority (and whose quasi-Sapphic love scenes with Séverine are played as if between two narcissistic nymphs) reiterates Buñuel's clear intention to have the Séverine/Deneuve persona ripped apart at the ideological seams by the sword of a sexually ambiguous – yet, like her, feminised – punisher.

Deneuve's underrated English-language vampire movie *The Hunger* deepens and extends the use of violent – this time fantastically so – lesbian representation to over-mythologise and simultaneously drain the aristocratically feminine Deneuvian star persona of substance. A simultaneously hyper-earnest and self-deriding 'lesbian vampire flick', famous for its brilliant opening sequence of the ice-cool Deneuve and David Bowie cruising for young flesh in London's nightclub 'Heaven' to the song 'Bela Lugosi's Dead', *The Hunger* is a truly astonishing addition to the subgenre, far outstripping any of its predecessors in its quality of production and direction and organisation of its thought.[11] Paramount in the film's success, though, is its shrewd use and abuse of its three utterly iconic stars, Deneuve, Bowie and Susan Sarandon.[12] By casting Deneuve as a vampire, a creature driven by inhuman rule, ritual and regulation, the film renders literally supernatural all the aspects of her persona which might, in other circumstances, be naively and unblinkingly accepted as natural, innocent and somehow organic. As in *Belle de jour*, Deneuve appears at first to be utilised in a rather predictable fashion that merely solidifies and props up her already existing star image as the quintessential lady. This is intensified still further by her Frenchness in the film's Anglo-American context, as she and her supernatural character Miriam take on a heavily-accented, decadent, 'old-world' sheen. As alabaster-skinned and flawlessly blonde as ever, Miriam/Deneuve is clothed in dresses of the utmost luxury and resides in a palatial house containing the most beautiful and precious of objects, oozing health, wealth, culture and privilege from every pore. We are told that she is of royal blood, certain brief images suggesting that she ruled even in Ancient Egypt. The casting of Bowie as Miriam's lover John Blaylock reinforces still further the film's apparent determination to associate Deneuve with a sort of fantasised, simultaneously ahistorical and specifically neo-Aryan 'breeding', relatively fresh as he was from his long stint in Berlin and his own constructed star persona of the Thin White Duke. Our brief glimpses of the courtship of Miriam and John, wigged and powdered in pre-romantic-era Europe, function as almost ludicrously excessive visual indices of the star couple's reinvention by cinema as inherent, eternal, natural aristocrats, still playing their eighteenth-century music in modern-day New York.

If Deneuve as Séverine was granted a male girlfriend in the form of Marcel/Clémenti, her scenes as Miriam of heterosexual activity with John/Bowie are similarly infused with a pseudo-lesbian quality that prepares us for the film's continual destabilisation of categories of 'natural' sexual identity. When the (suddenly) strong and powerful Miriam ritualistically carries the (equally suddenly) aged, weak and emaciated John to her mausoleum of former lovers the viewer is primed indeed for the film's systematic exposure of the sheer contingency of Miriam's desire, sexuality, and concomitant acts of authority. When the spectral lesbian role play of Deneuve and Bowie is converted into the more fully realised lesbian role play of Deneuve and Sarandon, the film is able to begin its steady disintegration of a Deneuvian persona we may have fantasised as embedded in unchanging privilege. From the minute that Miriam brings Sarah under her violently erotic spell at the latter's book-signing event, we are made aware of how the highly constructed *type* of femininity and power she wields cannot, in this film, be buried under the myth of some kind of natural order. Through Miriam's specifically lesbian courtship, seduction and fantastical domination of the very different 'type' of woman that is Sarah, the film draws attention to the way in which all social and sexual relations are marked – and power is created – by the artificial (but usually disavowed) exaggeration of difference. Thus, as Sarah, Sarandon is given a deliberately short, auburn, wavy '1980s' haircut, is clothed throughout in slacks and shirts, and is frequently filmed blushing, the pinkness and redness of her complexion insisted on by the film's lighting.[13] All this contrasts spectacularly with Deneuve's 'classic', straight (but pinned-up) blondeness, regal dresses and pallor. The heavy, dark mascara worn by Sarandon adds to her laboured physiognomic difference from the pale-lashed Deneuve. Sarandon's strident, forthright American tones provide a final, aural contrast with the sometimes barely audible regal drone of Deneuve. The film thus insists upon hyperbolic differences between Deneuve and Sarandon that are, in many ways, far more pronounced than differences between Deneuve and Bowie: it is through the comparison of two actresses on film, then, rather than that of an actress and an actor, that the social and ideological construction of difference and of power can be most clearly perceived.

Difference in type is increasingly articulated and performed by Miriam as an eroticised difference in status. Miriam's erotic conquest of Sarah is preceded by a subtly controlling assertion of a cultural superiority that is also a wooing (her classical piano-playing), and by the legend she narrates of an Indian princess and her female slave/lover. Miriam 's domination of Sarah is conveyed as much by the predictable dental penetration as by her repeated declaration, in formal terms, of the bond of non-negotiable ownership that now ties the two women together. Explicitly naming herself as Sarah's mistress and ruler she sets up a discursive framework of bondage to accommodate and render visible the women's hitherto unspoken relation of hierarchical difference.[14] Exactly as was the case with the film *Belle de jour*, in *The Hunger* the Deneuve character's silently smug enjoyment of her privilege-suffused persona begins to be dispersed and dissolved the moment that persona is articulated and performed as such within the new contract. It is with the clear appearance of a new and outrageously 'post-natural' form of power – symbolised, as in many lesbian vampire films, by the spurting together of the blood of two women – that the underlying structures that have all the while silently and invisibly facilitated that power can be seen, and perhaps dissolved.[15] The film's alteration of Whitley Strieber's original novel (in which the Miriam character lived on and prospered after Sarah's martyr-like suicide) revels in its purely cinematic discovery of how it is precisely once it has been formalised on-screen, with another woman, and as articulated contract, that the Deneuvian persona begins, in fact, to fall apart. Having lulled the spectator into a state whereby it seems inevitable that Miriam cannot help but vanquish the punily *ordinary* Sarah, Scott instead offers us a denouement in which it is precisely this slave figure who, having understood the workings of the contract imposed upon her by her mistress, will quickly usher in that mistress's demise, usurp her place as vampire queen, and become the (knowingly provisional?) owner of her own young female lover. In the new, contractual, sadomasochistic world that Miriam unwittingly sets in motion, the role of queen is replaceable: once the Sarandon figure has understood how 'Deneuve' functions she realises that she does not have to *be* Deneuve to fill it. *The Hunger* is, in many ways, a film that sadistically uses the 'aristocratic' icons that are Deneuve and Bowie to record, with an utter absence of sentiment, the dissolution of essentialised categories of privilege. Ghoulishly showing us how in a few short moments handsome young men can so quickly transform (as in Bowie's famous aging sequence in the hospital waiting-room) into emaciated corpses, it employs Deneuve as its limit case, its metamorphosing linchpin par excellence: exposed as a princess constructed not of magic but of discourse, in her final frame she is sadistically revealed as just one more cadaver.

François Ozon's 2002 film adaptation of Robert Thomas's long-forgotten murder mystery for the 1960s French stage, *8 femmes/8 Women*, will doubtless be remembered most for its almost arrogantly ostentatious casting, almost entirely composed as it is of French female screen icons of an overwhelming symbolic stature. Ozon's assertive injection of glamorous feminine iconography into his pedestrian theatrical source is heavily dosed with two more, no less crucial, supplements that are certainly not present in the original play script either: lesbianism and sadomasochism. Ozon's cinema is saturated with a specifically violent and abusive gay aesthetic: like Fassbinder he seems fascinated by what is starkly revealed about the workings of society as a whole and identity *tout court* when two males or two females come together in a sexual alliance of clearly expressed cruelty. In *8 femmes/8 Women* French cinema's leading actresses – and Catherine Deneuve in particular – are laughingly inserted into a horrifically cruel doll's house. Yet again a director of Deneuve orchestrates the effective disintegration of the Deneuvian persona through his cinematic exposure of her to the lesbian sadomasochist's contract; the difference with this film, though, is its suggestion (even if ironic) that on the other side of that disintegration might lie the potential for new, less fascistic bonds.

As was the case with *Belle de jour* and *The Hunger*, *8 femmes/8 Women* appears at first to use Deneuve's 'majestic' presence merely to reiterate the star's putative aristocratic superiority, and in that reiteration to contribute to the ideological naturalisation of the Deneuvian persona. As the film's *grande dame* Gaby, Deneuve is yet again wrapped throughout the film in the accoutrements of luxury, this time with a particular emphasis on heavy jewellery and fur. Her relations to almost all the other women/actresses of the household/film set seem predicated on an assumption – shared by both intra-diegetic characters and extra-diegetic audiences – of Gaby's/Deneuve's symbolic, social, racial, sexual, economic or aesthetic superiority over the others. Furthermore, these relations are performed in much of the film with the *casualness* that we noted earlier as a characteristic of *The Women*'s representations of hierarchy. When Gaby slaps young upstart of a screen daughter Catherine (Ludivine Sagnier) there seems to be something quite acceptable about such contemptuous violence on two levels: this is an exasperated mother hitting her annoying teenage offspring, but it is also the regal, middle-aged Deneuve asserting her rightful authority over the tomboyish *arriviste* of new French cinema screen that is Sagnier. When Gaby smashes a bottle over the head of her demented screen mother (Danielle Darrieux), again this violence seems comically justifiable within the logic of both the narrative *and* the 'real' world: the old woman had it coming to her, and Darrieux, even if we can remember her as a pretty young thing in *Club de femmes* (which most of us cannot), is frail and irritating compared to the still stunning, still powerful player that is Deneuve. The scenes of 'comic' contempt displayed by Gaby to her neurotic plainer sister Augustine (Isabelle Huppert) smack of the queen of French cinema having a quite feasible dig at a mere duchess, as much as they are a detail of the plot itself. And when we see the overweight, black and recently outed lesbian house-keeper Mme Chanel (Firmine Richard) on her knees before an implacable and disgusted Gaby, an inevitable (and rather uncomfortable if thought about for too long) conflation between the privileges of Gaby as character and Deneuve as superstar vis-à-vis Mme Chanel's/ Firmine Richard's relatively humble position both in the narrative's household and in the French film scene quickly takes shape.

These naturalised instances of Deneuvian domination are, once again, destabilised when they are commanded to declare themselves – explicitly, erotically and ritualistically – as desire-driven enactments of power. Gaby's prostitute sister-in-law (and the lover of Mme Chanel), Pierrette (played by Fanny Ardant), will of course eventually goad Gaby into an act of lesbian violence; the result is the famous fight/kiss engaged in by Ardant and Deneuve on the living-room carpet near the film's end. Of far more sustained significance, however, and entirely invented by Ozon's adaptation, are the repeated commands made to Gaby to embody eroticised authority; it is her mysterious maid Louise, played by Emmanuelle Béart, who issues these commands. Louise is a figure steeped in the paraphernalia of a specifically lesbian sadomasochist imaginary. Dressed as a fetish-ised chambermaid (complete with kinky boots reminiscent of those of Jeanne Moreau in Buñuel's *Journal d'une femme de chambre/ Diary of a Chambermaid*), it is suggested several times (again an invention of the film) that she is not a maid out of necessity, but rather a young woman who merely enjoys working and living in a scenario of perpetual domination and submission. Although she has sex with the master of the house, Gaby's husband, the apparently defunct Marcel, she makes it clear that her most ardent desires are channelled through the prospect of subjugation to the authority of the mistress, Gaby herself.[16] In the numerous scenes in which Louise demands, through lustful insinuation, that Gaby fully ritualise her elsewhere much-vaunted power in a sadomasochistic erotic union with Louise herself the result is, once again, transformational of the social status quo thus far: once again, we witness the authority of the Deneuve figure crumble. As the film progresses, the casual, infinitesimal, 'normal' gestures of dismissal and contempt that Gaby performs towards her domestic staff are transfigured by Louise's own exaggerated gestures of excited submission into a dynamic that, despite the mistress's attempts not to see it, establishes itself as resolutely ritualised. In the process of transforming Gaby's ongoing social and domestic affirmations of unchanging power into eroti-cised instances of contingent masochistic pleasure, Louise is able to bleed them of their substance and humiliating social force. By the last quarter of the film Béart as Louise is able – the only figure in the film to do so – to render Deneuve as Gaby a melting, shadowy cipher, a once-powerful mistress-lover whose ephemeral, contractual period of authority is over. Wearing her long, blonde hair loose, standing majestically under the portrait of Gaby/Deneuve when young, Béart as Louise asserts herself in *8 femmes/8 Women* as a new Deneuve, one that looks like her, smokes like her and can act like her, but who also accepts the pure masquerade of all these 'gifts'.[17]

The final frame of *8 femmes/8 Women* is, like so many of Ozon's final frames, a highly ambivalent image of a newly functional community reborn: the film's all-female cast dance in loving pairs to Danielle Darrieux's performance of the utterly depressing Georges Brassens song 'Il n'y a pas d'amour heureux'. However one interprets that particular Ozonian conjunction of blissful image and tragic soundtrack, it seems to me a fitting summing-up of Deneuve's entire cinematic relation to other women. We remember her in warm and tender embrace with female co-stars throughout her career: most famously, perhaps, with her late sister Françoise Dorléac in *Les Demoiselles de Rochefort/The Young Girls of Rochefort*, and (no less touchingly) as Björk's loving friend Cathy in *Dancer in the Dark*. But the sincerity of those gorgeous instances of cinematic female intimacy could not exist, perhaps, without their darker counterpart: the Deneuvian violence beyond whose explosion truly new relations sometimes emerge.

Notes

1 In this volume we find many analyses of the 'perverse' Deneuve, alternately 'frigid' (*Repulsion*), 'slave dog' (*La Cagna/Liza*), potentially
   incestuous daughter (*Peau d'âne/Donkey Skin*), sister (*Ma saison
   préférée/My Favourite Season*) and mother (*Pola X*). The way in which
   Deneuve's cinematic persona slips thus between (often self-consciously
   off-kilter) sexualities, at the same time as clinging, meaninglessly, to a
   discourse of 'purity', seems to anticipate much of the academic 'queer'
   theory of the 1990s (e.g. Butler, 1999), which emphasises the 'performative' aspect of sexuality. The lack of depth, or 'blankness' of many
   of her performances might be noted as itself a 'queer' feature insofar as
   it draws attention to the potentially limitless ambiguity of the identity
   she is apparently portraying. Camille Paglia comes close to this conception of Deneuve when she describes her as one of the 'affectless movie
   zombies' embodying 'emotional lifelessness ... psychological abstrac-
   tion, a masculine impersonality' (1990: 368).
2 The term 'queer' has traditionally been a (pejorative) term for 'homosexual' or 'gay'. It is only in a relatively recent academic and political
   context that it has been redeployed to embrace a whole range of
   non-normative sexual attitudes.
3 In Proust's *Un amour de Swann* Swann worries about rumours that his
   beloved Odette is deceiving him with female as well as male lovers, while
   in Laclos's *Les Liaisons dangereuses* part of Merteuil's interest in Cécile
   is clearly sexual in nature. It is interesting to note too in passing that
   both Proust and Laclos's novels display an outrageous (for their time)
   interest in the implications of a specifically lesbian sadomasochism.
4 Vincendeau's chapter 'Catherine Deneuve: from ice maiden to living
   divinity' and Austin's chapter 'Red woman/white woman: Jeanne
   Moreau and Catherine Deneuve' are, in any case, overviews of Deneuve's
   star persona and are not specifically interested in that persona's lesbian
   dimensions.
5 Deneuve famously sued the lesbian publication *Deneuve* because she
   was annoyed by its apparently flagrant use of her name for its own
   self-promotion. This action seems to dog her years later: even on the
   extremely mainstream British chat show 'Jonathan Ross' in 2005 the
   host (somewhat inanely, and with grinning asides about women in
   dungarees) quizzed her about the *débâcle*.
6 The 1995 *Advocate* interview in which Deneuve discusses all these
   issues can currently be accessed from the website www.toutsurdeneuve.
   free.fr . The French gay and lesbian student website www.degel.asso.fr
   also contains a useful article entitled 'Deneuve et nous'.
7 Deneuve was, as is so often remarked, the model for the Republic's
   Marianne. All the various 'weird' roles and highly publicised biograph-

ical facts (unwed motherhood, abortion, and so on) have not dented her essential centrality in French culture.

 8 Camille Paglia makes comically explicit Deneuve's alternative cultural function as lesbian sexual fantasy figure. When asked what she would do if she grew a penis she says 'I would [imitates Groucho Marx] go find Catherine Deneuve in a hurry!' (1994: 12–13).

 9 For an excellent French account of Deneuve as a star with a singular strength and clarity of vision see the 2004 piece 'Nom: Deneuve, profession: réalisatrice' in the magazine *Les Inrockuptibles*.

10 A veritable cultural studies debate, the fascinating implications of which cannot be analysed here, has sprung up over the past years, vis-à-vis the extent to which sadomasochistic practice is or is not subversive of the status quo. Where theorists such as Foucault, Bourcier, Anita Phillips and Gaylyn Studlar write convincingly of S & M's capacity for transformation, others such as Leo Bersani ('The gay daddy', 1995) and Slavoj Žižek ('Why perversion is not subversion', 1999) have (for quite different reasons) found fault with some of these claims.

11 Compare it with the awfulness of the lesbian vampire films of British Hammer Horror, or with Jean Rollin's art-porn lesbian vampire cycle. Still, only Camille Paglia really gives the film its due, though even she misses the point when she complains of its 'horrendous errors, as when the regal Catherine Deneuve is made to crawl around on all fours, slavering over cut throats' (1990: 268). A highly noteworthy addition to the subgenre is Abel Ferrara's 1997 film *The Addiction* (with Lili Taylor).

12 All three stars could be described as 'queer icons' (Bowie for the duration of his entire pop career, Sarandon as a direct result of *The Rocky Horror Picture Show*).

13 A very different image is cultivated for Sarandon in Louis Malle's *Pretty Baby* (1978), for example, in which her 'whiteness' and 'femininity' (in the racist, misogynist context of a 1920s New Orleans brothel) is relentlessly insisted upon.

14 Here the film is in keeping with many other lesbian vampire films, in which the chief lesbian vampire, herself usually aristocratic, preys on lower-class women, peasants and servants (Weiss, 2002).

15 Marie-Hélène Bourcier speculates at length on the wondrous artifice of sadomasochistic female blood, replacing the paradigm of 'natural' female blood and semen (2001: 76).

16 The allusion (via a dropped photo) to the image of Romy Schneider as a former mistress (in every sense) of Louise is fascinating when one remembers that Schneider played the maid Leni in Welles's version of Kafka's *The Trial*. Both Leni and Louise display the subversive characteristics of Kafka's maid-whore figures.

17 That Béart had already played Deneuve's daughter (as Gilberte Swann in *Le Temps retrouvé*) heightens this doubling effect still further.

Works cited

Les Inrockuptibles, Number 471, 8–14 December 2004.

http://toutsurdeneuve.free.fr/Francais/Pages/Interviews_Presse9099/Advocate95.htm

http://degel.asso.fr/culture/people/people101.php

Austin, Guy (2003), *Stars in Modern French Film*, London: Arnold.

Bersani, Leo (1995), *Homos*, Cambridge, MA: Harvard University Press.

Bourcier, Marie-Hélène (2001), *Queer zones: politique des identités sexuelles, des représentations et des savoirs*, Paris: Balland.

Butler, Judith (1999), *Gender Trouble: Feminism and the Subversion of Identity*, New York: Routledge.

Foucault, Michel (1997), *Ethics – Subjectivity and Truth: The Essential Works 1*, Harmondsworth: Penguin.

Paglia, Camille (1990), *Sexual Personae: Art and Decadence from Nefertiti to Emily Dickinson*, London and New Haven: Yale University Press.

Paglia, Camille (1994), *Vamps and Tramps*, Harmondsworth: Penguin.

Phillips, Anita (1999), *A Defence of Masochism*, London: Faber & Faber.

Studlar, Gaylyn (1988), *In the Realm of Pleasure: Von Sternberg, Dietrich and the Masochistic Aesthetic*, New York: Columbia University Press.

Vincendeau, Ginette (2000), *Stars and Stardom in French Cinema*, London: Continuum.

Weiss, Andrea (2002), *Vampires and Violets: Lesbians in the Cinema*, London: Jonathan Cape.

Žižek, Slavoj (1999), *The Ticklish Subject*, London: Verso.

10

Belle toujours: Deneuve as fashion icon

Fiona Handyside

Belle toujours

With Téchiné's film released in France, and a new perfume launched in the United States, Catherine Deneuve is drawing as much attention to herself as ever. Discussing, elegance, make-up, diet and fitness, she talks to us about beauty.

(Le film de Téchiné qui sort en France, un parfum lancé aux Etats-Unis, Catherine Deneuve fait plus que jamais parler d'elle. Elégance, maquillage, régime, forme, elle se raconte aujourd'hui en beauté'). (Demornex 1986: 69)

The creamy Norman skin has settled over the beautiful bones of her face as paint grows to a canvas over the years, enhancing its beauty. The eyes have lost none of their flash, the voice none of its cello timbre. Even at five on a rainy afternoon, her navy-blue Yves Saint Laurent linen pants suit is as crisp as a new banknote. (Baxter 1993: 150)

The above quotes from French *Elle* 14 April 1986 and Australian *Vogue* February 1993 are typical of the way in which Deneuve's image is constructed in the fashion press. In the former, her appearance in an auteur film is equated with the launch of a perfume: both activities are seen as of equal importance to the way in which Catherine Deneuve 'draws attention to herself', i.e. has a public image. It may also be noticed that for readers of this particular magazine, Deneuve is interviewed not about her role in Téchiné's film, but for her alleged expertise in the area of beauty. It is noticeable that in a shift of register, from the more mass-market *Elle* to the elite fashion magazine *Vogue*, a shift of language, and indeed, a shift in continent, has changed strikingly little in the terms of Deneuve's image, which is primarily concerned with her beauty (and implicitly her unruffled elegance, as symbolised by the crisp linen suit). Here, we have lost the reference to Deneuve's film career entirely, and her relation to Yves Saint Laurent works with other signifiers of a cultured Frenchness (Norman skin, painting, beauty) to evoke sophistication and style. For readers of *Elle* and *Vogue* magazines, despite the differences between them, Deneuve's persona remains one of flawless elegance. Deneuve circulates not so much as a cinematic icon, but as one associated with fashion and beauty. Beyond the constituency of the cinephile fan of auteur cinema, Deneuve functions in the global realm of female popular/fashion elite culture as an icon of eternal, elegant, sensual French feminine beauty. Profiles of Deneuve in film magazines such as *Les Inrockuptibles* and *Première* praise her adaptability, as they enumerate the many directors and co-stars she has worked with. In contrast, Deneuve's fashion persona is overwhelmingly identified with Yves Saint Laurent, with articles tracing the way she has worn his clothes throughout her life, such as *In Style* featuring her wearing Saint Laurent clothing to the Oscars in 1993 or while arriving in the south of France in 1968 to begin filming *La Sirène du Mississippi/Mississippi Mermaid* (Truffaut, 1969) (Hutchings 2000: 120). This chapter is especially interested then in why it is that while Deneuve's cinematic star persona is noticeable for its flexibility, her fashion icon persona remains remarkably consistent – as the title of the Australian *Vogue* profile proclaims, she is (sic) 'belle toujours' (Baxter 1993: 150), a play on words that recounts her most famous film role and turns it into a celebration of her beauty and longevity outside of that filmic sphere.

The off-screen persona: from reverence to relief

Star studies has characterised the star as a media text constructed from both on-screen and off-screen material (Morin, 1957 and Dyer, 1979). This off-screen material comes from a variety of sources, such as magazine interviews, film reviews, biographies and advertising. Classically, it is considered to highlight the discrepancy between the glamour of the star world and either the 'ordinary' domestic life of the star, shopping, cooking, caring for a family, or the 'desperate' life of the star, ill, addicted to drugs, losing or gaining weight (Geraghty, 2000). While film studies in general privileges the production and aesthetics of the filmic text over its reception contexts, star studies emphasises the interconnection between the film and its audience, as the star is a key way in which a film generates its audience appeal. The exact relationship between a celebrity's intertextual persona and its impact on viewing a particular film may be difficult to determine with certainty. But the star's strong social presence and ability to attract audiences allow us to draw two conclusions. First, a star is not merely present in film, but rather works to link films to a whole range of diverse production contexts and media texts. Second, while the presence of a star can help shape the meaning and audience reception of a film, their presence more widely in popular culture is equally worthy of serious consideration when we consider the meanings generated by a star image. Indeed, one can take a more polemical stance and argue that the meanings generated by the off-screen image are more powerful and important than those provided by an individual film, or even a body of film work. As Christine Geraghty argues, 'it is this duality of image [the on-screen and off-screen persona] which is deemed to mark the star' (2000: 185). In other words, it is the very fact of the existence of off-screen material that differentiates between a star and an anonymous actor. If the off-screen persona does not exist, the star cannot function, whereas films can function perfectly well without stars.[1]

When we come to consider the focus of this volume, the star Catherine Deneuve, some qualifying comments need to be made to this general model sketched above. Catherine Deneuve is not just known for her film work, prolific though that is. (She has made close to 150 in her forty-year career.) Deneuve occupies a role in international popular and elite cultural production that exists independently of and may even arguably be greater in shaping her international image than the diverse body of films that she has appeared in. This role is constructed through fashion and cosmetics, notably her long professional association with the couturier Yves Saint Laurent. Yves Saint Laurent designed the clothes for three films she starred in during the late 1960s: *La Chamade/Heartbeat* (Cavalier, 1968), *La Sirène du Mississippi* and most paradigmatically *Belle de jour* (Buñuel, 1966). She has worn his clothes at significant moments in her personal and professional life, such as to her son Christian Vadim's wedding and when she was nominated for an Oscar (for her role in *Indochine* (Wargnier, 1992)) in 1993. She models his clothes in fashion shoots, including in the high fashion magazine *Vogue*, such as a black and white fashion shoot entitled 'belle de nuit' and photographed by Ellen von Unworth in the September 2001 issue. She talks with passion and enthusiasm about his work in press interviews and in the catalogue from a retrospective of his work held at the Museum of Modern Art in New York, 14 December 1983 to 2 September 1984, and which included a broderie anglaise nightdress from *La Sirène du Mississippi*.[2] She accompanies him to various parties, such as the celebration of his thirty years in couture held in 1993 at the Opéra Bastille where she was photographed holding his hand and wearing a specially designed Yves Saint Laurent 'mermaid' dress with hand-stitched sequins. At his retirement party on 22 January 2002 held at the Centre Georges Pompidou in Paris she tearfully serenaded him with the song 'Ma plus belle histoire d'amour, c'est vous', an event that was widely reported in the press (see for example Anon 2002: 9). She has also advertised a line of beauty products for Yves Saint Laurent, 'Le Soin Précurseur de Beauté'. Alongside this complexly negotiated relationship with Yves Saint Laurent, her fashion-icon image is further enhanced by such events as the launch of an eponymous perfume in 1985; her advertising of L'Oréal shampoo and Chanel perfume; and her regular appearances on the covers of women's magazines including *Elle*, *Vogue*, *Madame Figaro* and *Paris Match* magazine in countries as far flung as America, the UK, Australia, Portugal and Spain, as well as France. Indeed, Deneuve herself signalled the importance of this work for her international star image when she suggested that she was better known in the United States for her Chanel advertisements than her film work and its enduring role in defining her star image in America (King, 2000). She comments that she continues to be seen as a 'blonde icon' in the USA despite starring in films that complicate her image (Gonzalez 2000: 176): this is hardly surprising, however, when one considers that the vast majority of her films have been made outside of Hollywood (she has in fact only made four films in Hollywood). So, in common with all stars, Deneuve's stardom depends on an off-screen and on-screen star image that work in tandem with each other. With Deneuve, however, it is the elegant, cool image established in advertising and fashion magazine interviews that overrides the more complex and ambivalent star persona that emerges from her films, certainly on the international stage.

The contrast between glamour and drudgery that we identified earlier as marking the on-screen and off-screen persona is reversed in the case of Deneuve. The contemporary on-screen works to figure Deneuve as ordinary or even ugly and abject: it is her off-screen image that emphasises elegance, sophistication, allure and appeal through its emphasis on luxury goods. Deneuve's film work, such as in Lars von Trier's *Dancer in the Dark* (2000) or Nicole Garcia's *Place Vendôme* (1998) has worked to hide the allure associated with her name. In the former film, she plays an immigrant factory worker, and in the latter a recovering alcoholic. This process is not just linked to her more contemporary (and therefore 'older woman') films, however. Her work with André Téchiné has emphasised her as ordinary, dressing her in drab clothing and filming her unmade-up in extreme close-up, from *Hôtel des Amériques* (1981) onwards. In *Agent Trouble/The Man Who Loved Zoos* (Mocky, 1987) she wears an unflattering drab brown wig. As early a film as Buñuel's

Tristana (1970) challenges her effortless glamour by making her a wheelchair-bound amputee. Even films which have allowed her a more glamorous role, such as *Le Dernier Métro/The Last Metro* (Truffaut, 1980) *Est–Ouest/East–West* (Wargnier, 1999), *Je rentre à la maison/I'm Going Home* (Oliveira, 2000), *8 femmes/8 Women* (Ozon, 2002) or *Rois et reine/Kings and Queen* (Desplechin, 2004) have problematised her star status. This has happened through a variety of devices. Often she has a small cameo role which reduces her to 'symbolic presence' (Vincendeau 1993: 21); her glamour is clearly marked as a performance as she plays an actress (Truffaut, Oliveira and Wargnier); she looks bored and annoyed when told she is beautiful (Desplechin); she performs a camp parody of neurotic French femininity and the publicised traumas of her own personal life as she rolls around on the floor with her on and off-screen 'love rival' Fanny Ardant in *8 femmes*. Such roles, which parody or render the star abject, would seem to undermine Deneuve's famous ice-cold glacial star persona and its association with elegant beauty. The contention of this chapter is that while many of her films work to undercut Deneuve's beauty and glamour and deviate from her pre-established star persona, the only reason they can do this is because her off-screen persona is so powerful. In other words, while her films may make Deneuve poor, ugly, ill, dowdy or grotesque, the audience still knows her to be beautiful, glamorous, rich and desirable. This is because while Deneuve's film career has showcased her versatility and the polysemic possibilities of her star image, her off-screen image has retained a remarkable continuity over more than forty years, in different countries, and across a bewildering variety of media texts (TV chat shows, fashion documentaries, statues, radio interviews, popular and high-fashion magazines, websites, advertisements).

Deneuve's status as a fashion icon emerged alongside her arrival as a major French film star. She starred in her first major role as Geneviève in Jacques Demy's *Les Parapluies de Cherbourg/The Umbrellas of Cherbourg* in 1964; appeared on her first *Vogue* cover in April 1962; and first modelled Yves Saint Laurent's clothes in 1965. Geneviève's appearance at the end of *Parapluies* on a snowy garage forecourt clothed in Chanel, the clothes symbolising her ascension into the bourgeoisie and rejection of her true love (and car mechanic) Guy for the more prosperous jeweller Roland, worked to establish Deneuve's image of cold, haughty bourgeois beauty reinforced and enhanced by the infamous *Belle de jour* where she wore Yves Saint Laurent clothing. In her Yves Saint Laurent films, the crisp careful neat styling and limited colour palette of the clothes (tan, black and white predominate, with the occasional splash of red or pink) create an image of constraint and control.

Recent analysis of the role of costume in film has drawn attention to the way in which it allows us to reconceptualise the classic position of the woman in film theory: that is to say, the object of a sadistic, fetishising male gaze. Stella Bruzzi (1997) has demonstrated that costume works to generate extra and alternative meanings to the narrative, allowing the fashion icon woman to undermine or disrupt the narrative that may seek to contain her. Jackie Stacey (1994) has argued that clothes were constructed as an important way in which female spectators could gain pleasure from the viewing experience. Rachel Moseley's (2002) study has illustrated the complex web set up by costume and female viewing and consumption practices as she interviews women who bought Audrey Hepburn dress patterns. Deneuve's fashion-icon status creates her as an ambiguous figure for feminist film theory, then. On the one hand, her clothes serve to reinforce the film's narrative, and act as an index of her bourgeois repression and sexual coldness. On the other hand, they also enable viewers to construct alternative viewing pleasures in the films (we can enjoy the clothes as well as, or even instead of, the body) and give Deneuve agency in the construction of her image as she wears Yves Saint Laurent clothes in different films by different directors.

As the above discussion shows, however, it is in the realm of fashion and women's magazines that Deneuve continues to function as a fashion icon, whereas her film roles from 1970 onwards (and certainly from the 1980s) have moved away from the image of icy elegance established by the films she made in the late 1960s. It is worth noting here how the magazines themselves remark upon this continuity: the comment made in *Vanity Fair* in April 2001 that she is '*still* one of the world's most beautiful women' [my italics] is typical as female magazines praise her ability to maintain her image of flawless beauty despite her ageing. Such is the emphasis on continuity in Deneuve's image it is not surprising that she was the actress chosen to be literally petrified as Marianne from 1985–1989. When Deneuve edited a special edition of French *Vogue* in December 2003, the cover, shot by celebrity photographer Mario Testino featured a close-up three-quarters profile of Deneuve, her blonde hair swept over her brow. It is a highly stylised cover shot through a red filter. It was a deliberate reference to the first *Vogue* cover Deneuve modelled in April 1962, shot by celebrity photographer Helmut Newton, which was also shot through a red filter and featured a blonde Deneuve in profile. The two covers reinforce the unchanging nature of Deneuve's image and status in the world of the fashion elite. In its editorial on the covers, *Vogue* reproduces all sixteen covers Deneuve has appeared on, further testament to her continuing elegance and fashionability in the face of both social and personal change. Finally, the comment that both covers are shot through a red filter as it is 'the colour of passion to seal a sincere friendship' ('la couleur de la passion pour sceller une amitié sincère') is typical of the way in which Deneuve's fashion image is constructed as a natural choice of friendship and pleasure (her 'friendship' with Yves Saint Laurent, to be discussed in further detail below) rather than as a commercial decision (Anon 2003: 49).

Her fashion-icon status has thus been maintained from the 1960s to the 2000s through fashion editorial and advertising. Deneuve's off-screen image then problematises the generally accepted argument in star studies that the contrast is between an appealing glamorous filmic life and an ordinary/desperate private one. Rather, it suggests we have to rethink these categories of stardom, especially in the face of the specificity of how French female stardom is constructed. The construction of stars in France differs from that in the UK and the USA partly due to France's strict privacy laws (Vincendeau 2000: 34). These were well used by Deneuve, who engaged a lawyer from the age of seventeen and a half to protect her from the press. In a radio interview on France Inter's Tam-tam programme broadcast on 4 March 2004, Deneuve argues that she is not a star as 'a star is absolutely American [...] I'm not a star, I'm a well-known actress. I'm very discreet, and am not photographed with my children. I don't want to become banal' ('une star est fatalement américaine. Je ne suis pas une star, je suis une actrice bien connue [...] je suis très discrète – on ne me prend pas en photo avec mes enfants. Je ne veux pas me banaliser').

Deneuve's comments address the difference of the French star system when it comes to our understanding of the off-screen star image. It is disingenuous for Deneuve to say she isn't a star, given the role that she has played in French cultural life for the past forty years. However, her stardom has a specifically French inflection, in which her off-screen image can be as carefully controlled as her on-screen image. Whereas her on-screen image functions within a government subsidised auteurist national cinema system that allows a star to take on a broader range of roles than would typically be available to a Hollywood star her off-screen image is managed to sell elegant French femininity and is less likely to be undermined by negative press intrusion.

This new paradigm could speculatively be applied to other French female stars whose on-screen roles emphasise abjection, degradation and grief but whose off-screen persona is based on an idealised notion of French femininity constructed through cosmetics, perfume and fashion, most notably Juliette Binoche.[3] The contradictions and differences of the off-screen and on-screen film persona are more complex than the classical model offered by star studies and the idea of an inherent glamour in French femininity exploited by global corporations in their promotion of cosmetics and fashion is not undone by a dowdy appearance in a film. Indeed, this image of French women, that they are sophisticated, glamorous and chic, has proved far more exportable than their films. The discourses that the advertisements key into appear far more stable than the individual film text and circulate more easily across nation states. Furthermore, these advertisements allow the star image to circulate to a wider fan base that may therefore read the star in a way that runs counter to a complex and ambivalent star image such as that performed by Deneuve on-screen. While star studies tends to emphasise the instabilities and contradictions that permeate the star persona and allow the possibility of 'resistant' readings from various sub-cultural groupings (such as gay appropriation of Judy Garland) by attending to the smooth homogeneity of Deneuve's fashion-icon persona we can begin to understand the ways in which personas can accommodate contradiction yet still work to maintain certain ideologically powerful notions, such as the innate elegance of French femininity (used to sell perfume and cosmetics). While Deneuve can be demystified in an auteur film such as *Hôtel des Amériques*, popular culture retains her as beautiful, elegant and exquisitely groomed.

Deneuve herself is well aware of the gap between her cinematic work and the image portrayed in popular culture. Although she discusses her elegance and style with monotonous regularity, she does also express frustration with the fixity of her image. 'Do you think the newspapers and magazines, apart from those dedicated to film, want photos of Björk and me in the film [*Dancer in the Dark*]? They want attractive, glamorous, sophisticated photos' ('Croyez vous que les journaux à part les journaux de cinéma voudraient passer les photos de Björk et de moi dans le film? Les journaux veulent des photos attrayantes, glamour, sophistiquées') (Gonzalez 2000: 176). Deneuve argues in an interview with *Les Inrockuptibles* that even her most glamorous roles such as in *Belle de jour* are more complex than the elegant stylish blonde persona of the fashion icon and this is worth quoting at some length:

> Damn it! These are films that have pretty mixed up people! [*Repulsion, Belle de jour, Tristana*]. But these roles get forgotten and people think of the icy blonde. I actually think that what remains in the collective unconscious is not my film image but based on my paper-image: interviews, magazine covers, the actress talking about her films [...] I haven't been an icy blonde in the cinema for a long time. Magazines always tell you they want to talk about something but at the same time they need a cover that will sell [...] I know in advance that what you read in the press will be in total mismatch with what's in the film. It's difficult, you have to play with it, take account of it, but not refuse everything [...] But when *Elle* dedicates a cover to your new haircut!

> (Mince, ce sont quand même des films avec des personnages assez décalés, assez tordus! Mais on oublie ces rôles et on ne retient que la blonde glâcée. Je crois aussi que ce qui reste dans l'inconscient collectif n'est pas mon image dans les films, mais mon image papier. Les interviews, les couvertures de magazines, l'actrice qui parle de ses films [...] Et je trouve que cette image je ne l'ai plus au cinéma depuis longtemps. Les magazines vous disent toujours qu'ils veulent bien parler des choses et en même temps ils ont cette exigence de couverture "vendeuse" [...] De toute façon, je sais à l'avance que ce qu'on lira dans la presse sera en décalage complet avec ce qu'il y a dans le film. C'est difficile, il faut jouer avec ça, en tenir compte, et en même temps ne pas tout refuser [...] Et quand *Elle* fait une couverture sur votre nouvelle coiffure.) (Bonnaud, 1996) [4]

While Deneuve clearly derives great pleasure from wearing Yves Saint Laurent clothes, as I will discuss below, here the mismatch between her fashion icon persona and her film work is experienced as a frustrating way of containing her meanings and her professional abilities. Ginette Vincendeau argues that Deneuve's cool elegant persona is undermined in films as part of a male sadistic fantasy – the purer the feminine image, the greater the desire to profane it. She memorably encapsulates this process as 'from reverence to rape in one image' (1993: 21). While this clearly has resonance in the context of *Belle de jour*, we can have a far more positive view overall of the 'profanation' of Deneuve's glossy fashion image in her film work. By attending to Deneuve's comments we can see how the filmic work acts as a way in which she can disrupt and problematise the sophistication and glamour of the fashion-icon image. This is not about male sadism but female ease, a melting in Deneuve's case. It is the dowdy appearance in the film, which allows Deneuve to suggest that the fashion-icon image is a fantasy construction also, and escape its constraints. *Elle* claims that 'the beauty lesson' Deneuve can teach all of us is that 'As soon as she shows herself in public, she respects both the public and her image. There is no question of letting yourself go. "You mustn't become lazy about your look", she says' ('dès qu'elle se monte en public, elle est la Deneuve qui respecte à la fois son image et son public. Là, pas question de se laisser aller. "On ne doit pas être velléitaire par rapport à son image" dit-elle') (Demornex 1986: 71). It is the films then that allow Deneuve to 'let herself go', to take pleasure in comfort rather than glamour, as she claims she likes to do in the same *Elle* interview. Not so much from reverence to rape, then, as from reverence to relief, allowing Deneuve to escape the constraining signification of beautiful public French femininity, even though she may usually benefit from it commercially and professionally.

Advertising and commodification in Deneuve's image

This complex web of meaning, in which costume comes to symbolise both pleasure and constraint for Deneuve, is typical of how fashion is analysed by academics. Costume was initially treated academically through a historical perspective but now attracts a wide range of feminist scholarship including Elizabeth Wilson, who argues against received wisdom that fashion is 'a seamless web of oppression' to claim that fashion also functions as 'the most wide-spread medium of women's self-expression' (1984: 3). Lesley Rabine similarly argues that fashion functions 'as a symbolic system which inseparably entangles signs of oppression and liberation within the fashionably feminine body' (1994: 67). Fashion, then, is argued to operate as a privileged vector of certain cultural ideas concerning femininity and its ongoing, inherently paradoxical, construction. Fashion both enables women to express their own individuality, yet also holds them within inscribed performances of femininity, a performance that is so naturalised that it is difficult to see it as performance at all. Deneuve as fashion icon embodies these very contradictions, being celebrated as a remarkable individual while exhorting other women to emulate her through advertising.

Deneuve's Chanel adverts are exemplary here. Running from 1969–1977, these took the form of print and television advertisements and were photographed by the celebrated fashion photographers Richard Avedon and Helmut Newton. Particularly striking is the similar way in which Deneuve appears throughout the seven-year campaign. Featuring a close-up of Deneuve's face and a bottle of perfume, they stress both Deneuve's idealised, ice-cold blonde beauty, and also suggest it is obtainable by any woman, as long as she can afford to buy a bottle of Chanel. The cinematographic style of the television adverts and the swept-back hairstyle of the print advertisements both draw attention to Deneuve's face emerging from the shadows. The advertisements were part of a campaign to re-establish Chanel's brand values that had been eroded by over-distribution and Deneuve's face was felt to signify such quality and elegance that her presence would work to this effect. In an interview with Christian Blachas on French television channel M6's *CulturePub* programme, Chanel's director of marketing, J. Helieu claims that Avedon decided that the television advertisements should have no *mise-en-scène* and concentrate purely on Deneuve (Anon, 2005). The qualities to be associated with the perfume can be culled entirely from her face: 'being French she gives an indication of good taste, sensuality and romance' (Gleason 2000: 32). The print advertisement is similarly dominated by image: usually the only copy is the brand-name Chanel. The perfume bottle and Deneuve's face are enough to evoke ideas of exclusivity, beauty, Frenchness and femininity.

In a televised interview between Deneuve and Larry King on CNN, he makes a small slip which rather misleads Deneuve, who is after all speaking English live, and that is rather delightfully revealing of how these adverts function. I quote King: 'And now you are a product? Do you still have products in your name?'. Unsurprisingly, Deneuve rather balks at this description/commodification of herself –'Products?' and goes onto claim 'I never worked for Chanel. I just did the publicity, the ad for the perfume you know. Perfume is the advantage of something very, very – it is not concrete you know, it is something. It has so much to do with imagination, and it is not a product for me, a perfume' (2000). King mundanely places Deneuve and her role in product placement – using her name and image to shift huge volumes of perfumes and other cosmetics – in a globalised commodity market place in which she is simply another product. Deneuve's relationship to commodification is multifold here. She explicitly constructs herself as ideal through using a commodity, the perfume. Furthermore, she constructs herself as a commodity, selling her image alongside selling the perfume. However, Deneuve denies this commodification, both of herself and the perfume ('perfume is not a product') and this denial is necessary, for the appeal to the ephemeral, the mysterious, the imagination, is partly what sells perfume. Deneuve simultaneously emblematises women's commodification in a capitalist patriarchal system in which the only relationship one can have to the feminine object is that of possession and yet remystifies it through an idealised reconsumption that takes place at the imaginary level of some idealised, ineffable feminine being. French femininity is thus characterised in these advertisements as enmeshed in capitalist systems of exchange and yet also imagined as ideal, beautiful, and unique.

It is hardly surprising considering his voracious appetite for all aspects of modern culture that the cultural theorist Edgar Morin turned his attention to fashion in his wide-ranging consideration of the impact of cultural forms on French life. He argued that the relationship between haute couture and popular culture was far more symbiotic than it may at first appear.

> Fashion constantly advances the new. This answers two needs. It stimulates consumer demand and through seduction affirms the individual. This explains why haute couture enters the mass market. Fashion descends from the elites to the feminine masses [...] And mass culture, through feminine fashion, reveals its own function. It gives access to the two mythical ideals of feminine seduction and feminine individuality. It allows mimetic identification. And at the same time it allows an abiding obsession with consumption whose importance to the economy is becoming ever greater in western society.

> (D'où reste une perpétuelle relance vers le nouveau [...] qui correspond à un double besoin: celui effectivement de la restimulation séductrice, celui de l'affirmation individuelle [...] C'est ce qui explique que la mode entre dans le cycle de masse [...] La mode descend des élites vers les masses féminines [...] Et la culture de masse, sur le plan de la mode

féminine, révèle sa fonction propre: elle donne accès aux grands archétypes 'olympiens', elle procure les prestiges de la haute individualité et de la séduction. Elle permet l'identification mimétique. En même temps, elle entretient une obsession consommatrice [...] dont l'importance comme stimulant économique se fait de plus en plus grande dans les sociétés occidentales'). (1962: 193–4).

According to Morin, then, fashion and its representations are privileged sites to explore how mass culture constructs the feminine ideal through individual aspiration and mimetic identification, both promised through the consumption of goods. The Deneuve–Chanel adverts operate in just such a dialectic. The consumption of the perfume promises the acquisition of ideal femininity based on notions of quality, sensuality and French beauty. In fact, all that is guaranteed is the sale of yet another bottle of perfume. Furthermore, perfume is how the couture house enters into popular culture while attempting to appear elitist. Perfume is the commercial lifeblood of couture houses, generating the majority of their profits, to the extent that the fashion can sometimes appear to be a way of publicising the perfume. When Yves Saint Laurent was sold to Elf-Sanofi in 1993, accounts showed that 80 per cent of its revenue of 3 billion francs a year came from the 'Parfums' division (Menkes 1993: 9). Deneuve may try and remystify her image with her talk of perfume being more than a product, but the linking of her face to Chanel perfumes and later Yves Saint Laurent beauty products (the adverts use a strikingly similar iconography of a close-up on Deneuve and the product with very little extra copy) seems to confirm her own objectification and commodification. The pleasures she gains from the advertisements, both the explicit one of using the product, and the implicit one of a large salary, confirm the problematic that constrains the female fashion icon. Her pleasure is always for sale.

Deneuve's whole relationship with Saint Laurent echoes this paradoxical combination of pleasure and commodification. The account of their meeting has the status of myth and is repeated with minor variations as follows:

> I needed an evening dress and it was just as a customer that I went to Yves Saint Laurent, for the first time, in 1965. Then he dressed me for films, I saw him working, I admired him, and from then on we had a more intimate relationship. I love his clothes and naturally I've always worn them. Nowadays, we're used to seeing certain actresses associated with certain fashion designers, often for marketing purposes. But my relation-

ship with Yves Saint Laurent goes back to 1968 or 1969 and things just worked out this way, in the context of a real relationship in which we are both colleagues and friends.

(J'avais besoin d'une robe de soir et c'est en simple cliente que je suis allée chez Yves Saint Laurent, pour la première fois en 1965. Puis il m'a habillé pour des films, je l'ai vu travailler, avec admiration, et dès lors nous avons eu une relation plus intime. J'adore ses vêtements et je les ai toujours naturellement portés. Aujourd'hui on est habitué à voir le nom de certaines actrices s'associer à celle des couturiers, souvent pour des raisons publicitaires. En ce qui me concerne, mes relations avec Yves Saint Laurent remontent à 1968 ou 1969 et les choses sont faites comme ça, dans le cadre d'une vraie relation professionnelle et amicale). (Lalanne, 2001).

As with the Chanel adverts, the denial of commodification is prevalent in the description of Deneuve's relationship with Yves Saint Laurent. She 'naturally' wears his clothes. They are characterised as intimate friends. In interviews discussing her agreement to advertise Yves Saint Laurent beauty products she continues the metaphor: 'our free love became a marriage – a contract linked us for the advertising visuals' ('pour que notre union libre devienne mariage – un contrat alors nous a lié pour les visuels publicitaires') (Zana 1995: 48), rescuing even this moment from the taint of consumerism although as Australian *Vogue* comments, 'no-one will talk money but obviously a great deal of it must have changed hands to win her involvement' (Baxter 1993: 155). Clearly admiration and friendship do work to link Saint Laurent and Deneuve: what is worth noting is the insistence that the relationship is beyond commodification when it is clearly heavily embedded within it, especially when it comes to the marketing of his beauty line. Deneuve, however, seems to suggest this only occurs in the relationship between other actresses and couturiers to whom she explicitly contrasts herself.

"Everything is lined in silk satin": private pleasures and public celebrations

As Vincendeau argues, there is indeed a long history of elegant French actresses modelling couture clothes, such as Michèle Morgan, Martine Carol and Danielle Darrieux. The difference with Deneuve is that she does not model the clothes in the films. Rather, they become part of the character she plays in the film. Vincendeau argues that

Deneuve's clothes in *Belle de jour* are used by Buñuel as an index of bourgeois repression (1993: 21). All three of the films where Deneuve is styled by Saint Laurent feature narratives of upper-middle-class sexual and romantic entanglements and feature Deneuve in understated garments which fit perfectly into their context: trench coats, pleated skirts and slim polo necks for day wear, stunning evening dresses for parties and theatre visits. Deneuve explains, 'Saint Laurent carefully reads the script, and with his clothes he creates an important expression of the role and even of the scene' (Saint Laurent 1984: 34). Saint Laurent's clothes then work in the cinema as subservient to the narrative, rather than drawing attention to themselves. It is the perfect fit between the clothes in the films and the characters Deneuve plays in them that set the context for the close identification between Deneuve and Saint Laurent over the next forty years and which is constructed as a love story, with the constant use of terms such as intimacy, friendship and marriage being used to describe the relationship between the designer and what may more conventionally be referred to as his muse (placing the relation into the realm of aesthetics and art) or his customer (placing the relation into the realm of commerce and finance).

Deneuve's comment that Yves Saint Laurent 'designs for women with double lives' neatly summarises his function in terms of how she is read as fashion icon and as cinema star: his clothes fit both roles perfectly. Rather more interesting, however are her accompanying comments to this remark: 'Everything [...] is lined with silk satin. That detail is emblematic of his total attitude towards women. He wants to spoil them, to envelop them in the pleasure of his clothes. He is also very protective [...] His day clothes help a woman confront a world of strangers. They permit her to go everywhere without drawing undue attention, and with their somewhat masculine quality, they give her a certain force [...] In the evening [...] he makes her seductive' (Saint Laurent 1984: 34).

There is a sense then that Saint Laurent's clothing functions as a protective layer for Deneuve. Through its masculine design (notably the 'smoking', the male dinner suit redesigned for women and named by Deneuve in *Vogue* (Lalanne, 2001) as the most elegant and quintessentially French item of clothing one can own) and its understated qualities, this clothing prevents Deneuve from symbolising only passive to-be-looked-at-ness: being the object of a desiring gaze becomes a position of choice for Deneuve (she chooses when she wishes to seduce). Furthermore, she emphasises the role of sensual pleasure in the wearing of Yves Saint Laurent's clothes: she takes her body outside of the realm of visual signification and explains the private pleasure she gains from the feel of the clothes, their touch on her skin. The ideas of pleasure, luxury and sensuality are reinforced in further interviews. 'It's not just a whim to have a Saint Laurent dress. It's a desire, a luxury to which I am very sensitive. I'm not blasé about it' ('avoir une robe Saint Laurent, ce n'est pas une caprice. C'est une envie, un luxe auquel je suis très sensible. Je ne suis pas blasée') (Zana 1995: 49). Deneuve as fashion icon no longer functions simply as object of the gaze but here emphasises pleasure, touch and protection as possible advantages of wearing Yves Saint Laurent clothing. Saint Laurent claims that he uses masculine-style clothing patterns for women as male suits are cut from 'a handful of basic shapes' and 'I've always wanted to give women the protection of a sort of basic wardrobe – protection from ridicule, freedom to be themselves. It pains me physically to see a woman victimized, rendered pathetic, by fashion [...] I love women' (Saint Laurent 1984: 21–2).

Yves Saint Laurent's clothing, as with the icon it clothes, becomes a matter of style rather than fashion, an unchanging elegance that works despite, not to express, social upheaval. Deneuve's fashion icon persona suggests that while society may worship physical perfection, it is rather tiring for the person who is thought to possess it as it becomes so difficult to signify beyond it: she is always a blonde icon for popular culture, whatever may happen in her films. Her image comes ready packaged, ready to be sold to the highest bidder. And yet ... although Deneuve may understandably sometimes wish to escape the very constraints of her own elegance, grace and flawlessness, just occasionally, Yves Saint Laurent's clothes allow her to do that too. When nominated for the Oscars in 1993 she wore a typically minimalist and understated black dress that was uncharacteristically trimmed with flamboyant vivid pink ostrich feathers. The dress thus played into the complex way Deneuve constructs herself in media texts, suggesting both her cool, controlled beauty (the black) and her desire to play with and disrupt that objectifying image. She commented that some people didn't like the dress, but 'if you can't wear pink ostrich to the Oscars, when can you?' (Hutchings 2000: 26). It is a final comment that allows us to enjoy the possibilities of pleasure, celebration and professional success contained in women's clothing, a moment when the fashion icon was permitted to change and to escape her frozen form of icy-blonde perfection.

Notes

1 The most notable example of this is probably Italian neo-realism, when the use of non-star actors was an essential part of the film's aesthetic, but also animation and documentary tend to be genres that do not require stars.

2 The exhibition, organised by the Costume Institute of the Museum of Modern Art in New York, was the first retrospective of a living fashion designer ever organised.

3 While further development of this point is beyond the scope of this chaper, it is worth considering how female Hollywood stars are also shown as glamorous in their private lives and in advertising compared to 'ordinary' or 'grotesque' in film. Two obvious examples are Renée Zellweger as Bridget Jones and Charleze Theron as Aileen Wournos.

4 The offending cover appeared 28 October 1991 with the headline 'Deneuve s'offre une nouvelle tête'.

Works cited

Anon. (2002), 'Les femmes en noir d'Yves Saint Laurent', *Le Monde*, 24 January, 9.

Anon. (2003), *Vogue* (France), December.

Anon. (2005), http://www.catherinedeneuve.free.fr/catherinepub5dechanel.usa.htm (last accessed 14 November 2005).

Baudot, François (1996), 'Yves, l'élégance et moi: 30 ans d'amitié avec Saint Laurent', *Elle* (France), 105–8.

Baxter, John (1993), '*Belle toujours*', *Vogue* (Australia), February, 150–5.

Bonnaud, Frédéric and Serge Kaganski (1996), '"Les acteurs devraient faire des films et disparaître"', *Les Inrockuptibles*, France, May, n.p.

Bruzzi, Stella (1997), *Undressing Cinema: Clothing and Identity in the Movies*, London and New York: Routledge.

Clark, Pascale (2004), 'Tam-tam', France Inter 4 March download at http://www.radiofrance.fr/chaines/france-inter01–emissions.tamtam/archives.php (last accessed 14 November 2005).

Demornex, Jacqueline (1986), 'La Leçon de beauté de Catherine Deneuve', *Elle* (France), 14 April, 69–71.

Dyer, Richard (1979), *Stars*, London: BFI.

Geraghty, Christine (2000), 'Re-examining stardom: questions of texts, bodies and performance', in Gledhill, Christine and Linda Williams (eds), *Reinventing Film Studies*, London, Arnold: 183–201.

Gleason, Dan (2000), 'Catherine Deneuve: never out of style', *Millionaire* (USA), September, 30–2.

Gonzalez, Christian (2000), '"Je ne suis pas une icône blonde"', *Madame Figaro* (France), October, 176.

Hogan, Michael (2001), 'First ladies', *Vanity Fair* (USA), April, 24–8.

Hutchings, David (2000), 'Belle Deneuve', *In Style* (Australia), November, 120–2.

King, Larry (2000), 'Larry King Live', CNN download at http://www. toutsurdeneuve.free.fr/Francais/Pages/Interviews/LarryKing00.htm (last accessed 15 August 2005).

Lalanne, Olivier (2001), 'Belle de nuit', *Vogue* (France), September, n.p.

Menkes, Suzy (1993), 'Elf-Sanofi buys Saint Laurent', *International Herald Tribune* 20 January, 9.

Morin, Edgar (1957), *Les Stars*, Paris: Seuil.

Morin, Edgar (1962), *L'Esprit du temps*, Paris: Grasset.

Moseley, Rachel (2002), *Growing Up with Audrey Hepburn: Text, Image, Resonance*, Manchester: Manchester University Press.

Rabine, Leslie, W. (1994), 'A woman's two bodies: fashion magazines, consumerism and feminism', in Benstock, Shari and Suzanne Ferriss (eds), *On Fashion*, New Brunswick: Rutgers University Press, pp. 59–75.

Saint Laurent, Yves, Diana Vreeland, René Huyghe *et al.* (1984), *Yves Saint Laurent*, London: Thames & Hudson/New York: Metropolitan Museum of Modern Art.

Stacey, Jackie (1994), *Star Gazing: Hollywood Cinema and Female Spectatorship*, London and New York: Routledge.

Vincendeau, Ginette (1993), 'Fire and ice', *Sight & Sound*, April, 20–2.

Vincendeau, Ginette (2000), *Stars and Stardom in the French Cinema*, London: Continuum.

Wilson, Elizabeth (1984), *Adorned in Dreams: Fashion and Modernity*, London: Virago.

Zana, Jean-Claude (1995), 'Eternelle belle de jour', *Paris-Match* (France), 45–51.

Index

Please note that all films are listed by director.

181

Index